Tornadoes
over Texas

Research publication in mental health
for the Hogg Foundation

Tornadoes
over Texas

A Study of
Waco and San Angelo in Disaster

By Harry Estill Moore

Austin
University of Texas Press

THIS STUDY was financed by grants
from the National Academy of Sciences–National Research Council, acting through their Committee on Disaster Studies; and from the Research
Council, the Institute for Public Affairs,
and The Hogg Foundation for Mental
Health, all of The University of Texas.
Academy–Research Council funds were
obtained from the Federal Civil Defense Administration; medical services
of the Army, Navy, and Air Force; and
the National Institute of Mental Health
(Public Health Service, Department of
Health, Education, and Welfare).

The conclusions herein are solely
those of the author and not necessarily
those of any of the sponsoring agencies.

Foreword

THE OPPORTUNITY to introduce both the director of a new research program and the author of the first book in a new monograph series is a privilege. Dr. Wayne Holtzman, associate director of The Hogg Foundation for Mental Health, is now in charge of research and is editor of the Foundation's new series of research publications. Dr. Harry Estill Moore, who has written several books and articles in the field of sociology, is the author of *Tornadoes over Texas*, the first monograph in the Foundation's series.

Unique as a permanent endowment given to a state university for mental-health education, service, and research, the Hogg Foundation has developed a program in keeping both with the request of the donors and with the purposes of an institution of higher learning. For a decade and a half, it has worked through departments and branches of The University of Texas to increase an understanding of mental-health principles by professional workers, to develop clinics, research, and teaching facilities, and to initiate new patterns of community organization and service. An increase in income in 1955 enabled the Foundation to expand and establish firmly its research function, which now represents one-half of its total budget.

Dr. Holtzman joined the staff of the Hogg Foundation as associate director in 1955, and has given wise and aggressive leadership to research projects undertaken directly by the Foundation and through work financed by Foundation grants. He brings to his assignment an excellent background of education and experience in experimental research and clinical studies, holding advanced degrees in psychology from Northwestern University and Stanford University. He continues his teaching and research in the Department of Psychology at The University of Texas.

Dr. Moore, director of the study which led to this book, conceived the idea for investigation of the resources of people and their insti-

v

Foreword

tutions for recovery from the disastrous tornadoes in Waco and San Angelo, Texas. He received initial encouragement from the President's Office, the Hogg Foundation, and the Institute of Public Affairs at The University of Texas, and from the Committee on Disaster Studies of the National Academy of Sciences–National Research Council. More substantial assistance came later from the National Academy of Sciences and the Hogg Foundation.

The author brought to this specialized community study years of research experience in social organization, community leadership, and mental health. *Nine Help Themselves,* published in 1955, reports a five-year analysis of educational leadership roles in community action. This volume was one of the several outcomes of the Southwestern Cooperative Program in Educational Administration, financed by a grant from the W. K. Kellogg Foundation to the College of Education. He was co-author with Howard W. Odum of *American Regionalism,* published by Henry Holt and Company, and collaborated with Ernest R. Groves on *An Introduction to Sociology,* published by Longmans, Green and Company. Dr. Moore has contributed articles to the professional journals in sociology and is editor of the *Southwestern Social Science Quarterly.*

The University of Texas and The Hogg Foundation for Mental Health are pleased to introduce the mental-health research series by this acknowledgment of the able leadership given the Foundation's research program by Dr. Holtzman and by this appreciation to Dr. Moore, professor of sociology, for contributing the first manuscript in the series.

Tornadoes over Texas is published through a co-operative arrangement with Mr. Frank Wardlaw, director of the University Press.

LOGAN WILSON, *President*
The University of Texas
ROBERT L. SUTHERLAND, *Director*
The Hogg Foundation for Mental Health

Preface

SUDDEN DISASTER has reduced man to impotence since the beginning of recorded time. Floods, earthquakes, fire, and tornadoes have wiped out entire communities overnight, striking terror to the hearts of countless victims. Slowly during the past few decades, progress has been made in controlling floods and in limiting the destruction of fire. Earthquakes and tornadoes are still completely beyond control but at least efforts are being made to understand and guard against the disastrous effects of such natural forces. Yet, somewhat ironically, just as man is beginning to find ways of dealing with natural calamities, he is confronted with the monstrous child of his own invention—the catastrophic annihilation of civilian populations by atomic bombing.

In time of war, there is no opportunity to study the sudden disintegration of communities and the impact of disaster upon the individual and his family. All one's energies are invested in a massive struggle for survival. In time of peace, one must wait for a natural catastrophe to strike before the social impact of such disaster can be investigated. And as likely as not, the social scientists best equipped for such study are deeply immersed in other activities or are so far removed from the scene of the disaster that it is all over before anything can be done. It is small wonder that little serious attempt has been made until recently to study the immediate impact of sudden disaster upon society.

Tornadoes over Texas: A Study of Waco and San Angelo in Disaster is the first thoroughly documented investigation of the social disorganization and recovery of major cities following disaster of catastrophic proportions. Led by Professor Moore, a team of social scientists carefully studied everything they could lay their hands on—from economics, government, and community structure to the individual, his family, and their emotional reactions—everything from the moment the tornado struck until years later when its impact was all but forgotten in the minds of most citizens.

This exhaustive study is rich in its implications for the development of a theory of social organization and disruption through disaster, whether one is interested in the complex structure of an entire community or the organization of the family. It is primarily descriptive in nature and makes no pretense of rigorous hypothesis-testing. Though very different disasters in many respects, both Waco and San Angelo were characterized initially by confusion, disorganization, and inactivity—Waco far more seriously than San Angelo because of badly damaged communication networks and severe destruction in the vital center of town. After this first period of shock came an intense outpouring of great generosity, selflessness, heroic efforts, and activity—some rational, some senseless—all reflecting a profound desire to "do something." With continued frenzied activity eventually came fatigue, depression, and the growing realization that no amount of effort would make things exactly as they were before the disaster. For some disillusioned, weary victims, frustration led to hostility and a search for a scapegoat. Slowly and painfully came acceptance of reality with a redefinition of goals, and the healing process commenced. The vigorous determination to recover and the optimistic faith in the future which characterized citizens of both Waco and San Angelo were indeed impressive testimony to the tough, resilient power of American communities when struck by overwhelming disaster.

Of all the natural calamities confronting man, the tornado is most like the man-made disaster of bombing civilian populations. The lack of forewarning, the complete helplessness of a community when disaster strikes and the wake of desolation and destruction which follows, the sudden, explosive fury of winds, and the brief duration of onslaught so characteristic of a tornado are also characteristic of bombing in war. Throughout the civilized world today there is a foreboding sense of urgency to gain new knowledge about community disasters. What social institutions prove most effective in minimizing chaos and facilitating rapid recovery? What forces in a community add to the confusion and delay recovery? What can a given community do to build defenses against paralysis and disorganization in a disaster? How can communication networks, the "nervous system" of society, be protected and effectively utilized? In this thorough study of two tornado-stricken cities, considerable light is shed upon these and other important issues pertinent to the survival of society. Is it too much to hope that we can learn such lessons before it is too late?

One particularly valuable feature of *Tornadoes over Texas* is the investigation of a second, similar disaster only thirteen months later in San Angelo. Of 150 families studied in San Angelo after the first tornado, 114 were interviewed again soon after the second destructive wind, providing valuable "retest" data. Unstructured interviews of a probing nature were tape-recorded for 22 families who had experienced the tornado and had then shown a serious degree of emotional disturbance following the second storm. Initial shock reactions, defensive behavior, and neurotic symptoms of a more chronic nature which had their roots in the tornado are amply documented in Chapters 13–15 by excerpts from these interviews. Striking similarities are apparent between the traumatic neuroses in bombed cities in the Second World War and the emotional disturbances manifested by some victims of the tornadoes.

More impressive, however, is the much larger number of victims who doggedly went to work to rebuild what had been destroyed. The determination to recover, the fundamental cohesiveness of families in disaster, their unfailing optimism toward the future, and the gratitude of those whose life was spared though property was lost are significant signs of strength which, if wisely nurtured in a society, can be a powerful defense against disaster.

Wayne H. Holtzman

Contents

Contents

Contents

Introduction and Acknowledgments

WHEN PORTIONS of Waco and San Angelo were devastated by tornadoes on the afternoon of May 11, 1953, members of the Department of Sociology of The University of Texas immediately became interested in the research possibilities presented. Informal discussion was followed by a series of staff meetings at which various possibilities were explored.

Through a suggestion of President Logan Wilson, contact was made with a colleague who had done research on disasters and, through him, with the Committee on Disaster Studies of the National Academy of Sciences–National Research Council. A token grant of $500 was offered. The Hogg Foundation for Mental Health also offered $500 for exploratory work.

A member of the department went to Washington and discussed plans more fully with the Committee on Disaster Research and with members of the research and planning division of the Federal Civil Defense Administration. At this meeting an agreement was reached whereby the Federal Civil Defense Administration made available to the National Academy of Science–National Research Council $5,000, which it in turn might pass along to The University of Texas to finance the study.

A windfall grant was obtained from the Institute of Public Affairs, of the University. An employee of the institute had resigned, and his salary for a portion of the fiscal year was available for other use. Arrangements were made for approximately $2,700 to be used on the disaster-research project.

As the research developed, initial data demonstrated the presence of problems that badly needed study. The Committee on Disaster Research and the Hogg Foundation made available additional funds —not so much as was needed, but as much as could be used profitably by the available staff.

Introduction and Acknowledgments

An entertaining, and perhaps illuminating, essay could be written on the interinstitutional relations established under this multiple sponsorship. One short section might be devoted to the intricacies of spending money—all of which was to further one project—from seven different accounts under four sets of regulations. Except for the patient understanding and help of the accountants of the University, this alone would have been sufficient to discourage any except the more foolhardy.

The recruitment of personnel was a problem mitigated by the fortuitous appearance of a former teaching fellow in the department, who was completing a tour of military service with the Human Resources Research Institute of the Air Force and who agreed to work on the study.

It might be assumed that, considering the lengthy prior discussion and formulation of plans, the actual research would have been sharply focused. But the project plan as finally developed was inclusive, rather than delimited. Without any sure guide or firm agreement about what it was feasible to study, we decided that the initial work should be descriptive, rather than incisive, believing that as exploration progressed, more specific focuses would be selected. But the factor of primary importance turned out to be the reaction of the persons interviewed. Almost without exception, they insisted on recounting their experiences in the tornado and its immediate aftermath. Perhaps it should be added that the interviewers were intensely interested in these accounts. As a result, much of what was obtained is excellent descriptive material that does not lend itself to rigorous analysis of a "research" nature. This is not to say that such data are without worth; they have high value. But they do lack focus and are not as directly related to the study of rehabilitation as had been planned.

A colleague discussing procedure in studying a disaster situation said that the first imperative is to throw out preconceived ideas as to "scientific method" and to see the setting as an interactive experience, adding that though this may not be statistically respectable, it is sociologically justifiable. Looking back over the years' work, it appears that we followed his advice, perhaps to a greater extent than was realized at the time.

Early data collected consist primarily of interviews and observations. Tape recorders were used in talking with officials of governmental and other agencies so that not only their words but something of the emotional overtones of their words might be secured. American

Red Cross and the two local disaster-fund committees made available summary records of their work with families, and from these sources data were secured on about 2,400 families who had suffered loss in the tornadoes. Federal Civil Defense Administration officials working in and with the cities supplied records of their actions. A subscription for a Waco newspaper provided a source of day-to-day clues. The state had entered the picture through the office of State Co-ordinator of Civil Defense and Disaster Relief, and files there were open.

Too much emphasis cannot be placed on the fact that private and governmental agencies, without exception, gave access to any and all requested information pertinent to the study, and did so without interposing the "red tape" that is supposed to require tortuous unraveling in such instances. What valuable data we failed to secure either did not exist or we did not ask for them.

Persons accustomed to reading social-science research reports are likely to be surprised, and may be displeased, at the paucity of statistical measures of significance and of footnotes in this study. These omissions were made because this is primarily descriptive research, designed to give, in semipopular style, an understanding of disaster and its consequences. This, of course, sets it apart from the more technical presentations of experimental or analytic testing of hypotheses commonly presented in learned journals.

Although there is a rapidly growing literature on disaster, little of it has to do with rehabilitation; most of it is concerned with the impact of the disaster and the events immediately following. For this reason we found no data with which we could compare that we obtained in Waco and San Angelo. Theoretical formulations are more abundant, as is evidenced by the relatively much greater number of footnotes in the chapter "Toward a Theory of Disaster" in this volume.

The significance of any statistical difference depends primarily on the size of the sample used. When the total number of cases involved—families or persons—is of the size range found here, and the percentage of this total number is in the range we used, statisticians estimate that normal probable error will run as high as from 10 to 25 per cent. This means, of course, that a difference of 25 per cent in some of the tables may be due entirely to chance, and has no real significance. But it should also be added that when a number of tables—no one of which in itself meets tests of significance—all point toward the same conclusion, the probability of that conclusion's being a matter of mere chance becomes very small indeed. However, it must be emphasized again that the aim here is to describe, not to claim that this or that probability has been demonstrated as correct. For this reason many tables are included that clearly do not meet customary statistical tests of significance.[1]

Someone has said that most social-science research must be content to illuminate an area of concern rather than to demonstrate the validity or falsity of a given proposition. If this report succeeds in illuminating the situations in which two cities found themselves after being struck by disaster, and the ways in which they strove to restore the sort of existence they had before those events, it will have served its purpose.

The dramatic qualities of the impact of a disaster so far outweigh the pedestrian efforts at rehabilitation that it is only natural for interest to focus on that early period. This was brought out in a two-day conference held on the campus of The University of Texas in mid-September, 1953, called to define more narrowly the research problems involved in this type of work. It was even more apparent in a "post-mortem" discussion held in Waco in August, 1953, where, without exception, the participants held their remarks to the impact period and the immediate problems it raised. Later, when the Columbia Broadcasting System became interested in a television presentation of the research project, it was found impossible to escape putting major emphasis on what had happened during and immediately after the tornado, with only an almost casual reference to the fact that research was being done on rehabilitation of the cities.

But fascinating and dramatic as are the data relating to the disaster itself, we had started out to study rehabilitation and felt we should do so because of both our agreement and our interest. Because the family is the basic social institution and because one of the sponsors of the research was particularly interested in interpersonal relations, the family was selected as the unit for more intensive study. Schedules were constructed, and interviews were held in Waco and San Angelo with fairly large samples of the affected families. Details of how this study was set up and conducted are found elsewhere in this report.

More directly concerned with rehabilitation was the application

---

[1] For an outstanding example of a social scientist of high repute presenting data obtained in interviewing and with no indices of statistical significance, see Samuel A. Stouffer, *Communism, Conformity, and Civil Liberties* (Garden City, N.Y., Doubleday & Company, Inc., 1955). Appendix D (pages 270ff.) contains an excellent simplified discussion of significance.

of Public Law 875, the federal statute under which funds from the national government are made available for reconstruction purposes. Analysis of this law and the manner in which it was executed in these two cities is recorded in another section of the report.

In June, 1954, a very heavy hailstorm struck that portion of San Angelo which had been devastated by the tornado only little more than a year previously. More field work secured data concerning the effects of this second storm on the victims of the first. These data differed from those previously gathered in that they included, in addition to information obtained by interviewers who filled in schedules, about two dozen intensive interviews in which victims of the dual disasters were encouraged to talk of the emotional stresses they had developed from their experiences. This material added a depth to the study it had lacked but badly needed.

What is the justification for the expenditure of funds and energy necessary to produce the study from which *Tornadoes over Texas* is taken? It might well be answered that no justification is needed other than that of studying a phenomenon of interest to the researchers and to those who supplied the funds. No other justification is demanded, for instance, of the astronomers who study the chemical composition of the atmosphere of a distant star. But such an answer is insufficient in social science; and perhaps it is fortunate that this is true.

Specific information has been recorded that has great value for those charged with the defense of the civilian population in event of warfare. Local and state governmental units familiar with the situations faced by these two communities have said they learned much from the grisly lesson. Perhaps others may learn a little by more indirect means. The same may be said for nongovernmental institutions and businesses that must act in disaster emergencies, whatever the source from which the disasters strike. A few persons received general training in disaster research and some in specific techniques. Most of the latter can be transferred to other areas of research.

Some of the ideas passed along from textbook-writer to textbook-writer were checked against the experiences of the persons, institutions, and communities studied. And it was found that some of these accepted ideas do not apply in these particular situations. For instance, victims of the tornadoes did not panic as had been expected, nor did many recover their emotional equilibrium within the short time medical literature has indicated. A few bald facts of this sort may bring about a change in the ideas interlacing our literature on human behavior under severe and unexpected stress. Perhaps this and other studies may aid in developing more trustworthy theory out of which may come more realistic and fruitful understanding of human behavior and planning for catastrophes.

Collaboration is a fortunate requirement of the growing complexity of our academic world. This study of catastrophes involved the joint efforts of many individuals, including a score of students at The University of Texas. Credit goes especially to Fred R. Crawford, who exchanged his title of Field Director of the Waco–San Angelo Disaster Study for that of Assistant Professor of Sociology at Texas Technological College in 1954. He was by far the most active and influential person employed on the project. By transmuting general ideas into specific activities and by directing and encouraging the efforts of the shifting remainder of the staff, he gave both direction and continuity to the effort. Mrs. Mary Elizabeth Powers, Mrs. Bettye Nelson, James Hankerson, and Ted Brannen performed major roles during the first year's work. Hankerson made a preliminary draft of a report on the legal and political problems of rehabilitation; Brannen made the initial study of economic consequences. Mrs. Powers gathered data in Waco; Mrs. Nelson served as office assistant.

During the second year of the study, Mrs. Margaret P. Nolle made a study of employment following the disasters, Joseph B. Perry studied building permits, and Tyrus G. Fain worked on statistical problems by teasing out factors of pertinence in explaining differences of impact on families of various types. Two husband-wife teams of psychology students—the D. W. Tylers and the C. B. Elams—did intensive interviewing following the second San Angelo storm. Material growing out of this event was worked over by Frank S. Stockwell, Mrs. Wilhelmina Perry, and Dr. Bernice Milburn Moore. Mrs. Frances J. Perry performed the nonglamorous but essential clerical and stenographic work, supplying both ideas and good humor when they were needed. Mrs. Colleen Warren and Mrs. Marjorie Heaton aided in preparation of the final manuscript.

Thanks are tendered the *American Sociological Review* for permission to reprint the chapter "Toward a Theory of Disaster," which appeared in that journal in December, 1956.[2]

The study of which this is a partial report was conceived only

---

[2] Vol. 21, pp. 723–727. Thanks are also expressed to The Free Press for clearing for publication materials developed in this study and used by Dr. Martha Wolfenstein in *Disaster: A Psychological Study*, which appeared in the spring of 1957. See p. 228 for an explanation of this anomaly.

through the united efforts of the staff of the Department of Sociology of The University of Texas. It was made financially possible only through the active co-operation of President Logan Wilson; Dean A. P. Brogan, director of the Research Institute; Dr. Stuart A. McCorkle, director of the Institute of Public Affairs; Dr. Robert L. Sutherland, director, and Dr. Wayne H. Holtzman, associate director, of The Hogg Foundation for Mental Health, all of The University of Texas. In addition, generous support from Dr. Hoyt Lemon, of the Federal Civil Defense Administration, and from Dr. Harry B. Williams, Miss Jeannette Rayner, and Miss Luisa Fisher, of the National Academy of Sciences–National Research Council Committee on Disaster Research, is most gratefully acknowledged.

No researcher has a right to ask for more than was freely given to this project.

More technical and more detailed reports on the research than are presented here have been filed with the sponsoring agencies and in libraries in Waco and San Angelo, where they may be consulted. This volume is an attempt to combine and synthesize the more pertinent portions of the longer reports into a more meaningful, less time-consuming, and more readable form.

This has been a co-operative project. Without such generous co-operation, the research underlying this report could never have been conducted, and the task of the director would quickly have been seen as impossible. Nonetheless, final decision was always reserved to him. Shortcomings or errors of fact or judgment belong exclusively to him.

HARRY ESTILL MOORE

Tornadoes
over Texas

1. Cities in Crisis

MONDAY, MAY 11, 1953, was a threatening day in Texas—and the threat became a more terrible reality than had been imagined possible.

Early that morning weather bureaus had broadcast a warning that masses of warm, moisture-laden air moving up from the Gulf of Mexico would meet a front of cold air somewhere near a line extending from Waco to San Angelo and that tornadoes were a possibility in that general area. During the early afternoon heavy rain began to fall. It was welcomed, as rain always is in Texas, especially in the growing season.

Storm warnings continued. They, and the rain, kept many persons from going shopping, it may be assumed. But it is also likely that the storm warnings did not create as much apprehension in Waco as they would have in other cities: Waco was immune to tornadoes, according to an ancient Indian legend repeated in a 1951 Chamber of Commerce publication.

Perhaps the immunization had run out; perhaps the Indian Spirit whose duty it was to protect the city nodded. Disaster dealt death and destruction that afternoon with a heavy hand. Waco and San Angelo bore the brunt of the blows.

Early in the afternoon a tornado twisted its way through Lake View, an area of small homes in the northwestern portion of San Angelo; late in the same afternoon a tornado swept across the entire city of Waco, venting its full fury on the downtown business center.

The Tornado and Waco

A local peace officer living some miles to the southwest of Waco reported after the disaster that he had seen a tornado funnel and had called the office of the county sheriff. But before he could give any details the connection was broken.

3

4

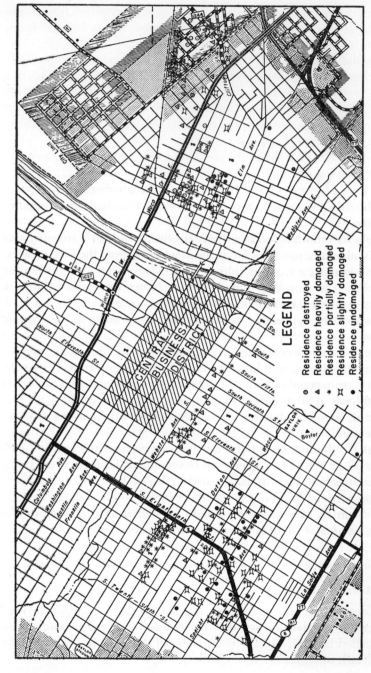

Fig. 1. Pathway of tornado and estimated damage to homes of sample families in Waco.

A spectator eight miles outside Waco saw a "monster" funnel, but stated, "It was so wide and the rain so heavy, it was impossible for anyone in the city to see the funnel approaching."[1]

Into the area swooped the tornado, dipping down into the Bell's Hill area on the southwestern flank of the city, bouncing along in a northeasterly direction, and then striking with full force in the very center of the business area. Coincidentally, the point of heaviest destruction from the tornado was the assumed target in case of enemy attack on the city.

In Waco the final death list contained 114 names. There were 145 others listed as having major injuries, and 952 with less serious ones. More than 2,000 families were reported to have suffered loss of some sort. About 2,000 automobiles were damaged, many of them demolished by falling debris. Fairly careful, but not exact, estimates place the number of homes destroyed at 150, with 250 others seriously damaged, and more than 450 damaged less seriously but requiring repairs. In the business area 196 buildings were classified as "demolished" or so severely damaged that they could not be repaired, and 376 others were placed on the "unsafe" list.

Estimates of damage to buildings and other material possessions run from $21 million to $36 million; total losses, including those resulting from deaths, injuries, unemployment, etc., run from $41 million to $63 million. Although no exact accounting can be made, a year later the consensus of those in position to know was that the total damage was approximately $51 million.

The downtown situation during the height of the storm was reported as difficult to believe even by those who witnessed it. Buildings, partly hidden by the driving rain, suddenly lifted and fell into the street in masses of splintered wood, bricks, and plaster; brick walls crumbled across parked automobiles; tons of plate glass flew through the air. Within seconds the former business district was a pile of rubble, its streets obliterated by debris. A survivor said, "I don't think the atom bomb could be any worse."[2]

---

[1] The research staff is happy to acknowledge its indebtedness to Dr. J. G. Brittain, of Harlingen, Texas, who made the tape recordings upon which *The Waco Tornado* (a mimeograph), a transcription of portions of the post-mortem discussions sponsored by the Director of Defense and Disaster Relief for Texas, is based. Throughout this chapter we have freely appropriated material from *The Waco Tornado* as well as from *The Waco Disaster* (Federal Civil Defense Administration, Southwestern Regional Office, Dallas, Texas, 1953). The staff assumes responsibility for the accuracy of all borrowed material.

[2] *The Waco Disaster.*

5

Persons in a fairly modern steel-frame building, whose foundation was securely tied to rock, watched, horror-stricken, as they saw an older building directly across the street collapse. The floors of this building were supported only by the walls. When a heavy water-tank on top of the structure blew off its foundation, it collapsed the roof. The roof collapsed the floor beneath it; that floor fell onto the next and so on until the whole building became a mass of rubble spilling across the street. Workers in another building reported that the roof was blown off with a "whoosh," and the front wall fell forward into the street as their building literally exploded. Buildings with skylights and large windows suffered only minor damage because the glass gave way to the intolerable pressure.

Damage varied from broken windows and twisted trees on the edge of town to the almost complete destruction of nearly two square miles of business houses in the high-value district of the city.

According to W. C. Connor, of the New Orleans Weather Bureau, who visited Waco and studied the wrecked buildings, the tornado funnel traveled from fifteen to twenty feet above ground, taking off second and third stories of buildings, but leaving the lower structures less severely damaged. Had it not been for this freak behavior, damage and loss of life would have been even more terrible. Here the tornado traversed the city, from southwest to northeast, a distance of some five miles, in comparison with a three-mile path through the Lake View residential area in San Angelo. This longer path, and the fact that it traversed the business district, made it inevitable that the loss would be much greater in Waco than in San Angelo.

Snapped telephone and electric lines added to the damage and made rescue work both slow and hazardous. Had heavy rain not followed the tornado, broken gas pipes and short-circuited electric wires would have set fires that would have greatly increased the loss of life and property.

The extent of damage to buildings depended largely upon their construction. The City Hall, the Amicable Building, and the Roosevelt Hotel, in the center of the tornado and adjacent to demolished buildings, received only minor damage. These are of modern concrete-and-steel construction. Most of the buildings nearby were older and were constructed of light sandy-clay bricks, with only the walls supporting the floors. Many of these buildings collapsed as the eye of the tornado created vacuums around them. What had been a business area became, in a matter of minutes, a scene of devastation, with dazed survivors unable to comprehend what had happened.

6

Army engineers expressed the opinion that the great majority of the casualties could have been avoided by as little as five minutes' warning, which would have given the victims time to take shelter in one of the modern steel-framed buildings that were within easy reach of all those in the downtown area and that came through the storm with only minor damage. They also said that death came almost instantly to most of those killed, judging from the crushed condition of the bodies.[3] Hence, more rapid rescue efforts and quicker medical attention likely would have been of no avail.

Survivors told harrowing tales of death and injury, as well as inspiring ones of heroism and sacrifice, among those who sought protection it was not possible to find. A newspaper picture shows a woman resolutely entering a wrecked building, in which her husband was trapped, while a group of men stand by in embarrassed and uncertain attitudes. But, all agreed, there was little panic. A few survivors wept hysterically, more appeared to be dazed and shocked, but the largest number began at once, and without direction, to dig at the ruins in an effort to reach those they could hear crying out from beneath the rubble or from within crushed automobiles. The immediate reaction seemed to be to attempt to put things aright again by using physical strength.

Most cases of severe emotional upset were of persons who knew that relatives or close friends were trapped, or who had seen them mutilated and killed. Social workers reported that, particularly after the first day, many came in for interviews, but "just sat," staring and expressionless. Those who never had asked for aid before seemed to have great difficulty in grasping the reality of their situation.[4]

Rescuers attacking the debris, which in some places reached a depth of nearly twenty feet and extended across the street, could hear cries and sometimes see bodies that might or might not be alive. In many cases rescue was effected quickly by removing superficial material; but when the sound of cries or of tapping came from the depths of rubble, would-be rescuers were helpless.

Traffic in the downtown area was immediately jammed. Persons attempting to enter it found their progress blocked by debris; survivors with cars that could be operated tried vainly to leave. Although police attempted to control traffic flow, they were unable to do so until a sufficient force of uniformed men had been recruited to man each street intersection in the area of heavy downtown damage.

[3] *Ibid.*   [4] *Ibid.*

For several days traffic management was one of the most difficult tasks faced by the authorities. The Chief of Police later asserted that traffic control and the maintenance of communications were the two most crucial problems in the early disaster situation.[5]

Bad as the traffic problem was, it almost certainly would have been worse had not the heavy rainfall and the failure of telephone communication prevented many people from learning of the tornado until several hours after it occurred. Many Waco residents received their first information of the disaster through their newspaper the morning following. The two radio stations went off the air, but both resumed broadcasting within less than two hours and performed most valuable services in relaying messages, ordering supplies for rescue workers, and giving news of the catastrophe to the outside world. "Ham" and military radio-station operators also performed brilliantly.

Because of the failure of power, radio, and telephone service, Waco citizens and officials alike were slow in learning what had happened. The Waco District Office of the Texas Highway Patrol received a report at 4:37 P.M. that a house in the southwestern portion of the city had been damaged by high wind and a few seconds later overheard a radio report from the local police that a second house also had suffered wind damage. A patrol car was dispatched to investigate. By 5:00 P.M. it was evident at the Highway Patrol offices that considerable damage had been done, though the location and extent of the storm were still not known. All patrol cars in the district were requested to report to Waco.

Almost simultaneous with the tornado, the switching equipment in the central downtown telephone office jammed, so that not even officials there knew what was happening until "a man came pounding at the door shouting that buildings were caving in." A telephone workman at once tapped lines to the radio stations to ask them to broadcast a plea for people not to use their telephones except in dire emergencies. Two employees then drove a mobile telephone car to the heart of the devastated area where they, with a mobile radio unit that arrived about the same time, became a communications center. Between 5:30 and 6:00 P.M. these mobile units were used for transmitting messages between the local police department and the Highway Patrol office. About six o'clock telephone communication was reestablished over one line, and this connection was held open until the jam on telephone switching equipment had been relieved.

[5] *The Waco Tornado.*

8

Luckily, an officer from nearby James Connally Air Force Base was in the downtown area when the tornado struck but was not injured. He succeeded in getting a telephone connection with the commanding officer of the base, who, after hurrying to the city to see for himself, dispatched another officer to the base with orders to bring ambulances, field kitchens, trucks, and heavy runway-building equipment, with necessary personnel, to aid in rescue operations. The base hospital was ordered to prepare for emergency cases and to set up operations to obtain blood for transfusions.

Air Force operations were hampered by lack of communications. Telephones were useless, of course, and Military Auxiliary Radio Service failed to function effectively. In the emergency, an attempt was made to establish a series of Air Police cars within sight of each other and to exchange messages between the city and the Air Force base by this means. But the Air Police cars could not get into the downtown area where the military command post was established. It was not until telephone service was restored about two hours later that effective communication was re-established. The military also had difficulty with "walkie-talkie" equipment. The batteries brought by Fort Hood, an Army tank base about sixty miles from Waco, were sufficiently different from those used by the Air Force as to be non-interchangeable. Rain put the batteries out of commission, making it necessary to send back to Fort Hood for new ones, as well as for new tubes. After communication was established with Fort Hood, additional personnel and heavy engineering equipment were sent in from there.[6]

Meanwhile, the Waco unit of the National Guard had been ordered into action. Men trained in first aid and rescue work searched the debris for bodies. Others were placed on police duty. A first-aid station was set up in the National Guard Armory. These military units joined forces with the police department of the city to guard exposed property, direct traffic, and rescue persons buried in the rubble. Though each unit at first worked independently, they brought about the first order in the chaotic situation.

In spite of the firm opinion of the Chief of Police that the primary duties of his men were the protection of property and traffic control, many officers yielded to the natural impulse to aid in rescue work and became members of loosely organized teams of mixed military and civilian persons.

[6] *Ibid.*

9

In the emergency many workers found themselves performing tasks for which they had no training. One person reported that he had been calling for and accepting offers of heavy machinery "... when I didn't know the difference between a front-end loader and a dragline. After it was over, I went around and looked at them to see what they are like." Nonetheless, it is reported that the man did an excellent job of securing and dispatching the machines requested.[7]

Partly because of the lack of communication facilities and partly, it would seem, because of inexperience, some responsible officials did not go into action promptly. The local Civil Defense organization had dedicated a control center less than a year previously, but it was not activated on the reasoning that, being on the edge of the city, it was too remote.

The previous August, a disastrous bus crash had given a test to Civil Defense forces. However, the director had later moved away, and his staff had been disbanded. A second director resigned after a few weeks, and the director at the time of the tornado, an insurance man, had received his appointment only on the preceding March 10, almost exactly eight weeks before the disaster. No urgency in reorganization had been felt, since citizens believed the city too small for A-bomb worries. The Mayor admitted to a general impression that Civil Defense and "ABC warfare" were too complicated for his town. He explained that efforts on the part of the Civil Defense Director to set up detailed plans had met with little success, though a "very nice organization had been set up on paper." This was true, he thought, because of lack of funds, because the plans were considered too elaborate, because nobody could get frightened at the prospect of an A-bomb's being dropped on the city, and because of a general lack of interest:

We hadn't been able to realize from a military point of view that we were in danger. When an enemy could attack Dallas, Fort Worth, or places down on the coast, we hadn't been able to visualize that enemy coming in here and attacking us with bombs. . . . We did realize the need in a disaster, but like so many others, we hadn't done anything about it much; we were all in the talking stage.[8]

The Civil Defense Director said:

Such organization as we had was strictly in the talking stage and on paper. Paper organization is a very dangerous thing because sometimes it

[7] *Ibid.*   [8] *The Waco Disaster.*

10

Cities in Crisis

leads people to believe there is an organization, when there actually isn't. The paper on . . . disaster organization . . . was old as well; so it was not a familiar thing. There was no organization.[9]

A banker explained the lack of a Civil Defense organization by pointing out that unless there is something to practice on, people will not go to a meeting every week or so. Several attempts had been made to activate a planning program, and a meeting of state, county, and city police officers had been held shortly before the disaster.

Aid requested directly from state officials in Austin was delayed until a check could be made with the district co-ordinator of Civil Defense—the district chief of the state police organization, whose office was on the outskirts of Waco.

Because of the lack of a single top headquarters or directing authority, chaotic conditions resulted during the first hours following the tornado. The National Guard commander, surveying the scene later, said, "There were thousands of persons milling around. It looked like the storming of the French Bastille." The next few paragraphs are abbreviated accounts of the actions and reactions of key officials in the city during those first few hours. They are given to show the situation as it existed during this critical period and, perhaps, the sort of situation that may be expected in other cities having a similar degree of preparation for similar crises. As an official later reported: "Little co-ordination between the many headquarters existed at first. Red Cross and other representatives, seeking someone in command, found nowhere to report." Or, as the Chief of Police put it more graphically: "For the first twenty-four hours we went around in circles in one direction; for the next twenty-four, we went around in circles in the other direction."

The Director of Civil Defense watched the tornado from an office in the Amicable Building. He was able to secure a telephone trunkline and immediately called the American Red Cross, the utility companies, the National Guard, and the State Co-ordinator of Civil Defense in Austin. In the excitement he forgot that the District Civil Defense Co-ordinator was at the state police headquarters in Waco and had teletype connections with Ausin. He reassured himself of the safety of his family by first telephoning and then by going home. Later he went to Red Cross headquarters, the blood bank, and Highway Patrol headquarters, where he conferred with the Mayor and Army engineers about 11:30 P.M. Still later in the night he joined

[9] *The Waco Tornado.*

11

others at disaster headquarters, first in the City Hall and later in the First National Bank quarters.

When the tornado struck, the Mayor was in his office in Baylor University Stadium, in the southwestern part of the city, about two blocks outside the path of the twister. He had a desk piled with work, and the telephone was quiet, so it was well past five o'clock when he made an effort to get in touch with anyone outside his office. He discovered his telephone was "dead" and left for home. After driving a few blocks, he came to an area of wrecked homes. He then went home, picked up his wife, and started out to see what had happened. When they arrived in the downtown area shortly before 7:00 P.M., traffic was so jammed that further progress by automobile was impossible, though persons in civilian clothing were vainly trying to direct traffic. The Mayor said that National Guardsmen, who had not had time to get into uniform and were attempting to direct traffic, were actually endangering their lives: "People get excited and, of course, they're curious and want to get down to the center of action. They don't pay much attention to anybody who is not in uniform. . . . But I would like to point out one thing and that is the public has a great deal of respect for a uniform and not much for anyone [else] who is trying to act in any official capacity; if he is in civilian clothes they will just run over him."[10]

The Mayor walked into the storm area; his wife returned home.

By this time, reported the Mayor, rescue operations were well under way, with heavy machinery moving debris while others worked by hand where it was thought there might be injured persons. Civilian contractors who owned needed machinery had brought it and had joined the military in operations on a voluntary basis.

The Mayor made his way to the City Hall, where he found police and other officials working without electric lights or telephone service. Communications at that time went by messengers, who could use automobiles for only part of the distances they had to travel. "The greatest lack was that of communications." This need was supplied during the early hours of the night by the restoration of telephone service, by police radio, and by mobile units furnished by the telephone company, the state police, and an electric co-operative, which sent in nine trucks equipped with two-way radio phones.

The Mayor checked at the Red Cross and Salvation Army canteens, the hospitals, and the funeral homes and found they were not over-

[10] *Ibid.*

12

whelmed. He then joined other leaders meeting about 11:30 P.M. at Highway Patrol headquarters on the outskirts of the city. Later in the night he conferred with the City Engineer, who was out of the city when the tornado struck but had returned immediately when he learned of it. A call was broadcast for engineers to come to the city to ascertain the safety of damaged buildings.

The City Manager was at his desk in the City Hall, over which the tornado swirled. Almost immediately, he reported, people from the wrecked buildings nearby began flooding the relatively undamaged City Hall, calling for doctors and other aid. As quickly as he could make his way through the crowd, he went to the police station in the same building, the only office with any communication facilities. He worked there with the police and others who came in until about 4:00 A.M., when he went home for a short time. Meanwhile, he had checked with his wife to see whether she was injured. She had not known anything unusual had occurred.

Civilian rescue "teams" were at first merely unorganized groups. Any member who lacked some article called out his need, and the request was picked up and amplified by loud-speaker trucks. From here it often went out over radio, connected to a state-wide hookup. As a result, roads were choked with assorted public and private conveyances bringing assistance, some needed and some not. An officer in command of some 18,000 soldiers was told, when he asked what aid he could supply, to "send everything you've got."[11] Fortunately, he did not take this demand literally and later discovered that no more than 200 of his men could actually be used to advantage.

The number of men needed decreased as the organization of workers into teams progressed. Intense, even frenzied, efforts of early rescue workers often lacked definite goals and still more often were not calculated to attain their purpose in the quickest or most effective manner. Later, the City Manager expressed the opinion that "in all probability, 5 men that were organized and knew who was in charge of what operation could produce better results than 20 men that were not organized. Therefore, we attempted to use organized groups."[12] He explained that for this reason unattached civilian personnel were worked in with military teams wherever possible. However, he also pointed out that a trained rescue team from Lake Worth and a group of organized steel workers from their trade union in Fort Worth did excellent work. Local labor unions and students from

[11] *The Waco Disaster.*   [12] *Ibid.*

13

Baylor University also formed effective teams. The lack of control over volunteer workmen was often dangerous, the City Engineer pointed out: "We had a lot of people working around and sometimes they were working on each other. In one spot we were trying to get a valve uncovered, but we had a heck of a time keeping others from throwing lumber down on top of us."[13]

The Chief of Police also emphasized the value of organized groups. He said that several nearby cities sent in groups of 8, 10, or 12 police officers with a leader and added: "We just talked to one man and told him what we needed most. Then we didn't have to think about those boys any more, because they went out there and got the job done."

Military workers brought organization to the rescue efforts by incorporating civilian workmen in their teams. By the second night these teams were commonly composed of 15 men under a leader and an assistant leader, with a walkie-talkie man to keep contact with headquarters and other nearby teams. Later, signs were put up showing the number of each team's area of operation so that trucks could be directed to those locations where debris was to be picked up. Previously, trucks had often waited in line at one site, while workmen were compelled to cease operations at another until accumulated rubble had been removed.

Gloves, essential for workmen handling broken glass and brick, became water-soaked and useless long before they were worn out. A downtown laundry met this problem by operating its drying equipment, not only for gloves, but for other clothing, so that such articles could be used each day.

The disaster destroyed the social organization of the city for a time. Lacking plan or direction, persons and groups moved in and tackled whatever problems they saw. Calls for supplies were broadcast and filled many times over—and needed to be filled again within a few hours. Rescue groups worked at cross-purposes. The immediate reaction was to "do something." Such a reaction probably served as much as a catharsis for the doers as it did as an aid in meeting the situation created by the destruction.

Co-ordination began to emerge at the meeting at state police headquarters, held shortly before midnight on the day of the disaster. The amazing outburst of energy on the part of officials and citizens began to be harnessed and controlled with results that brought praise from Civil Defense officials for the rapidity with which the situation

[13] *The Waco Tornado.*

was brought under control. Measures calculated to minimize danger and damage and to plan for rehabilitation were undertaken.

Discussing the preliminary meeting and the chaotic state of the city, the officer in charge of the state police in the area explained:

There came a time when somebody had to step out and say "We will wear the money." We finally organized a disaster committee, with the power to make the decisions and say "We got to do it one way or another; right or wrong, we got to do it this way." What finally boiled down was the Central Control Committee and they had, let's say, the authority to give or pass final judgment on any particular question. . . . No one man could do it all. Every man in a position of authority was intensely busy at the time. There had to be an organization that could operate in the new situation.[14]

Though a meeting had been held at the district office of the State Highway Patrol at 11:30 P.M. following the tornado, it was not until the next afternoon that an organization took shape. The Mayor later explained that he had not known that as the chief city official he was required to take charge. Realizing that there were, in his words, "better qualified" men to take over, he had side-stepped this responsibility. However, when the military insisted that they could act only on request and that the request must be initiated by the city, the Mayor reluctantly assumed authority. But this may not mean that the military actually did not exercise control. Later the Mayor commented:

The military people are a little bit modest in what they did, but I can tell you that if it hadn't been for the military, we would have been in a terrible shape—more so than we were. Don't let their modesty in telling you what they did have any effect on you. . . . They were invaluable help throughout this disaster from the very first.[15]

At an organizational meeting on the afternoon following the tornado, personnel work was assigned to the city manager, operations to the city engineer, and equipment and supplies to a man who had sold and serviced heavy-construction equipment. The city attorney was directed to work closely with the city manager and city engineer "in order that we might stay out of any lawsuits or legal entanglements that might result from unwise actions." State and city police and the local National Guard unit were asked to divide the patrol and property-protection work among themselves. The fire chief kept a close watch on some persons "who did not have tornado in-

[14] *Ibid.*   [15] *Ibid.*

15

surance but might have fire insurance. We wanted to be able to fight any accidental fires which might have started from broken gas mains."[16] The city and county health officer was placed in charge of health and sanitation measures, and an employee of the telephone company was asked to assume responsibility for restoring and maintaining communication facilities. In spite of the presence of many police officers, the force was not sufficient to give protection to merchandise, and the National Guard was assigned this task in large part.

The flood of donated supplies and equipment coming into Waco early provided a problem, for no provision had been made for a central place where such material could be received and dispatched to the points in need. The Chief of Police said many persons would call and offer types of equipment or even manpower and would be told to please come to Waco as quickly as possible, but "a little later they would call and tell us they couldn't get to a certain place in town or they couldn't get into the downtown area due to traffic congestion."[17]

As organization proceeded, three location points were set up at which personnel were to report, one on the north side of the devastated area, two on the south side. These check points greatly facilitated the use of volunteers. When a particular type of skill was needed, it was often found that a person with that skill was actually present at one of the points. Furthermore, this prevented a situation that had occurred several times: a person would volunteer for a particular type of work and be told he was not needed; later, when he was needed, those in charge of personnel were unable to locate him.

The absence of an effective organization during the first hours following the tornado was of particular concern to the commanders of nearby military posts. Although a military commander may initiate action in the case of a grave civilian emergency, he must at once inform his superior commander of what he has done and ask permission to proceed. Formal procedure requires the mayor of the stricken community to communicate with the governor, who in turn communicates with the commanding officer of the military area, who in his turn sends orders back down the line to the local commander. Military forces are to exercise no police power until the President has declared martial law. During an emergency period the military has authority only to aid in the saving of life and property. "As soon as

[16] *Ibid.*   [17] *Ibid.*

16

the rehabilitation phase commences, the Armed Forces aid must be withdrawn."[18]

In the case of the Waco disaster, military authorities at Fort Hood said they understood that the commanding general of the Fourth Army had been notified of the emergency and requested by the Governor to aid; hence, they had begun preparations for moving into the city. It was, however, 10:00 P.M. before authority to proceed was given and 11:30 when the first trucks with men and equipment got under way. They arrived between 3:00 and 4:00 A.M.

Speaking unofficially, a military authority commented: "For two hours from the time we received word that aid was needed here, we constantly added to, deleted, revised, and changed the make-up of the party and equipment to come up here, and even then, we went back and got additional stuff." The military complained that there was no area designated for their troops and equipment when they arrived:

Clear directions must come from somebody in charge. That is particularly true, if as the situation goes along, more critical areas are discovered and priority is given by taking people from one job and starting them on another. Therefore, there must be some central office which will govern that work. This is going to sound peculiar; but we do work only for you. It's necessary to satisfy the law. You ask us to do something and we will do everything we can to carry it out. But that request must come from somebody in authority.

Now in such operations, if you can tell us what you want, where it's to go, who is to meet us, give us a base in which to break up, marry up men and equipment, somebody to direct us, and tell us what to do, you will have no difficulty in getting assistance. Our assistance can get under way and begin efficient operation in as short a time as possible.[19]

By midnight police officers had fairly good control of traffic into and out of the devastated area, but not until two days later was a system of passes adopted that proved satisfactory.

The Air Force solved the problem of proper identification of persons and vehicles with permission to work within the restricted area by using wide strips of water-proof adhesive tape bearing numbers for each military team. This made it possible not only to identify the members but to separate them from the sight-seers. Paper passes were immediately printed—a pedestrian pass and a car pass—with the type of authorized activity specified. The 500 passes that at first

[18] *Ibid.*   [19] *Ibid.*

seemed sufficient grew to 1,000, and about 8,000 later became necessary. As the restricted area shrank, it was necessary to change the color of passes, as people with legitimate business in one area were found to be sight-seeing in others. Uniforms of any sort and official insignia on cars were usually honored without question, but in some instances public-utility workmen trying to close valves and restore essential services had difficulty moving about the area.

After control had been established, the most serious traffic problem came on the Sunday following the disaster, when it seemed that most of Texas arrived as sight-seers. Bumper-to-bumper for blocks, the cars attempted to get into the devastated area. Radio stations broadcast appeals throughout the day for persons to stay away from Waco but with no success. "It was worse than a football crowd," a tired police officer reported. "Airplanes buzzed over the ruins like buzzards, creating a sky-traffic jam." Many spectators broke through the cordon. The Chief of Police said the estimated 10,000 persons standing idly near the intersection of Fifth and Austin streets (where the greatest loss of life occurred) all but stopped the work in progress, since trucks were forced to "bull" their way through the crowds at a snail's pace. One police officer commented bitterly that it was practically impossible to get sight-seers out of the area. "Imagine having to take 5,000, 10,000 or 15,000 people by the hand and lead each one of them out individually. That is what you would have to do to get these people out once they had gotten in there."

Three Red Cross canteens were set up, at first mobile, later stationary, as supply trucks reached the heart of the town. Coffee and sandwiches were brought from the central kitchen. At no time was there any shortage of food; rather, an embarrassment of gifts poured in. A bank president, placed in charge of emergency welfare work, told of his difficulties:

One of the biggest problems we had was the food situation. It started rolling in and rolling in gradually from all over the state of Texas. If you stop to think about emergency food, what is the first thing you think about? When you think of food, if you're going to send it somewhere, it's sandwiches, isn't it? We had thousands of volunteers and the Army to whom we were trying to show our appreciation for the work they were doing. Well, they got fed up with sandwiches; so I finally got a report back that we were tired of sandwiches. If we could just have something to eat, it would help. We finally had to send out a call over the radio to ask the people to lay off the sandwiches for a while.[20]

[20] *Ibid.*

18

Proffered supplies were not confined to foods. Everything imaginable, it seemed, was offered in unlimited quantities. A city official confessed:

It may have been that some people phoned in, offered to give us assistance here in Waco, and they may have been told by someone, over long distance, that we didn't need any when in reality we did need it. But we were so disorganized that we didn't realize how much we needed. On the other hand, we had so much that we couldn't take care of what we had. It became embarrassing enough during the tornado having people call in and offering us things that we couldn't use. We regretted it very much, but it was embarrassing again to have to turn down some assistance that was offered.

So many and so varied supplies were sent into the stricken area that we really had the best mercantile store in Texas. Food supplies to canteens were regulated with the aim of keeping the supplies down to a point which would not interfere with the movement of the workers as happened in one or two feeding stations.[21]

More permanent kitchens also were set up, serving some 5,500 meals. About 600 persons were given shelter. Red Cross headquarters became a focus for food and clothing supplies which flowed in to such an extent that they threatened to crowd the workers out of their quarters. Finally, this agency asked radio stations to make no more appeals in its name.

This situation also had another side. Red Cross officials signed a purchase order for a city official for $700. Someone then ordered $4,500 worth of material from local merchants in the name of the Red Cross on the authority of the order. Two large vacuum jugs were sent to an unidentified recipient from the Veterans Administration Hospital nearby on an appeal in the name of the Red Cross. The agency paid in both cases to avoid ill will.

The Salvation Army in Waco was located well within the devastated downtown area, and fortunately the building was undamaged, except for a skylight. Four mobile canteens brought from other cities operated throughout the week of the tornado. In addition, meals were served continuously. Although no attempt was made to keep accurate accounts, it was estimated that more than 3,000 families were given food and clothing. An estimated $10,000 worth of groceries was distributed. No value was estimated for clothing, for appeals had brought such a staggering response that workers were al-

[21] *Ibid.*

most crowded out of the building. A full month after the tornado, shipments of clothing were still arriving for distribution by the Salvation Army. Although much of it was so badly worn it had to be sent to rag collectors, and other bundles required laundering (done free by local companies), there still remained a surplus of usable clothing.

Girls and boys sorted clothing, filled grocery bags, and helped to carry loads, while women drove automobiles, registered families, and prepared food. Some of the boys may have been a source of more confusion than assistance—one was discovered cavorting naked on a pile of clothing, amid cheers of comrades—but a great amount of work was accomplished. Clothing was sorted according to age, sex, type, and season, placed in boxes, and tagged for future use. After the disaster was over, some three tons of clothing remained on hand. This was made available to the various agencies in the city dealing with destitute families.

An unexpected need developed for bed linens and diapers. The storm hit on a Monday, catching many families with their washing on the line. One mother brought in a baby who had nothing left but the diaper he wore. At the same time, wet but undamaged sheets were being taken from rescue sites and thrown on the city dump, though laundries could have dried them easily.

No time was taken to certify applicants' qualifications for relief; all who sought food and clothing were given it, though workers estimated that a few recipients were not disaster victims. Even if their homes were not damaged, many of the poorer residents were put out of work when businesses were destroyed, and were cold and hungry, particularly since few people in this part of the country have proper clothing for a long spell of cold rain, authorities rationalized. Salvation Army workers recorded only the applicants' name, address, and size of family.

The Federal Civil Defense Administration was, of course, the federal agency most immediately concerned with the tornadoes of Waco and San Angelo. The activities of this agency are detailed in Chapter 3. However, various other federal agencies also made their services available.

The Reconstruction Finance Corporation set up headquarters for the purpose of making loans to aid in rehabilitation. The Small Defense Plants Administration sent in a liaison agent to advise plants having government contracts about the best way to get back into production and protect their contracts. The Department of Health, Education, and Welfare sent in several persons to work with local institutions. The Food and Drug Administration provided inspectors who helped protect food supplies and who also arranged for disposing of damaged food and drugs. The Public Health Service sent in workers to aid in the typhus-, rodent-, and insect-control measures.

The Bureau of Old Age and Survivors Insurance provided extra workers to take care of applications from survivors of those killed in the disaster. Some 70-odd of the 114 persons killed were insured. This unusually high percentage seems to be due to the fact that most of the victims were in the business district and were wage-earners rather than housewives or children. Staff members had secured names of the dead from funeral homes and had processed applications even before survivors appeared. Such promptness made it possible to make the first payments to survivors within a matter of two weeks.

The Office of Vocational Rehabilitation announced that some of the injured seemed eligible for assistance and aided in processing applications. The Bureau of Public Assistance worked through the Texas Department of Public Welfare in its public-assistance programs. Some three dozen employees of this state department were detached from their usual duties and put on disaster work.

The Surplus Property Utilization Division established a warehouse on the campus of Baylor University and operated it jointly with the state. From here lanterns, flashlights, ropes, and overcoats were distributed to rescue workers and other agencies.

At the request of Civil Defense authorities, the medical profession had prepared a fairly elaborate plan of action in case of disaster. Nursing teams had been designated for surgery and anesthesia, and locations for first-aid stations had been selected. When the disaster actually occurred, however, these plans were not acted upon, for here again communication was almost entirely lacking, and the emergency was met by physicians and other medical personnel going to the hospitals as they learned what had happened.[22]

A civilian medical authority said that, though there was no shortage of medical facilities, this was true more by accident than by plan. For example, he pointed out that the load on the hospitals could have been relieved tremendously had there been first-aid stations to

[22] This description of activities related to health is based almost wholly on *Waco Tornado*.

separate the seriously wounded from those not requiring immediate attention at the hospital, many of whom would not have required hospitalization at all.

Retail pharmacies and the medical corps of the military installations supplied narcotics and other drugs to first-aid stations and to hospitals as they were needed. A regional blood center in Waco had an ample supply of blood and blood plasma, but almost immediately after the tornado struck, persons began to queue up at the center and demand their blood be taken for use in the emergency. The same thing occurred at Connally Air Force Base nearby, and several cities rushed blood and blood plasma to the stricken city.

Sight-seers and those with no legitimate business in the area not only seriously hindered rescue operations; they also hampered the treatment of the injured in the hospitals. A "tremendous number" of people streamed into and through the hospitals, seeking families or friends they thought had been injured. As a medical person put it: "The hospitals became very quickly a sort of madhouse, with everybody running in to see what was happening. There was just no way to keep them out." Though it was realized that police had other duties which prevented their working with the hospital staff, he thought the city authorities should have delegated someone with law-enforcement power to control this "sight-seeing" traffic. "I don't suppose anyone ever counted how many sight-seers were there to see, but I imagine there were 5,000."

One authority said that a number of persons reporting to the hospital did not receive any attention for some time "because there were others who were much more serious. Of course, that is natural; they were taking care of the seriously injured and letting the minor injuries go." In spite of these difficulties, the medical fraternity was very proud of the fact that by one o'clock in the morning all persons brought to the hospital had been given preliminary treatment.

Of the 500 persons treated for relatively minor injuries and the 145 retained in hospitals for treatment, only one died. Several were dead on arrival or died in the hospital before treatment had progressed further than an initial examination. Physicians were relieved about the total absence of burns, since such an injury requires the services of eight to ten persons for proper treatment.

Except for being a short time without electric power, hospital facilities did not suffer. But word of the disaster did not get to the hospitals until victims began to arrive, just before 6:00 P.M. Then came a flood, not only of the injured, but of anxious friends and relatives seeking information. No attempt was made to get names or to make even a tentative diagnosis. Those in evident pain were given morphine, and this was indicated by adhesive tape attached to their foreheads.

Taxi- and ambulance-drivers took most of their injured to a downtown hospital, which was swamped before those at greater distance were filled. Still later, many injured, especially Negro patients, were taken to Connally Air Force Base Hospital some miles outside the city. The county medical society voted that no charge was to be made by any physician for treatment of victims. A Red Cross worker commented that this was unique in his experience.

In spite of grave dangers, no injuries more serious than blistered hands or pinched skin resulted from the rescue and demolition operations. The Mayor said he saw a steel beam fall within one foot of two workmen. This absence of injury was thought to be due largely to the fact that much of the work was done by military personnel and by civilians placed in crews directed by the military. But, also: "We were shot full of horseshoes all the way through. We sure were lucky. I guess the good Lord figured we were entitled to some good luck since we had so much bad luck."

The rumor spread that demolition work, with its use of bulldozers, "clam shells," and other heavy equipment, had resulted in the death of some persons trapped beneath the debris. Military authorities denied this. Their engineers reported that the rescue work could not have proceeded any faster with safety and would not have saved any lives even if it had been pushed to an extreme. As has already been pointed out, the condition of the bodies indicated that death had been practically instantaneous.

The City-County Health Office, like the hospitals, had no knowledge of the disaster until victims began to stream in. Only first aid could be administered there, for lack of facilities; but the health officer went to the hospitals and first-aid stations to check on the adequacy of supplies. He also checked the water system, the milk plants, and the slaughterhouses and found that they were not damaged, though they were without electricity for a time. He decided that the civilian food supply was reasonably safe. Supplies of perishable food in the disaster area were promptly distributed to Salvation Army and Red Cross canteens so that they would be used before they spoiled. Food-inspectors and nurses were dispatched to work with all food-dispensing agencies to make certain, insofar as was possible, that no contaminated or decayed food was used. One of their major tasks was the disposal of thousands of sandwiches before they became dangerous.

Only minor damage was sustained by the water and sewage lines, and those broken were sealed off temporarily. An early increase in flies and mosquitoes was combated by fog-spraying. Typhus-carrying rats were known to infest some of the wrecked buildings, but poisoned bait proved effective in preventing their invasion of other buildings.

The city-county health officer pointed out that one of his major problems was the spoilage of grain that had been made into feed-stuff and stored in buildings in the downtown area. It became water-soaked, spoiled, and formed breeding places for flies.

Hatcheries were a sanitary hazard of particular importance, since many chicks hatched immediately after the disaster and, though incubators were without electricity, some chicks continued to hatch for a week. The floors of wrecked hatcheries were soon inches deep in slimy water, dead and dying chickens, filth and flies, with owners not able to get to them to do anything about the situation.

But a month after the tornado, the health officer stated that he did not know of a single case of disease that could be attributed to the tornado.

To detail here the activities of all the numerous organizations active in Waco immediately following the tornado would carry this report into areas discussed elsewhere in this volume. It is sufficient to say that the American Red Cross, the Salvation Army, social-welfare agencies, hospitals, the medical profession, the various city departments, state and federal agencies, public-utility corporations, newspapers and radio stations, the Chamber of Commerce, the insurance companies, churches, and fraternal organizations—all moved into action with varying degrees of alacrity and all rendered services that drew praise from officials and the press.

But it must be noted that ordinary citizens working as volunteers furnished the manpower through which these organizations functioned. This matter of manpower was not without its problems, however. Many of those eager to serve did not have the required skills, and no organized means of utilizing the skills they did possess was in operation. The result was that many persons, skilled and unskilled, felt they were not allowed to make the contributions they were ready and eager to make. At first there were too many volunteers; later, too few. People rushed to the scene of rescue operations, found it already overcrowded, and returned home. Some twelve hours later, when the first volunteers were exhausted, the replacements were nowhere to be found.

At no time was there any surplus of volunteers in most of the specialized skills. Electricians, welders, heavy-equipment operators, and nurses were continually being sought.

Late in the week, when the military withdrew, a radio call for volunteers was made, giving the telephone number of a local milk company where contact could be made. The company was swamped and found it needed several telephones, registration desks, and information about the type of work, the type of clothing volunteers should wear, and other information. The telephone numbers and addresses of the volunteers were recorded and an attempt was made to employ as many as possible. There certainly was no lack of response on the part of the public generally; rather, the problem was to utilize the efforts of those who wanted to help.

If the social organization failed to meet the problem of using the manpower available in this crisis, it also failed in not having provided means for meeting other problems that arose a little later. In both instances, this failure seems to have resulted from an inability to foresee what would be required in such unusual and unplanned-for circumstances. How Waco and her sister in suffering, San Angelo, went about the task of re-establishing their social organizations and rebuilding their corporate lives is the more important consideration.

The Tornado and San Angelo

San Angelo was not without warning of the tornado that took 11 lives, injured 66 persons seriously, and left 1,700 homeless in the few minutes it swept across Lake View. About 320 homes had been totally destroyed, and 111 others so badly damaged that they could not be occupied until major repairs had been made; 88 more had been less seriously damaged, but required repair. Nineteen small businesses in the neighborhood were wrecked. The community school suffered damage estimated at just under $200,000. Almost 150 automobiles were smashed, though most were repaired later. The total cost, in terms of material possessions destroyed, was estimated at $3,123,000, plus an unascertainable loss in days of work missed, changes in occupation, and other such items not amenable to measurement.

Since the preceding afternoon the local weather bureau had issued warnings that conditions were favorable for storms and had continued these warnings through the day of the disaster. Explicit information on the approach of the tornado funnel was supplied by two

25

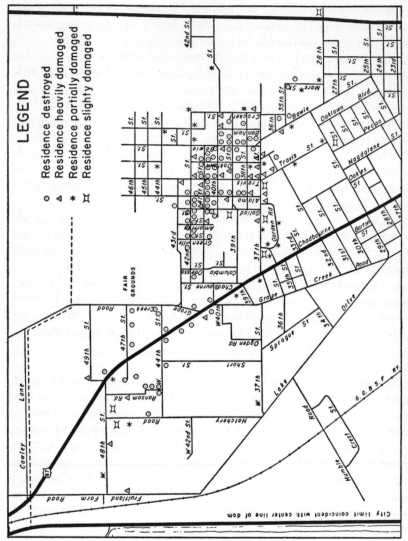

Fig. 2. Pathway of tornado and estimated damage to homes of sample families in San Angelo.

26

patrolmen of the Texas Department of Public Safety. These officers informed their San Angelo headquarters shortly after noon that they had sighted a funnel over Sterling City, forty-four miles to the northwest. Acting on instructions from the officer in charge at San Angelo, they had followed the funnel down the valley of the North Concho River as it approached San Angelo. They reported the forward speed as varying between 10 and 15 miles per hour. As the tornado and patrol car approached the city, the tornado changed direction, cutting across the highway less than a block behind the patrol car. The officers followed immediately behind the tornado into the area where it lowered and wrought such intense damage.

The San Angelo headquarters of the State Highway Patrol, meanwhile, had established connections with the local newspaper office in order to utilize the larger number of telephone trunk-lines available there. The newspaper, in turn, had warned the schools and the City Hall.

The funnel was not seen by most residents of the area it was to strike. Winds preceding the tornado proper had raised dust that limited vision severely. However, the overcast sky shortly before the storm struck gave some warning to those listening to the local radio station relay weather-bureau news.

During the ten minutes from 2:15 to 2:25 P.M., the funnel swept across the residential area, demolishing or severely damaging every building in a path about one-half mile wide and extending in a south-by-east direction through an occupied portion of the city—about three miles. Heavy hail and rain immediately followed the tornado, adding to suffering but effectively preventing the outbreak of fires from broken gas mains and electric lines.

Rescue efforts were under way almost immediately. The highway patrolmen who had followed the tornado into the area radioed their headquarters in the courthouse downtown and began seeking injured persons. Within a few minutes they left the scene with 2 dead bodies and later carried 12 injured to hospitals. Ambulances were on the scene within ten minutes. A city fire station well within the area of heavy damage and only about one block from the school got in contact with the central fire station by radio, and messages were relayed from that point to the police station, funeral homes, and other key points.

Because several hundred children were there, the Lake View School was the focus of immediate fear. However, school authorities, warned of the approach of the tornado, had ordered disaster drills.

Most of the children were gathered in hallways on the ground floor, and others crouched beneath desks; none were seriously hurt during the tornado. One child was cut by flying glass and another later stepped on a nail protruding from a board. The superintendent of the school was quoted by state Civil Defense officials as saying: "Had the Highway Patrol and the San Angelo Civil Defense organization not given me warning of the tornado's approach and had not my children been trained in safety drills which we immediately put into effect, 300 to 400 likely would have been injured or killed."

But the safety of the children was not known immediately, of course, and officials and anxiety-ridden parents converged on the school. As had been previously planned, the children, parents, and others were ordered to the community gymnasium, which served as a meeting and dispersal point.

The local unit of the National Guard assembled at the City Hall, and the first contingent of this force arrived in the disaster area about 3:15 P.M. At 3:20 the Mayor asked this military unit to assume command of operations in the devastated area. Troops from nearby Goodfellow Air Force Base arrived soon after news was received there at 2:35. The first contingent from this base brought three ambulances, carrying four physicians and four nurses, who immediately began work with civilian physicians and others in caring for the wounded. By four o'clock the Lake View School had been completely evacuated, and headquarters had been set up in the fire station to co-ordinate the rescue and protection efforts.

Casualties were sent to the three hospitals in the city, most of them going to the largest downtown unit. The hospitals had been alerted, and experienced no difficulty in handling the injured. However, friends and relatives seeking victims jammed the corridors of the large hospital, severely handicapping the movement of personnel and supplies for a time in the late afternoon.

By 5:00 P.M. supplies of clothing and blankets were on hand for distribution by American Red Cross and the Salvation Army, both of which had moved into the area and established facilities for food before six o'clock. Goodfellow Air Force Base supplied cots to the community gymnasium for the homeless, but so many offers of shelter were received from hotels, motels, owners of unoccupied rental property, and from families who shared their homes with victims that the cots were used only by relief and rescue workers. Field kitchens and personnel to operate them were supplied by the National Guard and Goodfellow Air Force Base in conjunction with the Red Cross.

28

Electric power and telephone service in the devastated area were unavailable, and commercial radio was not usable for the first few hours after the tornado. Communications were established through a radio network embracing the Police Department, the State Highway Patrol, the Fire Department, the sheriff's office, the Water Department, and the funeral homes. The National Guard unit used its own radio equipment.

Local and state police, firemen, and National Guardsmen set up patrols and made a systematic search of all ruins for dead or wounded during the night. So thorough was their work that only one injured person and one body were found the next day. Guards were stationed around the perimeter of the area, and persons without reasons acceptable to the guards were not allowed to enter. The following morning a formal system of passes was established.

At the local telephone-company office a special crew of switchmen and test-board operators was assigned to keep lines open for essential calls. Consequently, it was never impossible to get calls through to key personnel, except where cables or lines had been broken. Some 600 telephones in the storm area and some 6,000 in the city as a whole —of a total of 18,500—were silenced. Telephone communication with Goodfellow Air Force Base was interrupted about four o'clock, but radio was substituted.

The State Highway Department sent in 47 large trucks and 10 pick-up trucks, manned by 140 men, to aid in searching for victims and clearing away enough debris to permit the flow of traffic.

Plans for clearing out residential debris were put into operation also. A simple form was mimeographed, giving authority to the bearer to enter private property for clean-up purposes. The homeowner was asked to work with the authorities in sorting materials to be burned, salvaged, or hauled to a place of safekeeping. Open wells, many of which were being used for the domestic water supply, were chlorinated, and open toilets were filled. Dead animals were removed, and the entire area was fogged with disinfectant.

Two days after the tornado struck, it appeared that the emergency was under control, and the military forces were withdrawn.

As in Waco, one of the greatest handicaps to the persons working in the devastated area immediately following the disaster was the press of the morbidly curious. This became so serious that on the afternoon of the day following the disaster, a two-hour period was designated during which persons could drive through the area of demolition. The designated route was carefully guarded to prevent

29

persons or cars from leaving it. Between 5:00 and 7:00 P.M. it was estimated that about 2,400 automobiles and 10,000 persons toured the area.

Rehabilitation plans were begun on the day following the disaster. City officials took immediate steps to assure that the area would have facilities it had lacked in the past. The Salvation Army and American Red Cross continued their efforts to see that the victims had adequate food, clothing, and shelter for the immediate future, and the Red Cross began long-range planning with homeless families for restoration of their homes, health, and careers.

Donations began to pour into the city, and a committee was set up to receive them and to solicit others. This committee was composed of respected businessmen, serving under the chairmanship of Robert Carr, a well-known oil operator and philanthropist. Carr was chosen for the post not only because of his record of civic service and philanthropy but also because he had no business ties with the immediate community. It was thought, therefore, he would be in position to resist local pressures.

Goodfellow Air Force Base aided the local drive for funds for disaster victims by dropping ten thousand leaflets over the city, by using two sound-trucks to announce the campaign, and by supplying a band to provide music at a downtown street intersection during the concentrated drive.

San Angelo officials were positive in their belief that Civil Defense organization and drill greatly lessened the loss of life and hastened recovery. A simulated bombing attack had been staged in the city on Pearl Harbor Day, 1951. At that time it was assumed a school had been hit, and that all commercial communications facilities were rendered useless. All civilian and military organizations in the city that would be called on to function in a real emergency took part in the full-scale rehearsal.

This drill may have had an importance apart from its effectiveness in saving the lives of scores of school children. Although the devastation was much more complete in Lake View than in the residential area of Waco, for the total area struck by the tornado, the disorganization was not nearly so great. It seems logical to give some of the credit for this to the drill.

Other factors also entered in. Communications were not broken in San Angelo as in Waco; there was no time when messages could not be delivered by telephone or radio. City officials undertook emergency tasks almost immediately. The loss of life was much smaller.

All these factors, and perhaps others, worked to prevent the temporary lapse of governmental and other forms of social control, so that the picture presented by San Angelo is quite different from that shown by Waco. Just what weight should be given to the tighter Civil Defense organization in San Angelo, or to any other of the factors named, cannot be determined with any accuracy. But it is evident that in these two cities—well within a common cultural pattern—the meaning of the tornadoes, their effects, and the ways of meeting the crisis precipitated by them present widely different pictures.

2. Tornadoes Cost Money

Before the last body had been removed from the debris of wrecked Waco, plans were under way for rebuilding the economic life of the community. Most of the planning was by individuals owning or operating businesses in the devastated downtown area; but within a week architects had produced a plan to replace the dilapidated and unsightly structures facing the plaza in which the City Hall is located with an integrated and harmonious development. But Waco was not ready for such co-operative effort.

During its century-long existence, Waco had grown slowly, steadily, conservatively, almost effortlessly, as the market center for a rich cotton-producing and ranching territory. It showed no interest when opportunities were presented to secure more rail connections, manufacturing plants, or regional offices of nationwide corporations. Nonetheless, census surveys indicate that in 1947–48 there were more than 1,100 retail stores doing almost $100 million in business, 172 wholesalers with an annual business of $132 million, and 107 manufacturers who added some $60 million in value to the materials they worked. Chamber of Commerce estimates for 1952 were well above these figures, allowing an ample margin for growth. The local newspaper gave the city a trade territory of eleven counties, with more than 400,000 population.

Economists and journalists agree that Waco could have grown faster but did not do so because of the "Old South" economic conservatism of the controlling figures in the city. True, these were opposed, bitterly at times, by "Young Turks," who fought for more progressive policies. But the conflict produced little more than a division of opinion that found expression in political maneuvering and campaigning. The conservatives maintained control; Waco remained largely static until the Second World War forced prosperity on the community.

32

Even with the war-induced prosperity, reaction continued. There was opposition to the "waste of municipal funds" for employing a zoning specialist, for providing sewage lines to a new and undeveloped industrial area laid out to attract new businesses, to the building of a throughway to handle peak traffic loads, and to the requirement of more up-to-date plumbing and sewage facilities. One of the conservative leaders, who requested that he remain unidentified, asked: "Why should we pay $200,000 to run sewer lines to some vacant lots? The power company and other private utilities will do this because for them it's good business. That is no reason why the city government should spend the taxpayers' money to do the same thing."[1]

After the tornado this fundamental division made itself felt sharply at the political level. Once more a campaign was launched to change the form of municipal government and was supported by charges that city officials and their friends had failed to pay full and just property taxes and had gained other economic advantages unfairly. In less than a year after the tornado, the Mayor at that time had resigned his office and later left the city.

It must be emphasized that this controversy was not created by the tornado. Rather, the tornado and rehabilitation efforts were used to resurrect a fight that had been going on for some time. But before this took place, Waco had its shining hour in which all factions and all persons rose to magnificent performance to meet the emergency caused by the tornado.

For a short time, the ancient fault line that had for so long divided the citizens of Waco was cemented by overwhelming and unifying emotions of fear, anxiety, sympathy, and fellowship. However, the division soon reappeared in complaints that the military rescue workers did as much damage as had the storm by pulling down sound walls in their haste to search the rubble for victims, that the attempts of the city administration to enforce the building code were detrimental and unfair to those who suffered damage to their property, that the new tax-evaluation study which had been proposed, and resisted for several years, was discriminatory, and in other complaints. From the other side came charges that some of the businesses and

[1] Information about the economic situation of Waco was obtained from *Sales Management*, Vol. 662, No. 10 (May 10), 1951; *Editor and Publisher's Market Guide*, Vol. 28 (1952); U.S. Bureau of the Census, *Census of Business: 1948* and *Census of Manufactures: 1947* (Washington, D.C., Government Printing Office); J. Walstein Smith, "Which Way Waco?" (Waco, School of Business, Baylor University, 1952), *Baylor Business Studies*, No. 11, p. 19.

property-owners in the disaster area were sabotaging efforts to create a more modern community out of the chaos brought by the tornado by repairing the damaged buildings as cheaply as possible in order to re-create the same type of low-rent business area that existed before the storm. No regard was given, it was sometimes said, to plans developed for replacing the old with a well-planned business area. Such remarks as the following were sometimes heard with regard to the hastily repaired buildings: "I wouldn't enter some of these buildings. They are deathtraps in which the walls and roofs are liable to collapse at any time."

But the situation within the community was, in the last analysis, not the most telling factor in the rehabilitation of Waco. Perhaps no city, certainly not this one, could have faced such losses and survived if it had not been for the generous outpouring of aid from throughout the nation. And nowhere was this more evident than in the "hard-headed, nonsentimental business affairs."

Sjoberg has called attention to the increasing importance of extra-community influences in modern urban areas.[2] Chapin has also commented that "one of the perplexities of modern urban living is how to trace the threads of social relations through the close knit fabric of political and economic institutions. Where government leaves off and business begins is difficult to decide."[3] Firey adds:

An ever larger sector of community planning has been appropriated by agencies which lie outside of any given community and whose plans implicate a great many other communities. Thus, from the standpoint of a given community, a great many plans, often quite heterogeneous and even contradictory, emanate from remote bureaucratic agencies and converge upon that community.[4]

This condition is seen specifically in the disaster situations studied in this report.

Communities, like persons, do not live alone. They have interconnections and interrelationships with like units within the region and within the nation, so that what affects the community also affects the nation to some extent. Conversely, units outside the community—

[2] Gideon Sjoberg, "Urban Community Theory and Research: A Partial Evaluation," *American Journal of Economics and Sociology*, Vol. 14, No. 1 (January, 1955).

[3] F. Stuart Chapin, *Contemporary American Institutions* (New York, Harper & Brothers, 1955), pp. 10–11.

[4] Walter I. Firey, "Grenzen als factoren in der Gemeinderplaung," *Soziale Welt*, Vol. 5 (1954), pp. 114–21.

TABLE 1

Personal and Property Damage from the Waco Tornado

Personal

114	persons killed
145	persons with major injuries
952	persons with minor injuries
141	persons hospitalized
150	homes destroyed
250	homes with major damage
450	homes with minor damage
2,000	automobiles demolished or damaged

Business

196	buildings destroyed
376	buildings damaged beyond safety point

Institutions

7	churches damaged
1	college damaged

Municipal and County Public Property

Fire-alarm and signal system severely damaged
Streets, gutters, curbs, and sidewalks damaged
Bridge, twisted and damaged
Sewer lines clogged
Several buildings with minor damage
Farmer's Market demolished
Parks and swimming pool damaged
6 public schools damaged

Estimate of Dollar Value of Damage
 (by Federal Civil Defense Administration)

$23,500,000	businesses and buildings
700,000	utilities
700,000	public property
3,000,000	residential property
10,000,000	business inventories
600,000	household furnishings
1,000,000	automobiles
1,200,000	rescue and debris removal cost
2,500,000	business and employment loss
7,400,000	monetary value of lives lost
400,000	injuries
$51,000,000	Total

35

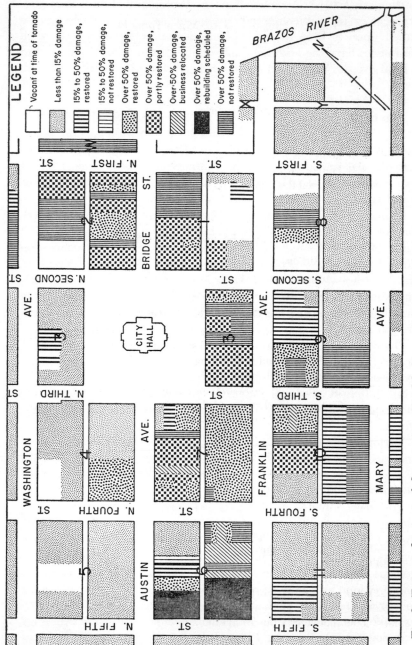

Fig. 3. Estimated extent of damage in central business district, Waco.

36

particularly where the connections are formal and strong, as in government or in multicommunity public-utility corporations—can be called upon to help in case of an emergency. Economically, such businesses have the additional advantage that any losses incurred in a local disaster may be spread over the various communities served.

The tornado struck at 4:35 P.M. on Monday, May 11, 1953. Normally the month of May is relatively busy, but Mondays, in Waco, are not the days of peak business activity. The time of day of the tornado was unfortunate for the business area, but, since it meant that no children were in the schools that were in its path, the time could have been much worse.

Damage to the downtown business area was somewhat scattered. One of the largest independent retail outlets in the city, located at Fifth and Austin streets, collapsed, causing the greatest concentration of fatalities. Except for the area around Austin and Franklin, and Fourth and Fifth streets, the area of concentrated physical damage was not to property in the center of the business district, but to buildings surrounding the city square, the business center of a generation ago.

Damage included loss of life and personal injury; collapse of all, or parts, of buildings; damage to utility facilities; destruction of automobiles by the storm or falling rubble; inventory loss occasioned by wind, falling debris, and water; loss of employment and sales; and the expenditure of effort on emergency tasks occasioned by the storm.

Various estimates have been made regarding the amount of damage caused by the tornado. The list of damages as shown in Table 1 is approximately an average of the estimate where several were available.

Loss data depicted by Figure 3 were primarily obtained by rapid estimates made by the University of Texas group. For the most part, the people of Waco were exceedingly co-operative and sought in any way possible to aid in creating an accurate report. However, this general attitude did not extend to the discussion of the amount of damage done to business property. Since the owners were unwilling to provide estimates of the percentage of damage, it was necessary to make such estimates by observing the condition of the buildings.

A point emphasized by Figure 3 is that modern methods of construction have greater resistance to stress and strain than do earlier techniques. Thus, there are buildings that received relatively small damage, while the surrounding ones were virtually demolished.

Storm destruction resulted in some businesses' re-establishing themselves in new areas. This occurred mostly in the transitional area between the business center and fringe. The usual pattern within the business center was to replace the old buildings with improved and modernized buildings or to use the space, at least temporarily, for parking lots. The pattern in the fringe area, on the other hand, was to return as quickly as possible to the conditions that prevailed before the storm. In many cases, buildings with partial damage received modern new fronts, but the intention was not primarily to provide a different type of building for a different type of business or to cater to a different type of clientele. The effect on the area suffering the greatest damage is thus somewhat mixed.

The reconstruction of business houses in the vicinity of the City Hall was slowed by two primary considerations. This oldest part of the city, as is often the case, had been occupied by businesses operating on a low margin of profit and thereby attracting customers from the lower economic levels. Property-owners faced two problems: If they rebuilt in accordance with a new and more stringent building code, could they expect to retain their tenants or attract others at the necessarily increased rentals? If "The Square" was rebuilt in more attractive form, would the shoppers who had used it continue to come there, or would they feel they could find better bargains in other shopping centers? Perhaps both questions can better be posed as one: Could the area change its character and retain its economic well-being?

Most of the buildings were old and deteriorated. Where there was more than one floor, the upper stories often were not being used. One building was in the process of being demolished at the time of the tornado to make room for a parking lot. Owners were understandably concerned over increasing or even replacing their investments in the area.

Perhaps as a rationalization, it was also argued that to change the character of the area would be a distinct disservice to the persons who customarily shopped there. It was pointed out that since most of these shoppers had only a minimum to spend, they needed a shopping center where overhead costs were as low as possible. Reconstruction on an expensive scale would increase the cost of serving these people and would increase the cost of living for those least able to afford it; therefore, repairs should be kept at a minimum and the appearance of the district be changed as little as possible. Indeed, in an effort to restore the buildings to usable condition as quickly and cheaply as possible and to resume receiving revenue from them, many of the two-storied buildings in this area were reconstructed

TABLE 2

Outside Funds Aiding Waco Economic Rehabilitation

Source		Amount
Federal government under Public Law 875		$ 212,945*
Other governmental aid:		
Social Security payments per month . . .	$ 4,500	
Unemployment claims	1,500	
National Guard payroll and equipment . .	19,200	
Army and Air Force	175,000	
Texas Highway Department	15,400	
Texas State Department of Health	2,000	
Total	. . . .	217,600
American Red Cross		382,091*
Private donations administered by the Waco Disaster Fund†		420,000*
Other sources:		
Property insurance claims payments . . .	$7,785,900	
Other insurance	700,000	
Church donations	42,400	
Salvation Army	15,000	
Fraternal and business organizations . . .	17,000	
Investments by outside interests	120,000	
Total	. . . .	8,680,300
Grand Total		$9,912,936

*Details of these amounts given elsewhere in this report.
† Estimates only. Final breakdown of expenditures of Waco Disaster Fund Committee had not been made in June, 1956.

with one floor only. Thus, several buildings now have walls consisting, in part, of new materials superimposed on the old sandy clay bricks, held together with lime mortar. The inadequacy of such construction was pointed up in a news item in the *Waco Times-Herald* for May 15, 1953:

The casualty list of Waco's tornado would have been slashed 90 per cent if the demolished and damaged buildings had been constructed under strict construction inspections based on a modern, rigid building code, Col. H.

Tumin of the U. S. Corps of Engineers said here today after completing a building-by-building survey of the damage. "Many of the buildings appear to be 100 years old, whether they were built that long ago or not. Construction methods used date them. There are no load-bearing walls . . ., no tie-in trusses to hold the walls together, no steel, no reinforced concrete. Most are just brick shells with a roof and floors stuck into the piles of brick."

Attempts to enforce a rigid modern building code while many of the damaged buildings were being repaired were not wholly successful. Consequently, there is some concern over the sometimes overly economical manner in which repairs were made.

One important factor in the rapid economic recovery was the availability of funds from outside sources. The Red Cross, the Waco Disaster Relief Fund, Reconstruction Finance Corporation loans, and insurance settlements provided some of the funds that allowed damaged establishments to return to normal operations. Funds supplied by the Federal Civil Defense Administration greatly aided the repair of municipal facilities.

Outside capital also aided in the rebuilding of the city. One bank made available as much as $5 million to be used for loans in reconstructing damaged buildings, and other banks offered to finance repairs and rebuilding operations. Without such funds, the recovery would have been considerably slower, and some firms which promptly resumed operations would have been unable to recover at all. A summary of funds available for reconstruction is found in Table 2.

Commercial Agencies in Disaster

If disaster consists essentially of the disruption of the social fabric, then it follows that rehabilitation consists primarily of the resumption of activities as nearly normal as possible. Governmental efforts usually are directed at the more "human" tasks: rescue, the recovery of bodies, maintenance of discipline, providing creature comforts, and, later, the reconstruction of necessary public facilities. As regards public utilities, government and privately owned facilities come into much the same area of activity.

In the Waco disaster, governmental agencies performed the heroic task of rescue and the removal of most of the debris resulting from the collapse of buildings. However, the job of restoring public-utility services, communication facilities, and of providing much of the expendable material used by rescue workers fell upon private enterprise. The reconstruction of buildings, both commercial and residential, also fell upon private owners after the emergency period was over and rehabilitation work began.

Gas, electricity, transportation, and communication are essential to the functioning of the modern large community. They are commonly supplied by privately owned utilities, or, in the case of government-owned facilities, through operations somewhat apart from other governmental activities. Usually monopolistic, they have no fear of competition within their own communities. Often, also, they are tied in with systems that supply the same services to many communities within the region, or, as in the case of the telephone corporations, throughout the nation. This extracommunity affiliation serves to set apart such utilities from the ordinary businesses of a community— businesses such as the neighborhood drugstore or the grocery store. Although some department stores belong to regional or nationwide chains, such businesses are looked upon as being "local" in most instances. Their extracommunity affiliations tend to give to agencies representing the federal government, regional or nationwide utility corporations, and similar organizations a universalistic philosophy as opposed to the more particularistic approach of the purely local businessman.[5]

This multicommunity character of utility corporations is valuable in case of emergency, for a ready supply of workmen from other communities can be rushed to a stricken one. This is true because the work is so highly standardized that the experience of a workman in one community fits him to work in any other community served by his corporation. The techniques, procedures, and materials are likely to be identical or very similar. Furthermore, such workmen may very probably have been shifted from community to community by their corporation and so have come to know the slight variations found in procedures or materials.

One other advantage utility workers have in disaster situations is their experience in dealing with minor emergencies. Since hailstorms, high winds, floods, and other destructive natural phenomena very often interfere with the smooth functioning of public utilities, workmen are trained to meet such crises. Hence, when they are called upon to cope with a major disaster, their very considerable training stands them in good stead.

These factors add up to a social structure in which the workmen become efficient bureaucrats devoted to their jobs and to seeing that

[5] See Richard T. LaPiere, *A Theory of Social Control* (New York, McGraw-Hill Book Company, Inc., 1954), pp. 307–308.

the job is done in the prescribed manner rather than having their attention distracted by extrajob or extracorporation factors or even, to a great extent, by relationships with the persons, families, or communities they are serving.

So thorough had been the training of employees of the gas company serving Waco that no men were called in from outside. All company employees were immediately put to work on an emergency basis, cutting off lines, inspecting meters, making sure that valves operated, and restoring the flow of gas through mains found to be safe.

The multicommunity electric corporation supplying power to Waco, foreseeing the need for disaster planning, had drawn up a detailed plan to be used in case of a major calamity. This plan was put into operation immediately and seems to have worked excellently. For example, without any specific authorization from the company, one man quickly made a purchase of $4,000 worth of raincoats for linemen. This was one of the things he had been instructed to do when and if the emergency plan went into operation. Some persons immediately bought flashlights and other critical materials. Others placed emergency generators at strategic points to take care of such places as freezing and cold-storage plants and hospitals.

The immediate task, of course, was to make sure that live wires were not exposed. Workmen traced the major lines throughout the affected areas, and as soon as the emergency had been taken care of, began restoration of service.

Foreseeing that living space for the local men plus a large number of outside workers might not be available in an emergency, this company had also prepared for meals, bedding, shower facilities, and had stocked clothing to be passed out to the workmen. One truck was assigned to supply the working crews with hot coffee, sandwiches, cigarettes, and chewing gum.

These two utilities and the telephone and telegraph corporations are examples of how local agencies operate under the control of municipal authorities and under a legally defined authority within their own system as well. Employees of such a system are commonly recognized as having a high degree of autonomy, so when they appear and go about their work, few, if any, questions are asked by either municipal authorities or the citizens. Their quasi-legal governmental status permits such activities as breaking pavement, digging ditches across streets, and removing branches or whole trees where they interfere with power lines. Accustomed to working in public and with a quasi-public authority, these corporations and their workmen met the situation in Waco promptly and effectively. In fact, it appears that they maintained their social organization more effectively than did the municipal government or other agencies of the city. Because of their more effective organization, they were also largely self-directing. The agency rather than the government made the decision as to what should be done, which area should be serviced first, and how this was to be done.

The bureaucratic features characteristic of multicommunity corporations also apply to military organization and may go far toward explaining the effectiveness with which the military meets emergencies.

The orientation and activities of other businesses, particularly of retail outlets, were in direct contrast to those of the public utilities discussed. In some there was immediate activity following the tornado. Several merchants, for example, remained in their stores or reopened them for the express purpose of supplying materials needed by rescue workers. One merchant in the heart of the disaster section later presented a claim to the Waco Disaster Fund Committee for some $4,000 worth of work clothing he had handed out during the rescue period. Other merchants supplied large numbers of flashlights. Hardware stores distributed all sorts of tools, and any materials needed by rescue workers were either given by stores or were freely appropriated from them.

However, there are critical differences between such actions by retail outlets and those of the utility corporations. None of the retailers demanded or even asked for any assurance that the materials they distributed so freely would be paid for by the persons receiving them or by any agency, governmental or private. Thus, they were not following their ordinary goal of selling goods for a profit, nor were they continuing, or preparing to resume, their normal activities. Rather, they were operating in the role of citizens aiding citizens in an effort to meet a grave emergency. Further, most of these merchants were later denied access to their places of business until rescue operations had been fairly well completed.

Once the emergency period had passed and the merchants had regained possession of their locations, there remained the long task of restoring their businesses. This was impossible for those whose buildings had been utterly wrecked either by the tornado or, as in some instances, by rescue operations. Such apparent misfortune was not always an economic loss to the operators. Some of the old build-

43

ings destroyed by the tornado were of such a character or in such disrepair that the owners actually profited by having them leveled in this fashion rather than by having to pay wreckers to do the job.

Changes in land use and in the structure of damaged buildings also occurred, particularly in the Square area. In general, heavily damaged two-story constructions were rebuilt with but one level. Several taller buildings destroyed by the storm were not rebuilt; their sites became parking lots. However, of fourteen known cases, six relocated within the downtown area, and eight moved farther from the center of town. The over-all pattern of land use changed little, however. It was evident that businesses with unusual architectural structures—theaters, hotels, and factories, for example—would find it most difficult to relocate. Without exception, buildings of these types were repaired and utilized in the previous way.

The problems confronting the commercial agencies of Waco were largely defined by their relationships with governmental and corporate social structures. The speed, ease, and effectiveness with which rehabilitation was accomplished were determined primarily by these relationships. In general, those having close integration in larger units, and with more bureaucratic structures, fared better than the independent units forced to depend on their own local resources.

Personal funds played a predominant part in the reconstruction of homes in both cities. How large a part such funds played in the reconstruction of commercial property in Waco is not known. Returns from a sample of families interviewed show that 69.5 per cent of the respondents whose homes were rebuilt or repaired said they had financed this work from their own resources. In San Angelo this proportion was 44.3 per cent. Banks, savings and loan associations, federal agencies, construction firms, and individuals also made available funds for reconstruction. But, apart from personal funds, the most frequently used source was the American Red Cross and the local disaster-relief committees.

While there is no possible means of depreciating the remarkable efforts made by the people of Waco on their own behalf, it must also be pointed out that these efforts were aided to a considerable extent by voluntary contributions of funds and labor from sources outside the community:

1. Relief funds exceeding $400,000 came into the community. Almost half of this amount was used directly for the rehabilitation of businesses destroyed or badly damaged.
2. Some of the buildings destroyed or damaged had deteriorated to

44

the point that they would have been replaced in any case. In such instances, destruction by the tornado and subsequent removal of the rubble by military and other forces simply saved the landlord the expense of this operation.

3. In some instances, insurance payments were of greater value to the landlord than the damaged property had been prior to disaster. This was particularly true where it was desired to use the space for other purposes.

4. Volunteer workmen, using equipment largely supplied by the military or other outside organizations, donated well over 20,000 man-days of labor. Much of this was aided by heavy equipment loaned to the community and operated by persons not residents of the city. Certainly the value of such work ran into hundreds of thousands of dollars.

5. Some firms were spurred by the disaster into moving to locations that allowed an increase in business and in prices and profits because of the higher economic level of their customers. This, of course, does not apply to all the damaged businesses. Many of them were of such a character that they neither could move nor could have benefited by the move had they been able to do so.

Measuring the Economic Blow

In spite of generous aid, it is obvious that the destruction of property to the extent present in Waco and San Angelo and the disruption of business in Waco presented most severe problems of rehabilitation. The economic fabric of the city was disrupted no less than the social fabric. Hence, one of our tasks was to find sensitive indices of the economic dislocation and rehabilitation. We selected, largely on the basis of availability, employment, numbers of business establishments, and retail sales. Information on these was readily obtainable through the co-operation of the Texas Employment Commission and the Bureau of Business Research of the University of Texas. The *Waco Times-Herald* carried much data on economic activities following the tornadoes, and this source was also utilized.

Much of the material on economic change appears in the form of percentages of change rather than totals. This form seems better for our purposes than gross figures since it is the change that is important for an understanding of what happened.

The year 1953 was not one of great prosperity in Texas. In fact, indices of business activity show a steady, though not drastic, decline for the entire year. Hence, when information is presented indicating that certain business or economic activities lessened during that part of the year following the tornado, the likelihood should always be kept in mind that there would have been some lessening regardless of the disaster.

The economic situation in San Angelo, unlike that of the state as a whole, appeared to be improving in the spring of 1953, primarily owing to good rains that had interrupted a five-year drought. The increased economic activity and higher prosperity level following the rains did much to mask any possible effect of the disaster on the economic life of this community.

Since tornado damage in San Angelo was estimated between $3 million to $4 million, it was expected that there would be a considerable in-migration of workers, primarily in the construction trades. Some increase in construction employment did occur but not so much as had been expected. Repair work was very active, but it appears that much of it was done in addition to regular employment on other jobs and that much of it was done by friends, relatives, or owners of damaged, but not destroyed, dwellings. Similarly, utility workers stayed on the job longer and increased their income through overtime by repairing disrupted facilities. Official records, however, did not show this as additional employment.

Although the Texas Employment Commission office in San Angelo offered to co-operate with other agencies to facilitate recovery, it reported later that it had been called upon for very few additional workmen. Similarly, it had few persons filing unemployment-insurance claims.

Since the evidence in terms of all the indices is negative so far as San Angelo is concerned, it appears that in the case of this community the economic disaster was important on a family rather than a community basis. Unfortunately, these aspects were largely covered up or smoothed out in the statistics available.

The situation in Waco was entirely different. In evaluating recovery there, it is important to remember that some 8,000 outside persons were added to the number of those working immediately following the tornado. About 7,200 of these were soldiers from nearby military installations. Utility companies brought in more than 600 others and the State Highway Department and the State Highway Patrol supplied somewhere in the neighborhood of 200 more. These workers not only engaged in rescue activities but with their heavy machinery cleared the downtown area of rubble in approximately one week's time. This was a tremendous accomplishment. Without

46

this aid, the economic rehabilitation of Waco would have been much delayed and would have been far more costly to the property-owners and to the community through its municipal government than it was.

Employment in Waco shows a clear effect of the tornado. The Waco office of the Texas Employment Commission maintains an unpublished forecast of expected employment and unemployment that normally is exceedingly accurate. Its prognostication for May and June—made prior to the disaster—was far from the actual development in those months. Table 3 shows the pretornado forecast for May and June as these figures were predicted and actually reported.

TABLE 3

Forecast and Actual Employment, Waco, 1953

Type	May		June	
	Number Forecast	Number Reported	Number Forecast	Number Reported
Total nonagricultural labor force	45,361	44,895	46,560	45,615
Nonagricultural unemployment .	2,100	3,300	2,400	2,900
Nonagricultural employment . .	43,261	41,595	44,160	42,715
Per cent of nonagricultural labor force unemployed . . .	4.6	7.4	5.3	6.4

Source: Files of Texas Employment Commission.

Thus, presumably because of the tornado, the Waco nonagricultural labor force was 446 lower than estimated for May, and, even with the smaller force, there were 1,200 more workers unemployed than had been forecast for May. It may be estimated, therefore, that had the storm not occurred there would have been approximately 1,666 more workers employed in May. Similar figures for June show the actual labor force to have been 945 below the estimate and the number unemployed to have been 500 more than forecast. Therefore, on the basis of the Texas Employment Commission estimate for June, it appears there would normally have been 1,445 more workers employed.

Several of the larger firms that suffered damage carried work-stoppage insurance; consequently, an unknown number of workers who were in fact not on the job were reported as employed, since their income was not disrupted. It is also apparent that a consider-

47

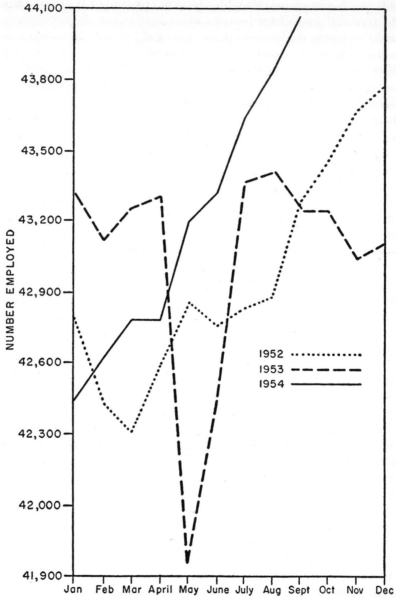

Fig. 4. Impact of tornado on employment in Waco.

able number of persons withdrew from the labor market shortly after the tornado, presumably persons who found it necessary to work at home repairing damage or taking care of the injured rather than to remain employed or seek employment that would bring in cash. The diverting of workers from their normal tasks to those that would have been unnecessary but for the tornado also had its effect upon employment, though the number of persons employed by firms and government agencies devoted to rehabilitation and rebuilding in the disaster area diminished steadily during the year of this study.

Several factors account for the rapid return to normal levels of employment, one being the shift of a part of the labor force from nonagricultural to agricultural employment. The rains accompanying the tornado caused increased agricultural activity in the area surrounding Waco. Because of the five-year drought in the area, the use of agricultural labor had been considerably reduced, and the replanting and increased farm activity resulting from the rains increased the need for agricultural workers who would not have been employed otherwise. Another factor is the speed with which some of the damaged businesses moved to permanent or temporary locations outside the disaster area.

The general pattern, of course, does not apply to employment in construction. It had been predicted that this industry would drop several hundred employees in May or June. On the contrary, there was such an increase that the net difference between the prediction and the actuality was about 1,200 persons, many of whom may have come from the 1,400-odd unemployed who formerly had worked in manufacturing. This seems highly possible in view of the fact that 24 manufacturing plants and 40 major retail establishments were put out of business by the tornado. Although the number of jobs available in construction increased by more than 40 per cent during the month of the tornado, the local labor supply was adequate. Since a great many construction workers entered the labor market in Waco, not all of those seeking work in construction were able to find it.

As was to be expected, employment continued its upward trend through June and July and into August, the peak employment month. However, contrary to predictions, employment declined steadily after August. The expected activity in construction and trade did not continue, and this raises the possibility—perhaps the probability—that the tornado had effects less obvious but more lasting on the economic life of Waco than have been recognized. This implication was clear in December—traditionally the busiest month for trade in the cotton area—when retail store sales were off 11 per cent from the year preceding. It may be of particular pertinence that sales by automobile agencies were off 22 per cent for this period.

The economic condition also manifested itself in the number of persons seeking employment. In May, the labor force in Waco underwent a drastic drop of about 1,700 persons, but 1,100 were added in June and another 1,000 in July, bringing the total above that of the previous year and above the pretornado number.[6]

The effect of the tornado on the employment picture in Waco is shown graphically in Figure 4. The very dramatic drop in employment in May, 1953, is clearly shown in contrast to the fairly even trend of employment in May of 1952 and 1954. But perhaps the most important aspect shown by the graph is the decline in employment beginning after July and continuing until December, 1953, when there is a slight reversal. This decline is in distinct and startling contrast to the trends of the year before and the year after the tornado.

In Waco, normally about 4.2 per cent of the total labor force had been unemployed. In May, 1953, this figure rose to 6.5 per cent, an increase of more than 50 per cent. In April it had been anticipated that there would be some decrease in employment in May, June, and July, but the actual drop was about 1,500 greater than had been predicted. For example, in manufacturing employment, where it had been expected that there would be an increase of 264 employed in May, there actually was a decrease of 1,204. In June and July the percentage of unemployed dropped so that by August it was at about its usual level.

Unemployment-insurance claims in May rose to more than 250, but even this number was much smaller than had been expected, for there had been an increase in the unemployed of 1,200 or more and a drop in the labor force of 400 or more. This indicates that about 1,000 persons who were entitled to unemployment insurance did not enter claims. About 1,500 textile workers were thrown out of employment by the tornado, most of whom were women. It is tempting to speculate that many of the 1,000 persons who did not seek unemployment insurance were these workers, who employed themselves in their homes rather than in the labor market. At any rate, it is evident that unemployment insurance was not utilized by the stricken community as fully as might be expected.

[6] These and other figures on employment, the labor force, and the number of business establishments were taken from records of the Texas Employment Commission and the Bureau of Business Research, University of Texas.

Data on the number of business establishments operating are another index to the general state of economic prosperity of any community. As might be expected, the number of construction contractors in Waco greatly increased immediately following the tornado. However, the raw figures cannot be accepted, for a large federal construction contract had been finished in April, and apparently many employees formerly on that job became contractors.

In the construction industry the initial demand was for roofers and carpenters rather than for general-construction workers. Interpreted, this means that repair, rather than reconstruction, accounts for most of the initial activity. Furthermore, the boom in building that had logically been predicted following the tornado did not develop. The Texas Employment Commission Labor Market Report for July stated: "A surplus of housing is causing rents and sales prices to be reduced." Some building-owners reported that they planned to defer reconstruction until 1954 in order to obtain income-tax savings which the delay would make possible.

The number of both retail and wholesale establishments dropped greatly in May, but in July there was a sharp rise in the number of retail stores. The number of wholesale stores rose more slowly; in neither case did the number rise to the pretornado level until near the end of the year. In the manufacturing industry, the plants for nondurable goods seem to have suffered much more than did those for durable goods.

The effects of the disaster upon plants manufacturing nondurable goods stands out as an extreme case in the employment picture. In this industry the number of workers employed in the early part of 1953 was just short of 5,500. The May tornado plummeted this figure to 4,068, a decrease of 27 per cent. But during the July–October period the number climbed to 5,786. During the last two months of 1953, employment in this category dropped once more, but only to 5,472. It seems reasonable to say that the rise to slightly more than average employment represents the satisfaction of demands accumulated during the May–June period, when plants and goods were not available. The 98 establishments in this category at the time of the tornado dropped to 75 in May, went up to 84 in June, and to 99 in July.

Retail employment also showed a dramatic change. An initial drop of 10 per cent in the number of retail workers occurred immediately after the tornado. Figures for June through October were from 5 to 6 per cent below normal employment, with a slight upswing in December to 96 per cent of normal. Employment apparently had been increased in anticipation of business that did not materialize.

On the whole, it may be said that finance, insurance, real estate, food and related products, and retail trade in general recovered rapidly. Plants manufacturing durable goods, wholesale trade, and business and personal services recovered more slowly. Medical and professional services, transportation, and contract construction were most definitely stimulated by the disaster. Increases in these categories served to mask to some extent the general slump in the number of business establishments when taken as a whole.

One of the best illustrations of the ability of the business community and the consumers of Waco to overcome some of the worst effects of the disaster in a minimum period of time is provided by the retail-sales index published by the Bureau of Business Research of the University of Texas. The normal seasonal trend of retail sales for Waco (and the state as a whole) is to reach a peak in May and to experience a substantial drop in June. Presumably as a result of the tornado, Waco sales dropped 3 per cent in May, 1953, from those of the previous month and 12 per cent from those of May, 1952. June, on the other hand, showed a rise of 1 per cent over May, 1953, and 12 per cent over June, 1952. The 12-per-cent drop in sales in May, 1953, from those of the same month of the previous year, followed by a 12-per-cent rise in June over those of the same month of the previous year, indicates that neither the usual May peak nor the June decline occurred in 1953. Instead, sales for the two months remained rather steady and reached approximately the same average for the two months that they would have reached had the normal peak and drop occurred.

Bargain sales in several of the older and larger stores about June 1 met with extraordinary response. One merchant was jubilant: "It's like the Saturday before Christmas." Others reported they were forced to close their doors and admit only as many customers as their salespeople could handle.

These special sales, in addition to the more numerous salvage sales of damaged stocks—and some merchandise brought into the city for the occasion—released the pent-up buying power accumulated by the forced closing of many retail stores during the latter part of May, and may have played a large part in the rapid recovery of retail business. The immediate recovery is also due in large part to the fact that the business area undergoing the greatest damage was a part of the area in which income is spent, not made. Had the tornado

caused greater disruption of the income-producing areas of the city
—for instance, the industrial area—normal consumer purchasing-
power would not have been available, and the business area as a
whole would have suffered more, in terms of sales, than it did. Data
gathered and published by the Bureau of Business Research indicate,
also, that the ratio of credit sales to total sales was not appreciably
affected by the tornado. However, the rate of collections on out-

TABLE 4

Business Trends, Waco, 1953

Categories	Percentage			
	April	May	June	July–Dec.
Employment*				
Durable-goods manufacturing . .	109	112	112	111
Nondurable-goods manufacturing .	97	74	83	103
Retail trade	101	91	97	98
Wholesale trade	103	92	95	99
Business establishments*				
Durable-goods manufacturing . .	86	82	83	86
Nondurable-goods manufacturing .	94	72	80	94
Retail trade	95	89	90	94
Wholesale trade	90	83	84	86

* January–March average equals 100 per cent.
Source: Records of the Texas Employment Commission and the Bureau of
Business Research, University of Texas.

standing debts dipped in May, normally a month of above-average
collections.

Medical and professional services show a rather startling effect of
the tornado. During May, there was an increase of 90 establishments
in this category, making a total of 390, and an increase of about 100
in number of those employed, suggesting that of these, from 80 to 90
were professional persons. For the June–August period, there was an
additional increase of about 460 workers. Although the increase in
employment is small compared to the approximate 5,500 in this category, it occurred at a time when a drop in the number employed was
expected and when there was an actual drop of 5 in the number of
establishments. This seems to indicate a direct connection with the
tornado.

There is another aspect of the employment picture that must be considered. The evidence is strong that in both wholesale and retail business the small operators suffered more than did the large ones. The percentage of loss is greater in the number of establishments than in the number of employees. However, in retail trade, this effect was reversed by late summer, and thereafter percentage losses in

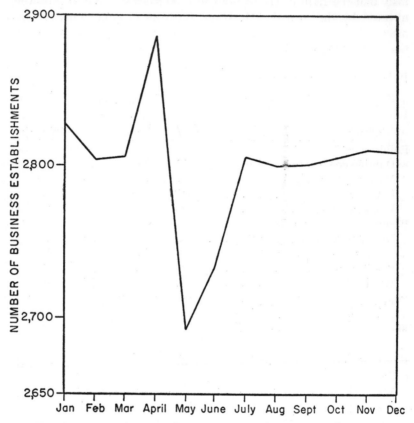

Fig. 5. Impact of tornado on number of businesses in Waco.

number of employees exceeded those in number of businesses. In May, 60 business and personal-service establishments closed. About 15 reopened during or after June. The change in number of employees strongly suggests that the 45 businesses that did not reopen were small and that most of them had been operated by their owners. This hypothesis is supported by data shown in Table 4 and Figure 5. It will be noted here that the index of the number of establishments is consistently lower than the index of employment, indicating that more persons were being employed by a smaller number of establishments. The employment figures more clearly reflect the disruption caused by the tornado. After July, employment appeared to have recovered to a large extent, returning almost to the pre-April level for the last half of the year, but business establishments failed to recover fully from the April and May decline. Apparently a new employee-to-business ratio developed. Those businesses that opened in and after July appear to have absorbed all or most of those out of work because of closed establishments.

Building Permits as an Index to Recovery

Building permits, employment figures, statistics on the number of businesses, and the volume of business would seem to be the best indices to physical and economic recovery. They give a fairly complete, if not wholly accurate, picture of the economic consequences and rehabilitation of a modern community recovering from a disaster.

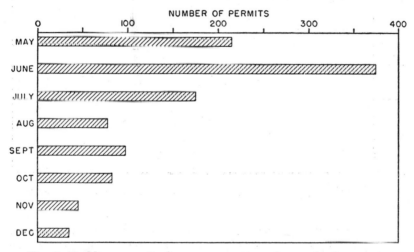

Fig. 6. Building permits for reconstruction of tornado damage in Waco, 1953.

Fortunately, data on building permits are easily available in almost every city, and an examination of these records offers answers to important questions. For example, to what extent would the normal construction in a community be affected after a disaster? Would it drop below the expected level for the time necessary to replace disaster damage, or would there be a greater effect? It might be supposed that the reconstruction of damaged business establishments would occur more rapidly than the reconstruction of residential areas, and that the highest-class white residential areas would rebuild at a more rapid rate than the lower-class areas.

In both Waco and San Angelo every effort was made to get reconstruction under way as rapidly as possible. In San Angelo, the city government announced that no fee would be charged for issuing building permits. In Waco, the city announced that persons working on repairs of storm damage could obtain building permits at a later date, though it later amended the statement to read that "temporary

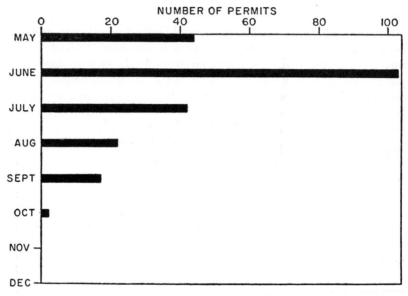

Fig. 7. Building permits for reconstruction of tornado damage in San Angelo, 1953.

repairs for safety reasons may be done without a building permit, but . . . all other jobs should not be started until a building permit is issued by the city inspector." This had the effect of suspending the operation of the building-permit system for about three weeks following the tornado.

In San Angelo, we secured data on the issuance of building permits directly from the file at the City Hall; in Waco, it was feasible to accept these data as reported in the *Waco Times-Herald*. In both cities we considered all permits for construction within a clearly delineated area as the results of the disaster, a practice that undoubtedly introduced some error. However, in San Angelo practically every building within the tornado pathway was wrecked or damaged. In Waco, much of the tornado area was an old part of the city in which it seemed likely there would be but little new construction. Some of the families whose homes were destroyed unquestionably rebuilt in other parts of the city, but what distortion of the picture may result from this relocation may in part be offset by the fact that construction within the affected area was sometimes new or better than before.

In San Angelo, the last disaster permit was issued during the twenty-first week after the tornado. In Waco, building in the devastated area continued through the year, and our figures cover the period from the time of the tornado until December 19, 1953. During the period for which we have data for San Angelo, 230 disaster permits were issued, with a total value of $797,058. It was estimated that about 320 homes had been destroyed or badly damaged. A discrepancy of 90 between the number of permits issued and the number of homes damaged indicates that much of the repair work was done without the formality of securing a permit or that some of the buildings were not replaced. It is known that a few of the dwellings in the area were not replaced. When rebuilding was done by members of the family and by their friends, the owner most likely did not consider it essential to secure a permit.

The rate of rehabilitation is indicated by the fact that by July 25—eleven weeks after the tornado—80.8 per cent of the rebuilding permits had been issued, and these represented 84.9 per cent of the total value of all the disaster permits issued. During this period, permits issued for reconstruction of residential properties amounted to $606,400. This gives a mean of $2,732 per residence repaired or reconstructed. In addition, 8 permits issued for business establishments within the area amounted to $190,658.

A detailed analysis of the rebuilding situation in Waco may be obtained from Tables 3 and 4. It is sufficient to note here that it was not until the third week following the disaster that rebuilding—as indicated by the issuance of building permits—really got under way, and that rebuilding was most intense during the four weeks following that time. After the first month and a half, the rate of building fell off rapidly, but there were occasional spurts later on during the period studied. The over-all picture is one of intense activity beginning less than a month after the disaster, reaching its height rapidly, and then slowly dissipating. Tables 5 and 6 test the reliability of the idea that disaster will so depress normal construction patterns within a community that such construction will be postponed until the reconstruction necessary to enable the community to resume its essential basic activities has been completed.

TABLE 5

Deviations from Expected Trends in the Number of Building Permits Issued in San Angelo after the Tornado

	1952	1953				1954
Month	No. Permits Issued	Estimated Normal No.*	No. Nondisaster Permits	No. Disaster Permits	Actual No. Issued	No. Permits Issued
May	109	113	132	44	176	117
June	193	150	84	103	187	107
July	153	138	121	42	163	123
Aug.	150	174	121	22	143	197
Sept.	120	132	114	17	131	144
Oct.	129	136	135	2	137	142
Nov.	84	113	104	0	104	142
Dec.	88	89	127	0	127	89
Total	1,026	1,045	938	230	1,168	1,061

* The normal number of permits that could have been expected to be issued in 1953 was 1,045, a figure obtained by averaging the 1952 and 1954 monthly figures of permits issued. Actually, 123 more permits were issued than were estimated, and 105 fewer nondisaster permits than were estimated for 1953.

Sources: University of Texas Bureau of Business Research and records in San Angelo City Hall.

In order to get an estimate of the number of building permits that might normally have been expected in 1953, we averaged the monthly number of permits for 1952 and 1954 in the belief that any effect of the disaster had been entirely dissipated by 1954. This appears to have been a more accurate assumption in the case of San Angelo than Waco, for in San Angelo, no disaster permits were issued in November or December, whereas this is not true for Waco. Hence, to the extent that disaster-caused construction was still going on in Waco during 1954, our estimate is in error. San Angelo issued a total of 1,168 building permits during the period from May through December, 1953. It had been estimated that the number would be 1,045. This seems to indicate that the tornado increased the amount of building in San Angelo for this period by 123 buildings. However, of the total number of permits issued, 230 were disaster permits. The logical conclusion, then, is that the tornado had the net effect of reducing the amount of normal construction by approximately 100 residential buildings, if we consider all disaster permits as essential replacements only. It is to be noted that beginning in September the number of permits actually issued falls very close to the number estimated, except for the final month of the year, when for some unknown reason 38 more were issued than had been predicted.

TABLE 6

Deviations from Expected Trends in the Number of Building Permits Issued in Waco after the Tornado

	1952		1953				1954
Month	No. Permits Issued	Estimated Normal No.*	No. Nondisaster Permits	No. Disaster Permits	Actual No. Issued		No. Permits Issued
May	344	261	200	215	415		177
June	178	221	255	374	629		264
July	185	243	172	176	348		301
Aug.	205	206	177	78	255		200
Sept.	226	251	191	97	288		276
Oct.	223	237	154	82	236		250
Nov.	181	189	121	46	167		197
Dec.	155	160	114	34	148		164
Total	1,697	1,768	1,384	1,102	2,486		1,829

* The normal number of permits that could have been expected to be issued in 1953 was 1,768, a figure obtained by averaging the 1952 and 1954 monthly figures of permits issued. There were 718 more permits issued than were estimated, and 384 fewer nondisaster permits than were estimated for 1953.

Sources: University of Texas Bureau of Business Research and the public-notices section of the *Waco Times-Herald*.

This discrepancy of 105 between the annual number of permits estimated and the number issued for normal construction in San Angelo is somewhat puzzling. Many of the disaster permits were issued for homes rebuilt with funds supplied by the local disaster-relief fund and American Red Cross. There also was more than the usual amount of money in the community because of insurance payments, federal aid, and the general prosperity resulting from the construction financed from donations and the increase in trade due to the replacing of furnishings. It would be expected, then, that once emergency construction had lessened, normal construction would have risen to the expected height or perhaps beyond. This did not occur.

One of the hidden costs of the disaster is the 105 buildings that would have been constructed but were not, apparently because of the tornado.

Building in Waco presents a similar pattern. During the period from May to December, 1953, the estimated number of building permits was 1,768; actually, however, 2,486 building permits were issued —718 more than was expected. The number of nondisaster building permits was 1,384—384 fewer than would have been expected had it not been for the tornado. After the number of disaster permits began to drop, normal construction approached, but did not reach, the expected level. It will be noted from Table 6 that in May, June, and

TABLE 7

Number and Value of Building Permits Issued, 1952–54

	1952		1953		1954	
	Permits	*Value*	*Permits*	*Value*	*Permits*	*Value*
San Angelo	1,698	$ 5,587,818	1,634	$ 5,472,710	1,608	$ 8,333,301
Waco	3,072	12,178,308	3,425	11,249,325	2,660	14,562,306

July immediately following the tornado, more disaster permits were issued than normal ones. That is, during these months most of the construction in Waco was an attempt at rapid rehabilitation.

Table 7 shows that in both Waco and San Angelo the total value of construction as measured by permits issued was considerably lower for the year of the tornadoes than for either the preceding or following year.

The conclusion is that normal construction patterns were depressed at least for the remainder of the year in which the disaster occurred. Whether this depression lasted only long enough to replace tornado damage, or whether it had a permanent effect is hard to determine, though the evidence in San Angelo certainly supports the latter condition.

In order to get at differentials in rehabilitation in various types of urban areas, the path of the tornado in Waco was divided into five districts (see Table 8 and Fig. 8). Waco only was used in testing this notion since in San Angelo all the damage occurred in a residential area of remarkable homogeneity. Area I is a Negro residential section of some 50 blocks. The mean value of homes in that area was placed by the U.S. Census in 1950 at $5,720. There were 117 disaster permits issued for this area, with a total value of $116,781, or a mean value of $998 per repair or reconstruction job.

Area II is a section occupied by white families living in homes with a mean value of $4,303. In this district 183 disaster permits were issued, having a total value of $199,778, or a mean value of $1,092. It will be noted that this area has a definitely lower value than Area I but that the reconstruction permits averaged slightly higher. This may or may not be due to a difference in the ability of whites and Negroes to finance rehabilitation.

Area III is the business district, some 51 blocks. Here 296 disaster permits were issued, with a total value of $1,533,689, or a mean value of $5,181.

Area IV is a Caucasian-Negro area. The mean value of residence units in this area was $3,868. Here 220 disaster permits were issued, with a total value of $219,464, or a mean value of $998.

Area V is a white section with a wide range of economic levels but containing some of the better homes of the city. In this area 286 disaster permits were issued, with a total value of $236,910, or an average of $828.

Table 8 shows the varying rates at which reconstruction proceeded in the five areas. Although all the permits accumulated during the first three weeks following the tornado are accredited to the third week in Table 8, it is notable that in Area III—the business district— 29 per cent of all the permits issued during the year for that area were issued in this period. This is a much higher initial percentage than in any of the other four areas.

Although the business area jumped into an immediate lead in its reconstruction, Area V—which is the residential area of highest economic value and in which damage from the tornado was lightest as compared with other areas—was also quite active the fourth week. This area had taken out a higher percentage of the total number of permits it was to receive during the year than any other of the five, and in the sixth week it passed the 50 per cent mark. At that time Area I and Area IV were also slightly ahead of the business district in the percentage of total reconstruction under way. Thus, it appears that in the business area those firms entirely sure of their plans went into action at once, whereas others—for any number of possible reasons—proceeded more slowly, with the result that the rate of reconstruction within the business area slackened after its fast start.

An indication of the relationship of economic level to the rapidity

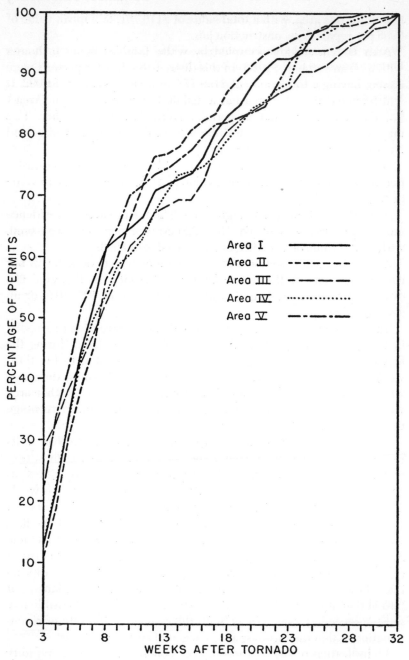

Fig. 8. Rates of reconstruction by socio-economic areas, Waco.

62

TABLE 8

Weekly and Cumulative Percentages of the Total Number of Disaster Permits Issued in Each Area in Waco, May 25 to December 19, 1953

Weeks after Tornado	Area I		Area II		Area III		Area IV		Area V	
3	12.8*	12.8†	10.9*	10.9†	29.0*	29.0†	13.2*	13.2†	22.7*	22.7†
4	9.4	22.2	8.2	19.1	3.7	32.7	8.6	21.8	11.2	33.9
5	11.9	34.1	11.4	30.5	5.7	38.4	11.4	33.2	7.7	41.6
6	10.3	44.4	7.7	38.2	4.7	43.1	10.9	44.1	10.1	51.7
7	7.7	52.1	7.1	45.3	4.1	47.2	5.9	50.0	4.5	56.2
8	9.4	61.5	10.9	56.2	5.4	52.6	3.6	53.6	5.2	61.4
9	1.7	63.2	3.8	60.0	4.4	57.0	5.0	58.6	3.5	64.9
10	1.7	64.9	6.0	66.0	5.1	62.1	1.8	60.4	5.2	70.1
11	1.7	66.6	5.5	71.5	1.7	63.8	2.7	63.1	1.7	71.8
12	4.3	70.9	4.9	76.4	3.7	67.5	4.1	67.2	1.7	73.5
13	0.9	71.8	0.5	76.9	1.0	68.5	3.6	70.8	1.0	74.5
14	0.9	72.7	1.1	78.0	1.0	69.5	2.7	73.5	1.4	75.9
15	0.9	73.6	2.7	80.7	1.0	69.5	0.5	74.0	1.7	77.6
16	2.6	76.2	1.6	82.3	3.0	72.5	0.9	74.9	2.4	80.0
17	4.3	80.5	1.1	83.4	5.7	78.2	1.8	76.7	1.7	81.7
18	2.6	83.1	3.8	87.2	2.7	80.9	2.7	79.4	0.3	82.0
19	1.7	84.8	2.2	89.4	1.7	82.6	2.3	81.7	1.0	83.0
20	3.4	88.2	2.2	91.6	1.4	84.0	2.7	84.4	0.7	83.7
21	2.6	90.8	1.6	93.2	1.4	85.4	0.9	85.3	1.0	84.7
22	1.7	92.5	1.1	94.3	1.4	86.8	2.3	87.6	3.5	88.2
23	0.0	92.5	1.1	95.4	1.0	87.8	0.9	88.5	3.8	92.0
24	0.9	93.4	1.1	96.5	2.7	90.5	6.4	94.9	2.1	94.1
25	3.4	96.8	0.5	97.0	0.0	90.5	0.5	95.4	0.0	94.1
26	0.9	97.7	1.1	98.1	1.0	91.5	1.4	96.8	0.0	94.1
27	1.7	99.4	0.0	98.1	1.7	93.2	0.9	97.7	0.3	94.4
28	0.0	99.4	0.0	98.1	1.7	94.9	0.9	98.6	1.4	95.8
29	0.9	100.3	0.5	98.6	1.0	95.9	0.9	99.5	0.7	96.5
30	0.0	100.3	0.5	99.1	1.7	97.6	0.5	100.0	1.7	98.2
31	0.0	100.3	0.5	99.6	0.3	97.9	0.0	100.0	1.0	99.2
32	0.0	100.3	0.0	99.6	1.0	98.9	0.0	100.0	0.0	99.2
Total	100.3		99.6		98.9		100.0		99.2	
Total Permits	117		183		296		220		286	

* Percentage of permits by week.
† Cumulative percentage by week.
Source: Waco Times-Herald.

of reconstruction of homes is revealed in the significant differences between the percentages of permits issued for Area II—lower-class homes—and those for Area V—a mixed section containing some of the higher-value homes of the city. During the first portion of the period studied, the higher-level district led. This means that the less prosperous district had postponed its reconstruction activity so that, percentagewise, it was crowded into the latter weeks of the period.

When Area I, occupied largely by Negroes, was compared with Area V in an effort to get at any significance of racial differences, the

TABLE 9

Weekly and Cumulative Percentages of Residential Disaster Permits and Their Value: San Angelo, May 14 to September 28, 1953

Weeks after Tornado	Number of Permits	Percentage of Permits by Week	Cumulative Percentage by Week	Value of Permits	Percentage of Total Value by Week	Cumulative Percentage by Week
1	4	1.8	1.8	$ 6,290	1.0	1.0
2	13	5.9	7.7	37,400	6.2	7.2
3	25	11.2	18.9	71,500	11.8	19.0
4	23	10.4	29.3	62,650	10.3	29.3
5	23	10.4	39.7	68,646	11.3	40.6
6	31	14.0	53.7	91,525	15.1	55.7
7	18	8.1	61.8	50,796	8.4	64.1
8	13	5.9	67.7	35,335	5.8	69.9
9	10	4.5	72.2	38,002	6.3	76.2
10	13	5.9	78.1	43,150	7.1	83.3
11	6	2.7	80.8	9,690	1.6	84.9
12	5	2.3	83.1	11,735	1.9	86.8
13	5	5.0	88.1	27,240	4.5	91.3
14	3	1.4	89.5	4,250	0.7	92.0
15	5	2.3	91.8	15,300	2.5	94.5
16	3	1.4	93.2	3,350	0.6	95.1
17	2	0.9	94.1	775	0.1	95.2
18	5	2.3	96.4	13,866	2.3	97.5
19	6	2.7	99.1	8,400	1.4	98.9
20	2	0.9	100.0	3,500	0.6	99.5
21	1	0.5	100.5	3,000	0.5	100.0
Total	222	100.5		$606,400	100.0	

Source: Building permits on file in the San Angelo City Hall.

64

rates of reconstruction were not sufficiently different to meet tests of significance.

A study of Table 8 does not give conclusive evidence about the net result of reconstruction, but the indication is that the business area and the residential area of highest economic level were the areas of the most rapid physical recovery.

This analysis of building permits supports the conclusion that the disasters seriously depressed the construction industry in San Angelo and Waco in spite of a boom immediately following the catastrophes; or, it may be, they delayed the construction of many homes for at least a year.

What general conclusions emerge from this analysis of statistics related to the economic life of these two communities in distress? Although there obviously was serious economic displacement, this effect is not always clearly attributable to the tornadoes. Official statistics did not give the precise measurement needed to assign definite causal effects to the storms. This indefiniteness raises an interesting question: Are such statistics an accurate means of studying the economic effects of disasters such as these? Since the statistics presumably reflect the general level of prosperity of a city, and since employing them fails to indicate any appreciable effect of the disaster in San Angelo and only inconclusive effects in many areas in Waco, the answer seems to be that they are not.

The statistics reflect general prosperity in the form of economic activity. Normally the correlation between economic activity and the prosperity level would seem to be almost perfect. But in disaster situations it is apparent that much economic activity is nonproductive. It merely brings the economic apparatus back to its state before the disaster. Hence, such activity is a result of the disaster, not of normal creative economic forces. In the two cities studied, for example, bank loans increased, real estate sales were stimulated, and construction boomed for a time. These activities increased the rate of flow of money in the economy, provided jobs, and resulted in indices that bespeak a healthy, prosperous economic situation. But there is still the fact that Waco suffered an economic loss of $50 million or more; that San Angelo was poorer from $2.5 million to $3 million. These losses do not show in the indices of business activity. On the contrary, the losses themselves stimulated activity that may give a false picture of economic well-being.

Hence, it is suggested that such indices as are customarily used to denote economic well-being do not truthfully reflect a disaster situation; on the contrary, they seem actually to mask the disastrous effects of such a calamity. It appears, then, that we need to develop and use other economic indices for studies such as this.

3. Legal and Intergovernmental Problems

Disasters of the magnitude of those that hit Waco and San Angelo impose tasks far beyond the power of any person, or community, or state to meet. A national effort is essential. At the same time, such disasters reveal to even a casual observer the complex of interdependencies of person, community, state, and nation that is modern civilization.

The more obvious and more easily foreseen interdependent relations in society have been subjected to social controls, ranging from custom to law. Political entities operate by virtue of legal enactments and are bound in their operation by the laws that create and regulate them. But they function also through custom, ideas of justice and equity, and the prevailing mores of the society and morals of the men who interpret and apply these laws.

National Activities: Public Law 875

Public Law 875 was the legal authority for the use of federal power to relieve suffering and aid rehabilitation in Waco. The Federal Civil Defense Administration (FCDA) was the agency officially designated to use the authority given the President by this law. But the men from the regional office of FCDA and other agencies who worked with Texas and Waco officials in using the authority of Public Law 875 found themselves doing far more than reading an act of Congress and finding in it the answers to the problems they faced in attempting to aid a community rehabilitate itself.

The regional FCDA office sent officials to Waco on the day the tornado struck. Thus four days prior to the May 16 Presidential proclamation declaring Waco a major-disaster area, a federal task force had been organized and was at work. Five federal agencies contributed personnel to this task force. From the regional FCDA office, various staff members formed the nucleus of the team headed by

Colonel E. V. Hardwick, deputy administrator. The Housing and Home Finance Agency, which had been responsible for the application of Public Law 875 before January, 1953, was represented by A. C. Allen, Larry Ramsdell, and James K. Singleton. General Services Administration sent Keith Johnson. The Department of Health, Education, and Welfare sent Harold J. Stafford, Dr. William Ossenfort, Paul Henderson, William Driskill, Harry Emigh, and George Hogan. The Veterans Administration was represented by Lewis W. Tynes. Additional workers from FCDA and officials from other federal agencies participated from time to time.

Congress, realizing the vulnerability of American communities to disasters, enacted Public Law 875 in 1950. It states in part:

> It is the intent of Congress to provide an orderly and continuing means of assistance by the Federal government to states and local governments in carrying out their responsibilities to alleviate suffering and damage resulting from major disasters.[1]

On Saturday, five days after the tornadoes struck, came the President's proclamation, carrying a tentative allocation of $250,000 for relief purposes. On Friday, May 22, the President extended the disaster designation to include San Angelo and fringe areas of both cities, with $115,000 added to the original allocation. Public Law 875 was in operation.

At the time of the Presidential proclamations, city, county, state, and federal units were all working in the disaster areas. Rescue operations had been more or less completed, but rehabilitation was only beginning. Paramount was the need for solving the more pressing financial problems created by the tornado destruction and rescue operations. Under Public Law 875, most of the activities of the federal officials were to be directed toward this need. Hence it is not surprising that one of the first actions of the Waco task force of FCDA was to make a financial analysis of the city and school district. It also gave its attention at once to the rehabilitation of the sanitary facilities in the stricken area, to the public facilities, and to the public-school system. The first federal grant—$27,603—was for the restoration of sanitary facilities and for other health measures. As early as May 18, agreement had been reached about requirements for this, and on May 27 the check was presented to Mayor Ralph Wolf by Federal Civil Defense Administrator Val Peterson.

The expedition with which this amount was agreed upon and the

[1] Pub. L. 875, 81st Cong., 2d sess., c. 1125, H. R. 8396, § 1.

restoration project carried through set many precedents and required considerable action not only by the FCDA but also at state and local levels. At the time of the tornadoes, no application form for disaster aid had been created, and the development of such a form was one of the early tasks accomplished in Waco. Hence it was of vital importance that FCDA officials decided to work directly with city and state officials in producing acceptable applications in the shortest possible time, rather than wait for local officials to attempt to develop an acceptable form before they could file it. It was their hope that such procedure would eliminate or minimize the possibility of claims being amended or eventually disapproved. It may be noted that this procedure placed federal officials in the position not only of interpreting the law but of applying it as the applications were developed. That this was accepted as an essential procedure is indicated by the comment of one of the Waco officials most intimately concerned: "We didn't try to interpret the law. We said to the federal officials, 'Look, you tell us what to apply for—we surely don't know.' We took advice and interpretations from any and all of them, but they couldn't always agree among themselves. There were a lot of arguments."

Here it must be emphasized that these were the first disasters to come under FCDA supervision. The administration of Public Law 875 had been in the hands of the Housing and Home Finance Agency until January, 1953; hence interpretations of the law had to be made without benefit of experience as situations arose. It was almost inevitable that there would be conflicting recommendations from various officials, and compromise was frequently necessary. In some cases questions were referred to Washington for decision. Such unsettled procedure undoubtedly left local officials confused, for they could not know exactly what to do or whose advice to follow.

Throughout the negotiations federal officials were necessarily in a dominant position. The responsibility for interpretation of Public Law 875, its application to the local situation, the final assessment of the extent of damage, and the amount of funds that could be supplied by the federal government for rehabilitation fell upon their shoulders. It should be added at once, however, that there was no discernible tendency for federal officials to impose their judgment. It would seem rather that they were most careful to seek a settlement that would be as satisfactory as possible to local officials, while remaining within the limits set by the law as interpreted by federal attorneys. In some instances FCDA representatives appear to have urged officials to file claims about which there was some uncertainty and then to have aided in processing these claims through the various levels.

Public Law 875 provided that federal funds should not be used to rehabilitate revenue-producing facilities owned by municipalities. One member of the task force wrote in a memorandum regarding the municipal water system and the City Market in Waco that both were revenue-producing facilities and therefore their eligibility to participate in the disaster-relief funds was questionable. In another memorandum another member of the group observed that although the City Market was operated by the city and leases were made to local farmers, "this City Market is not operated by the city for revenue," and that since Public Law 875 provided for making emergency repairs to public facilities operated by municipal governments, it followed that funds might be allocated for emergency repairs to the City Market. He supported his position with the argument that a municipality is prohibited from operating a private enterprise or assuming any function that is not in a legal sense a public enterprise and therefore the public market was unquestionably a "public facility" as the term was used in Public Law 875. The request was finally denied.

This reasoning, however, was not applied to the Water Department in an opinion offered by still another member of the task force, who wrote: "Since the Water Department is self-supporting, its debts self-liquidating, and its operations profitable even at a low monthly rate, it is not considered eligible for aid under Public Law 875." Variations in interpretations of the law are apparent.

An early agreement between the Waco city engineer and one of the federal officials indicated that the city fire-alarm-box system and the traffic-light system were both eligible for repair by federal grants under the provisions of Public Law 875. A request was made on the basis of this agreement. Later, however, this opinion was modified, and the grants were cut down to about one-third of the original amount.

Undoubtedly, the thorniest problems of interpretation were in regard to what constituted a "reasonable" local contribution to "repairs to and temporary replacement of public facilities." The complexities of interpreting these two provisions of the law were highlighted in the case of the East Waco Elementary School, which had been so badly damaged that it was felt it would be neither safe nor economically practicable to make repairs. Permanent reconstruction

70

was considered almost, if not entirely, essential. School authorities pressed for the use of federal funds to rebuild the partly destroyed structure.

FCDA attorneys ruled that reconstruction was beyond the provisions of the statute. At the same time, they admitted that it was highly inequitable to deny relief if the school board insisted on restoration rather than making repairs on a temporary basis. Justice seemed to lie with the position that certainly the local board might use as much money for permanent reconstruction as it would have been entitled to had it decided to make temporary repairs.

In ruling that the school was not eligible to receive funds for restoration, FCDA attorneys were bound by policy interpretations previously developed by federal agencies. In FCDA's *Disaster Interim Operating Procedures,* a policy statement reads as follows:

Emergency and temporary work to be performed will be considered as the minimum necessary to provide for or to establish either shelters or facilities or replacement necessary to restore facilities on a temporary basis long enough to allow for provision of permanent facilities. In such cases the intent of the law will be strictly adhered to and serve as a paramount determination as to the extent that federal assistance should be made available.

In the Waco situation, Val Peterson, administrator for FCDA, issued an administrative ruling which said, in effect, that it was not the intent of Congress to prohibit using for permanent reconstruction the amount of federal funds that would be allocated for making emergency or temporary repairs. In July, 1953, partly as a result of the Waco experience, Public Law 875 was amended, with the term "restoration" being used in regard to ways in which public facilities might be aided. This, of course, superseded the former opinions of attorneys that permanent repairs could not be made with funds supplied under this law. However, FCDA *Advisory Bulletin 154,* dated October 21, 1953—several months after the amendment had been made the subject of *Advisory Bulletin 144*—does not mention "restoration" of public facilities, but emphasizes the subsection of the law relating to emergency repairs and temporary replacements. It states, however, that at the request of the state or local community, a grant equal to the agreed cost of "minimum protection or temporary replacement or emergency repair" may be applied against the cost of permanent repair or replacement of facilities. Thus the amendment to the law validates Peterson's ruling.

TABLE 10

Federal Funds Made Available under Public Law 875 (Waco)

	First Estimate of Repair Cost, etc.	Adjusted Cost Estimate	Request for Aid	Applicant's Share	Aid Granted
Public works and engineering					
Sanitary sewer	$ 23,700	$ 11,500	$ 10,000	$ 1,500	$ 10,000
Debris removal	15,000	314,400*	14,000	300,000	14,000
Walks and curb repairs	15,000	5,510	5,250	260	5,250
Bridges	75,000	12,000	12,000	......	12,000
City streets	25,000	38,023	26,213	11,810	26,213
Traffic lights and fire alarms	......	25,600	7,800	17,800	1,380
Building protection	......	12,150	8,550	3,600	8,550
Bridges (supplemental)	......	......	5,395	......	2,502
Repair to City Hall	1,000	4,574	3,844	......	
City parks	44,040	49,300	42,640	6,660	
Overtime for police	......	57,400	7,400	50,000	
Water system	7,500	Tentative application withdrawn			
City Market	30,000	Tentative application withdrawn			
County facilities	3,000	Tentative application withdrawn			
Health and sanitation	36,253		27,603	8,650	27,603
Educational facilities					
Repairs to five schools	63,695	33,180	10,197	22,983	10,197
East Waco Elementary School	360,948	100,630	95,250	5,380	95,250
Total	$700,136	$663,867	$276,142	$428,643	$212,945

* Includes total cost of debris removal and military, volunteer, and city contributions.
Source: Figures in this table were brought up to date and verified by fiscal authorities of the City of Waco and the Waco School District in the summer of 1956.

This matter becomes complicated when an attempt is made to distinguish between "emergency repair" and "restoration." Is an emergency repair one designed to serve for only a matter of months? Or is it one that will satisfactorily meet the emergency created by the disaster? Further, is the interpretation of "temporary replacement" restricted to the use of facilities "temporary" in the sense of their being highly impermanent, or does it also include the temporary use of permanent facilities that may be rented, for example, for the period during which regular facilities are being repaired or restored? These and similar questions need further interpretation before what is and is not permissible under Public Law 875 becomes entirely clear.

The question of local contribution to the cost of rehabilitation was even more difficult to solve. Waco school authorities pointed out that they had no unallocated funds in their treasury. They had recently issued $3 million in bonds for building purposes, and they felt they were under moral obligation to use the funds for that purpose. Furthermore, if the money was not so used, there was no time to issue more bonds to provide for the anticipated enrollment in the schools the next year.

Federal officials pointed out that the Waco School Board had at that time something more than $400,000 in a building fund earmarked for remodeling and replacing certain school buildings and argued that some of this money might be allocated to rebuilding or repairing storm-damaged buildings. It was further argued that the expenditure of building funds to repair damaged buildings would yield more school capacity per dollar than could the same expenditure on the construction of new buildings.

Countervailing arguments were that the school system was in desperate financial plight and that the destruction of property due to the tornado would undoubtedly reduce tax revenue for the next years, making it very difficult to operate the schools.

A compromise was worked out whereby the school authorities were to furnish part of the equipment and labor crews as their fair local share of the total effort. Actually, the matter was settled somewhat dramatically after prolonged negotiations when school officials and FCDA officers were discussing the matter in Dallas. In the words of a school official:

One FCDA man there kept asking me the same question over and over, "How much is your share in this rebuilding going to be?" I finally insisted that he telephone Washington. He did and in less than one minute the

73

requested figure was approved. Then I was worried for fear the Dallas people would renege on this so I suggested an immediate press release. This was done and I think it saved the day for us.

Local federal officials took the position that the federal government helps those who help themselves. "This is not just a giveaway program," said one.

Public pressure appears to have been important in the settlement of this particular problem. The *Waco Times-Herald* had commented after the first meeting of the school board with FCDA officials that, although no official opinion had been expressed, there was a feeling that the federal men "took a dim view" of the school district's not contributing directly. The chief of the task force promptly denied this, pointing out that no complete application was before him and therefore he had not approved or disapproved any application and did not take any sort of view—particularly not a dim one—of any application. He commented, "We will fulfill absolutely the provisions of Public Law 875." Since this law requires that local authorities make a "reasonable contribution" to the total effort, the difficulty lay in determining what a "reasonable contribution" was under the particular circumstances surrounding this specific disaster.

In San Angelo, FCDA representatives first told the Lake View School officials that their school was not eligible for federal assistance; later, other FCDA workers urged them to apply for aid under Public Law 875.

Lake View School officials took the position that because insurance took care of "practically all" of their loss, they were reluctant to ask for federal aid. They finally did make application and received $10,681. This amount was placed in a special account until the spring of 1956, when it was returned intact to the FCDA with the explanation that the very favorable insurance settlement left the school board without any just claim for federal aid.

The distaste for federal aid often found among the residents of San Angelo was undoubtedly one factor in the refusal to accept and use the money for rehabilitation of this school system. However, another telling factor was the sheer burden of preparing the required forms. For example, one part of the application for aid required 18 copies of the 42-page single-spaced typewritten contract under which the building had originally been erected—no small task for a school superintendent with one part-time secretary.

As already stated, the development of an application form for aid was one of the early tasks accomplished in Waco, and there were complaints also about the amount of time taken to process applications after they had been presented in proper form. Quite often, local officials said, the work for which aid had been requested would be completed before a final decision on the application was made; hence payments were in effect a reimbursement rather than an aid to begin work. As one Waco official put it, "The emergency period was over before the applications were even made." Under the pressure of the emergency this was perhaps inevitable. Local officials also complained of the complexity and cost of keeping the accounts required by the federal government.

The initial estimates of the cost of rehabilitating municipal and school facilities in Waco were in excess of $700,000. Later this was scaled down to $664,000 and requests for aid amounting to $277,000 were actually filed. The total amount of grants was $213,000. The applications show the local share in this rehabilitation cost as $428,000, $300,000 of which is credited to the removal of debris. This work, however, actually was done largely by military personnel, working in conjunction with volunteer people and trucking concerns of the city. In other words, it was done not at direct expense to the municipality. Another item in the applicant's share shows $50,000 for overtime work of the police force. This was real work of a valuable nature performed by the police, but it did not represent an out-of-pocket expenditure of $50,000 by the city. Negotiations continued into 1956 in an effort to determine how the costs of damage and destruction should be divided between the city and national governments. In the summer of that year, Waco officials were still hopeful, though decreasingly so, of favorable action on a greatly reduced request for funds to meet part of the costs of repairs to the City Hall.

City officials in Waco commented on the thoroughness with which the federal government checked the expenditure of funds. At least five sets of auditors or investigators looked into the accounts and at least one municipal official reached the opinion that the city would be asked to refund a considerable portion of the money it had received from the government.

San Angelo applied for and received $700 to aid in repairing a fire station and $1,500 for partial repairs to the Fair Grounds. The San Angelo press and civic leaders had long been advocates of no federal "interference" in local and state affairs. A member of the City Council at the time of the disaster reported that he had argued against accepting any federal assistance for rehabilitation. We have not been told whether such an attitude significantly affected the behavior of other local officials or not. However, suspicion and even hostility toward federal representatives were apparent in the activities following the disaster.

A study of the laws, policy statements, agreements, and advisory bulletins under which federal relief may be given in cases of major disaster could constitute a minor branch of legal preparation, it would seem. Neither the intent nor the probable consequences of certain provisions are apparent to a nonlegally oriented mind. Two illustrations suffice. One curious provision of the law delineating the conditions under which federal property may be used in local disaster relief is that a State Surplus Property Officer is required to keep a catalog of all federal surplus property available and in emergencies must make application for its use. Federal officials are prohibited from initiating such action. It would seem more feasible to require only a statement from state officials about supplies needed and have a designated federal official then locate such property and determine whether it could be classified as "surplus."

There is a second provision of the law that calls for brief comment. After stating that surplus supplies may be used for the restoration of public facilities, the law adds "and essential rehabilitation of individuals in need as the result of such major disasters." Before the law was amended, it permitted the use of such materials only by state and local governmental units. The later provision seems to give authority for such supplies to be distributed directly to persons suffering disaster losses, in addition to their distribution through municipalities, institutions, and other agencies. If this is correct, it opens the possibility of an entirely new arrangement.

State Activities

The State Office of Defense and Disaster Relief, headed by William L. McGill, went into immediate action following the tornadoes. All other state units having emergency responsibilities also began work at the disaster scenes within a day or less. The importance of these activities cannot be overemphasized, but with reference to state, federal, and local relations, obstacles had to be cleared. The FCDA's *The Waco Disaster* (p. 37, A) notes:

The State of Texas made no special appropriations or other donations of funds for the Waco disaster, other than an appropriation of $25,000 for pay and rations of the National Guard in San Angelo and Waco. State

76

assistance was furnished in the form of personnel and equipment from state departments, sent to the area to aid city authorities.

The state's estimate of its costs and contributions in helping to alleviate the suffering and need in these two disaster areas totals less than $100,000. Its contribution consisted of furnishing trained personnel, physical equipment, and legal and administrative assistance —coupled with legislative action to meet the emergency—rather than grants of money. By a most fortunate coincidence, the legislature was in session when these disasters occurred, and it promptly adopted laws that cleared up some disputed legal points. The state-federal agreement provided in part that the state pledge itself to "utilize all available resources for the purpose of alleviating the damage, hardship, or suffering." The federal government agreed to supplement the relief efforts of state and other governmental agencies by using federal equipment and personnel, by aiding in clearing away debris, by aiding in making emergency repairs to public facilities that were destroyed, by providing temporary housing for displaced families, and by financial assistance amounting to $365,000.

In view of a law passed in 1951, which had been designed to restrict the accepting of gifts from the federal government, the question was raised as to the legality of the state's accepting federal funds for disaster relief. Attorneys from Civil Defense and the office of the State Attorney General studied the question and agreed that it would be safer to secure passage of legislation specifically providing for the acceptance of disaster relief. Two identical acts—one in the House and one in the Senate—were introduced and passed without opposition. They became effective when the Governor signed them on May 27. This new legislation provided that in case of a major disaster the governor, on behalf of the state and the executive officer of any political subdivisions of the state, had authority to accept gifts of funds, services, or supplies for use in meeting the disaster situation. When gifts are made directly to the state, the legislation gives the governor, or a person designated by him, the right to transfer such gifts to any political subdivision of the state. Perhaps it should be emphasized that the legislation provided authority for the state and political subdivisions to receive and use such gifts only in a disaster situation.

As FCDA *Advisory Bulletin 154* makes clear, Public Law 875 is intended to supplement, not supplant, local aid when it is beyond the ability of local governments to cope with disaster damage. But neither the law nor the policy statement goes into the question of how total costs shall be divided among the various governmental units. This leaves a wide field for the exercise of discretion by the officials charged with the administration of Public Law 875, a latitude probably essential to equitable administration.

Estimating the local and state contribution to disaster rehabilitation is difficult. In the cases involved in this study, the federal contribution was largely in money—a commodity easily assessed. But local and state contributions were largely in manpower and the use of supplies and equipment that would have been used elsewhere. This poses the question of how a calculation can be made that will separate that part of on-going expenditures chargeable to the disaster operation. State highway patrolmen were diverted from their customary duties, for example, and assigned temporarily to the disaster areas. Should their salaries, then, be made a part of the state contribution? State highway-construction equipment was diverted for use in the disaster situation, with consequent postponement of the construction or repair work on which it had been engaged. Should this expense be charged to disaster operations? Medical supplies for regular activities of state or local departments of health were used in the disaster area for mosquito or rodent control. Is the cost of such material legitimately a part of the contribution made by the state or local government? Finally, it was argued that donations to relief funds by citizens of the city or state represent contributions of the city or state. Is this a proper and allowable procedure in calculating the portion of the total cost borne by nonfederal sources?

Texas Attorney General John Ben Shepperd was of the opinion in the summer of 1953 that state funds could not be made available for disaster relief. In an opinion on drought relief he said, "Under the present law [Civil Protection Act of 1951] powers appear to be limited to expenditure of state money only for administration and co-ordination of disaster-relief activities." He suggested that this law be amended. This interpretation of the law seems to mean that until enabling legislation is enacted to make direct relief permissible, state participation in disaster operations must be limited to the use of facilities of the various state departments that may be pressed into service.

A Council of State Governments' committee at its 1952 and 1953 meetings recommended that a sum of money be made available to the governor of each state for use in civil defense or disaster situations. Recognizing the varying abilities of states to appropriate such funds, the committee suggested that $150,000 plus $0.25 per inhabitant of the state should be sufficient to begin a program that might later be supplemented by local and federal funds.

It is obvious that bothersome questions will continue to arise. It is equally obvious that it would be impossible, or certainly impracticable, to set hard-and-fast rules governing the amount of contribution or percentage contribution to be made by either the local, the state, or the federal government. As a general thing, state and local units will have resources of labor and supplies that may be made immediately available and used effectively. The federal government may have military manpower and surplus goods available if there is a military installation in the area. (If there is a military installation, there are likely to be supplies of surplus goods.) Hence, it appears that in most disaster situations the local contribution would be the manpower and supplies locally available, and the federal contribution would be in funds, plus such manpower and supplies as might be available within the particular area.

It has been suggested that some formula should be constructed by which the ability of state and local governments to contribute to disaster relief could be ascertained and applied when needed, with allowances made for the exigencies of a particular emergency. Such a formula has been developed in several states (Texas included) by which to calculate the ability of local school districts to support education. A study of formulas such as these might prove profitable in the preparation of administrative policies regarding disaster relief.

Local-Government Activities

In San Angelo, the FCDA representatives who came to consult with school and municipal authorities met a cool reception. Somewhat reluctantly applications for two projects were filed by the municipality and one for aid in repairing the school building was filed by the Lake View School District. As related earlier, the municipal grants, though small, were received and were used. The larger school grant was received also but later was returned.

In Waco several local officials described the early relationship with the Civil Defense officials as "confusing." Hardly had the task force set to work, it was said, before there was disagreement about what could be done under Public Law 875. One local Waco official reported that he felt the attitude of some members of the task force was suspicious and accusing.

It should not be forgotten that these Waco officials themselves

79

were under a great strain. Their city had already been operating at a deficit, and now they saw the heart of the business area devastated and the entire community facing a tremendous task of rehabilitation. It was almost inevitable that they would be unduly sensitive. "If Waco is entitled to anything," one of them told a member of the task force, "we would like to have it. If not, make the situation plain and we will not apply. We are not begging for anything although we need help badly."

The human-relations difficulties were by no means one-sided. When a federal engineer wanted to make a survey of damage to streets and gutters, he was told there were no city officials available to work with him. Later, when negotiations were under way in an effort to agree on the amounts for which applications should be filed, some local officials said that task-force members sometimes attempted to keep the amounts as low as possible and at other times encouraged them to request amounts not wholly justifiable by local standards. They construed delays as "stalling tactics." One local official said: "Haste is the best policy; any delay causes the amount of federal aid to diminish greatly."

Federal officials on their part pointed out that it was imperative to examine the applications carefully to make sure that they conformed with the terms of Public Law 875 and this necessarily took time. Similarly, federal workers had difficulty in securing separate and accurate accounts for funds already granted. Conversely, local officials expressed considerable trepidation as to future complications that might arise when government auditors began to examine accounts.

The total picture that emerges from a consideration of the application of Public Law 875 in the Waco and San Angelo disasters is one of uncertainty and confusion at the federal, state, and local levels.

It appears that this disorganization was inevitable for various reasons. Certainly it is not to be expected that Congress can, or should, enact a law defining in detail the exact areas in which disaster relief may be granted; the exact proportion of federal, state, and local funds to be expended on such relief; or the exact procedures required for participation in such relief. To do so would result in such rigidity that peculiar requirements imposed by the local situation could not be effectually met. And the local situation can be expected to vary from community to community. Hence the wisdom of providing enough latitude that those making and disposing of applications for federal aid may use their discretion. But whenever discretion is allowed, debates are likely to arise about the limits and the manner of using it.

For example, there is genuine doubt about when a given loss should be charged to disaster damage. In Waco, it was imperative to clear out clogged sewer lines immediately after the tornado and the heavy rains following it. Was this clogged condition a result of the heavy rains that swept small bits of debris into the lines; or was this a situation in which the lines, though still usable, were already so badly clogged that they could not accommodate the extra load placed on them as a consequence of the heavy rains plus debris? If the latter is true—and there is no evidence one way or the other—should cleaning the lines be chargeable to disaster damage and, if so, to what extent?

The same equivocal situation is further illustrated in the damage done to streets by the heavy equipment used in clearing away the debris of wrecked buildings. If at the end of the operation it is necessary to do extensive repair on the streets, should this work be categorized as disaster damage and, if so, to what extent? It is entirely possible, of course, that the extra load which was undoubtedly the result of the disaster may have been more the occasion than the cause—the proverbial last straw.

In situations such as these, the only guarantee of fair dealing is the personal integrity of officials of the local, state, and federal governments. Lacking this element, it would be easily possible for a local government to make claims for repair of conditions which had been faulty but not critical for some time and which it would have been forced to remedy at its own expense in the future. It would be equally possible, of course, for representatives of FCDA to insist that since the condition existed to some degree prior to the disaster, nothing more than a minor aggravation was caused by the event and therefore only a minor contribution should be made under Public Law 875. There appears here a fairly wide area of indeterminancy.

Businessmen were immediately concerned with all the problems raised by the disaster but particularly with discovering what had happened to their merchandise. The police cordon thrown around the area of devastation in the business district at first prevented anyone not engaged in rescue operations from entering. The merchants resented being excluded. The records are not entirely clear, but it seems that as early as the day following the tornado exceptions were made to this order, and some tenants of business buildings were allowed to enter for inspection. One of the primary purposes in refusing access to the area was, of course, to protect exposed merchandise from looting.

Weeks later a businessman, thinking back over the situation, offered this commentary:

When anything like this happens there are several phases. The first phase is when the people are so badly shocked they don't know what hit them; but when they begin to realize what hit them, a perfectly human reaction sets in. There are bodies to be dug out, there are people lost in there, debris piled all over. At that time, that phase of disaster, people are pretty noble; they are pretty high-minded; they will dig in and work twenty-four hours a day; they will do anything in the world they are called on to do; they just want to know what they are supposed to do. But soon that romance, that excitement wears off. The streets begin to be cleaned up a little bit, and things begin to look a lot better. Then some of the boys begin counting the effect of the disaster on their own personal interest. I am talking about businessmen and merchants; unfortunately in Waco. Lots of people thought they had insurance to cover this thing, and when they went to look at their insurance policies, they found that they did not have extended coverage. They may have had fire insurance, but they didn't have extended coverage. The boys that had the insurance were pretty calm about the whole thing. They felt that they were going to be taken care of; and in many cases they did all right. But, the merchants and people who did not have extended coverage got pretty panicky.[2]

Two days after the tornado, business leaders began to demand that persons having businesses in the area be admitted and allowed to do what they could to salvage merchandise. That evening a large group met to voice their disapproval at not being allowed to resume control of their business houses and stocks. The immediate response of city authorities was that none of the damaged structures would be permitted to reopen until they had been declared safe by the owners.

This situation presented a dilemma to city and military authorities. By regulation military operations were restricted to rescue work and the removal of hazards to public safety. City officials became convinced that they ran a serious risk of incurring liability for further destruction of buildings and merchandise. No thought had been given this question of liability in the first days of the emergency when rescue of the injured and the removal of corpses were paramount. On the other hand, no meeting of the City Council had been called to give authority for demolition work, and it was argued, therefore, that all such work was done on the volition of the military forces, private contractors, or other rescue workers. However, three days after the tornado many of the occupants of the damaged build-

[2] Brittain, *The Waco Tornado*.

ings said they were certain no injured persons or dead bodies were on their property.

Faced with this problem, the city authorities placed on the property-owners the responsibility for continued search for bodies. They were asked: "Are you positive there is no body or bodies in your building?"[3] If any doubt was expressed, the property-owner was then asked whether he was willing for the city to make a search. A search meant almost certain loss of merchandise and probable destruction of the building. Unless specific permission was granted, no further search or clearing of debris from the premises would be undertaken by the city or the military authorities. At the same time, it was emphasized that the property-owners would be held responsible for clearing away any danger to health or property of others if they resumed control of their buildings.

All but a few of the businessmen took the responsibility and resumed control of their property. This brought to a stop the work of the military. Personnel and equipment were withdrawn the following day with this tart caution from a military figure, "Gentlemen, I must warn you against leaning against many of the walls we are leaving standing." This withdrawal, of course, resulted in property-owners' being forced to spend private funds for work that might have been done at public cost. This realization came as an unwelcome surprise to some, but the decision had been made and one problem was solved.

This question of liability loomed large in the thinking of the military. Early in the Waco experience, military officials asked that their role be made very clear. "Military forces can properly serve only as labor forces in a civil disaster. . . . The Army can protect federal property such as the post office, and can shoot to kill in protecting it, but it cannot guard any other type of property." Thus, the military declined to serve as law enforcement officers or to aid in enforcing roadblocks or to send out antilooting patrols. In Waco, National Guard troops were assigned police duties, and this also brought some confusion, for federal military officers insisted that neither they nor their troops could operate under command of the National Guard.

Army Regulations 500-60 give authority to military commanders to act promptly in disaster situations to protect life and property but forbid "assumption of functions normally performed by civilian authori-

[3] *Ibid.*

ties." After the President has declared a "major disaster," the situation changes. Army participation then will be "as directed or requested by the agency acting as the President's designated representative." Executive Order 10427, dated January 16, 1953, gives Federal Civil Defense Administration, as the agent of the President, power to "direct federal agencies to provide assistance in major disasters." This seems to place top authority in the hands of FCDA in such situations. However, military men serving in the disasters in Waco and San Angelo expressed the opinion that their activities were so restricted unless martial law were in effect that there was grave danger of their exceeding their authority and placing themselves in jeopardy of being disciplined. In both cities there appeared to be a desire on the part of the military to retire from the scene as quickly as possible to avoid this possibility.

The removal of bodies from the wrecked buildings posed a knotty legal problem. In some cases, dismemberment was necessary to extricate bodies from the wreckage, and the question arose about whether this could legally be done without the consent of next of kin. This interposed the additional problem of getting the next of kin to the scene in order to make identification certain. This was often impossible and always involved delay. There was also the question of whether a body could be removed without the legal authority of a justice of the peace. (In Texas, justices of the peace act as coroners and are legally required to render a verdict as to cause of death when no registered physician has been in attendance.) Obviously, it is impossible to conform with these provisions in time of major disasters, and there is need for further local or national legislation. To ignore these provisions leaves unsolved the question of who is liable for damages in case of suits by relatives and what they are liable for.

Buildings damaged but still standing presented another problem. Immediately after the tornado in Waco, the city engineer and a corps of volunteer engineers made a building-by-building survey of the downtown area and placed public notices on all structures considered unsafe for occupancy. Later, property-owners engaged other engineers to survey their buildings and give an opinion about their safety. Frequently the two opinions did not concur, raising the question of whether the action of the city-sponsored engineers amounted to condemnation. It was feared that lawsuits would result, and if a court later held that the building had actually not been unsafe but had been destroyed because the city had ruled it dangerous, the city would be liable for the value of the structure and its contents. On the other hand, it was argued that the city had a responsibility to warn the public of dangerous buildings. But, it was pointed out, failure to do so would not entail liability. Hence the city removed all such warning signs and adopted a "hands off" policy regarding all private property not an obvious danger to persons in the street.

A third problem with perplexing legal aspects had to do with the disposal of materials taken from damaged buildings to the city dump. A large amount of this was salvageable merchandise. Who owned such material? To complicate the matter further, the city had a contract with a local person giving him the right to salvage all ferrous metals from the city dump. He claimed the right to salvage materials from the rescue and demolition operations. The city attempted to solve this problem of dumped materials by issuing a notice that persons whose stores had been entered in rescue operations might obtain permits to reclaim any merchandise they could identify. Many merchants took advantage of this offer and salvaged some durable items. One enterprising person purchased salvage rights from several merchants but was barred from the city dump on the grounds that since he had not originally owned the merchandise he could not positively identify it and that ownership of the property passed to the city since it had been abandoned by the true owners. The city health officer declared the city dump a serious health menace and demanded speeding up salvage operations. But before they were completed, fire swept through the dump, effectively ending, if not solving, the problem.

An even more vexatious legal and political problem arose in the interpretation and enforcement of the building code, adopted about a year before the disaster. This code was much more stringent than the one it replaced. Some objected that the new code imposed undue burdens on property-owners, pointing out that under provisions of the old code buildings could be constructed that would be better than they were before the tornado and that this would give needed relief to persons who had suffered extensive loss. Further, it was argued, rigid imposition of the new code would make it unprofitable for some of the property-owners to rebuild at all. Since most of the buildings in the vicinity of the City Hall had one or both walls in common with buildings on either side, failure or inability of one owner to agree to reconstruction plans effectively prevented the other owner from rebuilding if any use was to be made of remaining remnants of such walls. Moreover, failure to reconstruct would affect adjoining property-owners adversely.

Several damaged buildings in the business and residential areas were not repaired, and they were considered to constitute clearly a menace to public safety. To handle this situation, the city adopted an ordinance setting up a quasi-judicial Building Safety Committee, with power to hold hearings and make recommendations to the City Commission. This committee was composed of the city engineer, fire marshal, and county health officer. The City Commission asked for action by the committee, a public hearing was then called, and evidence was heard as to whether a particular building constituted "a serious hazard to life and property." After the committee had examined the building, it then attempted to reach an agreement with the owner to demolish or reconstruct the building if it was below reasonable standards. If no such agreement was reached, the committee then made a formal report to the City Commission, and a second hearing was held and a second attempt to arrive at agreement was made. If this attempt also proved unsuccessful, the city attorney had power to file a condemnation suit for demolition.

This ordinance was adopted in an effort to escape the costs in time, money, and ill will indigenous to condemnation suits. Such suits were considered hazardous because the laws governing condemnation proceedings were vague. The ordinance was also a means of dealing with substandard residences in slum areas after the tornado emergency had passed.

The creation of the Building Safety Committee and the manner in which businessmen and property-owners were given control of their damaged buildings at the termination of rescue work seem to indicate that the city government preferred to use quasi-legal procedures and instrumentalities rather than to rely on its own authority. Both decisions seem to have been made on the grounds that the municipal government was less likely to be in the position of being liable for financial damage if responsibility was shifted to property-owners.

The tornadoes that struck these two cities precipitated seemingly innumerable exigencies in the relationships between local, state, and federal governments, many of which had not been foreseen and for which there was no legal provision. Indeed, only the federal government had taken action of this sort.

Because of the many administrative units involved, questions of authority inevitably arose. Disagreement and delay might have been avoided had there been a provision setting forth distinct levels of authority, or, perhaps, even had there been a strict application of the existing federal law. But such inflexible procedure most likely would have created many more problems than it could have solved. Theoretically, it would be easy to draft a law particularizing the proportionate sharing of disaster costs by the three levels of government, but such a provision would almost certainly work out inequitably for one or two of the levels necessarily involved. Hence, the attractiveness of the conclusion that, though the law did not provide answers to all problems, nor even a smoothly operating procedure by which problems could be solved, it probably operated as fairly as a more detailed statute or a more literal interpretation of the existing law could have provided, and with greater equity.

The general impression gained from information gathered on the events following the tornado in Waco is one of stunned disorganization in which persons acted as individuals, almost entirely free of the normal aspects of social control and group pressures.

This phase was followed quickly by intense activity designed to reestablish the customary institutional controls, particularly in government, and to establish new working relationships between such institutions within the city as the city government, the American Red Cross, and the Waco Disaster Fund.

When it is said that formal controls and group pressures were not exerted on the behavior of persons immediately following the tornado, it is not meant that these persons acted without reference to accepted social and group norms. Certainly they did. But the point to be emphasized is that they acted in terms of norms only because— and to the degree that—these norms had been incorporated into their personalities, not because overt pressures were exerted on them at the time of action.

The fact that Waco police report little looting when objects from jewelry-store show windows were scattered over the sidewalks is perhaps as good an indication as could be asked for of the degree to which social norms had become part of the personalities of those who abstained from pocketing watches or other easily secreted merchandise. It is not true, of course, that no looting took place. It is not true, perhaps, that anybody acted wholly in terms of the group or community norms. But it does seem to be true that in general the majority did, and to a large degree.

From the evidence it seems fair to say that in this situation controls from without gave way and were replaced, temporarily, by controls from within. But, at present, this is no more than a hypothesis.

4. Families in Distress

IT WAS EVIDENT from the beginning of the Waco–San Angelo study that if any true comprehension of these tragedies was to be gained it would be necessary to pay special attention to their impact on the families in the areas across which they swept and to the means by which these families worked out their rehabilitation. Tragic and gigantic as was the loss in the business area of Waco and important as was this loss to the business life of that city, it was only in the residential areas that what happened to the families and their members could be uncovered. In San Angelo almost all the damage was in a residential area. Hence, again, the need to compare the effects of the tornadoes in terms of the affected families only.

But still another reason for intensive study of the families appeared. As interviewing and data-gathering continued, it became increasingly apparent that it would be impossible to understand what happens to a community in disaster without knowing in very considerable detail what happens to families in disaster. Hence, we decided to do as intensive a study as possible of those families, with particular attention to the more perceptible effects in housing, incidence of illness, and economic factors. It was also evident that additional important material might be uncovered by a study of the changes in attitudes, opinions, and feelings of the family members who had gone through these experiences.

Choosing the Sample

In carrying out this portion of the study, one obvious classification of families was available: those still living within the pathways carved out by the tornadoes as they swept across the cities. We recognized, of course, that this group was not completely representative of all those involved in the tornadoes. For example, the shoppers and workers who were in the business area of Waco at the time of the

88

disaster were not included in our sample unless their residences also happened to be in a stricken area. Too, injuries and emotional disturbances to persons in the downtown area during the tornado may well have affected their family situation to a greater extent than was true of some of the families directly in the path of the tornado. But even if it had been possible to locate all these persons, the cost would have been prohibitive. Hence, they were not included. The Waco sample also excluded those persons living in cheap hotels, flop houses, or in the less substantial structures in the older portion of the city on the flank of the business district and near the river. This was done in the belief that most of the people in these places at the time of the study were probably not the ones who had been there at the time of the tornado; hence, their inclusion would detract from the validity of the sample.

In both cities, the path of destruction encompassed an elongated ellipse, with the streets serving as crosshatching. Physical destruction was confined almost wholly to the actual path of the funnel. Area sampling seemed to be the most satisfactory way to obtain an adequate representation of impact ranging from complete destruction to minor damage. In Waco, the funnel did not cut a clean swathe over the whole route, but "bounced" from block to block, skipping some completely. Thus, area sampling in Waco also included homes undamaged but still in the tornado area.

To secure the information in the shortest possible time, the areas of residential destruction were divided into sections and assigned to interviewers separately. Interviewers began on designated streets at an arbitrarily designated house and then took every fourth house on the street in the direction toward the tornado-area boundary. If two interviews in succession involved residences with no storm damage, the interviewer began on another street. Since the primary aim was to obtain information about the effects of the disaster on its victims, this procedure seemed justifiable. Moreover, it eliminated to a large extent those living in the areas in Waco within the pathway of the tornado whose homes it did not strike. Hence for the most part the families secured by this plan constitute a sample of those who experienced the destruction of their homes rather than of those in the pathway of the storm but whose homes were undamaged.

The interviewer substituted the home immediately to the left of the sample house, as he faced it, if no one was at home in the selected house on each of two visits or if the selected resident was antagonistic or inhibited in any way toward completing the interview.

Several interviewers reported that they occasionally ran into antagonism until they explained the nature of the project and its purposes.
How successfully the interviewers handled their job is reflected in the
fact that only two respondents in Waco and none in San Angelo refused the interview. In both cities, a few respondents became so
emotionally upset during the interview that it was unwise to continue it.

To decide upon the size of the samples, two figures were used. Best
available estimates of damage in Waco indicated that from 850 to
900 homes had been damaged in a five-mile strip. We decided that
300 families—roughly a third of those affected—would be a fair
sample. In San Angelo, devastation was very intense for approximately two and a half miles, and the Civil Defense head there estimated that 530 homes had been damaged. Here we decided upon 150
families—about 28 per cent of the affected homes—as adequate.

The total sample was covered in San Angelo, but in Waco only 283
interviews—17 short of the proposed 300—were completed, representing 19.4 per cent of the affected homes. Of the 283 Waco interviews completed, 20 were with families whose residences had not
been damaged. However, in the analysis we used the total Waco
sample of 283, since those homes not damaged were located in the
tornado's pathway, and occupants of undamaged homes were subjected to many of the same stresses as their less fortunate neighbors.
But the inclusion of persons living in undamaged houses probably
mitigated the severity of the suffering shown in the Waco sample to
some extent, though the error is almost certainly on the conservative
side.

The Method

In San Angelo, three well-trained and mature persons each completed fifty interviews between November 20 and December 18,
1953. The interviewing in Waco lasted from February 2 to April 8,
1954. Through the co-operation of the Department of Sociology of
Baylor University, twelve advanced students were employed for the
project.

So that one interview would be comparable with any other, interviewers in both cities used the same schedule, which demanded specific information in specified sequence. The schedule was developed
from knowledge about the tornadoes gained by our research staff
through interviews with local people of all walks of life in both cities,
and also from a study of related materials supplied by members of

the Michigan State University research staff; from Bradford B. Hudson, Rice Institute; and from other studies of disasters. It was designed to investigate six basic areas pertaining to the family situation: (1) background factors; (2) predisaster and postdisaster housing; (3) effects on the health of the family; (4) economic consequences; (5) attitudes and opinions of the families as related to the disaster; (6) cultural factors related to rehabilitation. A total of 100 items was included, 78 of which were precoded so that the information could be transferred to IBM cards directly from the schedule. The schedule was pretested in San Angelo and Waco and some revision made.

As a means of ascertaining the types of families studied and particularly of determining whether there were essential differences between Waco and San Angelo families, several items concerning background were included in the schedule. The families were fairly similar but there were some differences, though only one was sufficiently marked to be statistically significant: in Waco, 77 per cent of the families interviewed were Anglo-American; 19 per cent were Negro; and 4 per cent were Latin-American. In San Angelo, all the families interviewed were Anglo-American. Other data revealed differences too small to be significant. The average size of the family in Waco was 3.52 persons; in San Angelo, 3.64. The Waco families were a little more likely to have members over 65 years of age and, conversely, those in San Angelo a little more likely to have children under 15. Waco families were somewhat more likely to have been broken by death, and those in San Angelo showed a higher rate of divorce and remarriage. But, again, none of these differences were great enough to be statistically significant, though it is possible the slightly greater number of young children in San Angelo families may have some bearing on the greater emotional distress observed in that city.

Statistics on religious affiliation upheld Waco's reputation as a religious center. Relative to San Angelo, the proportion of persons affiliated with the Baptist, Methodist, and Catholic churches was higher. San Angelo had a higher percentage who were members of the Church of Christ and a much higher percentage who professed interest in some undisclosed denomination or who were not actively religious. Between 50 and 60 per cent of the persons in the sample in each city were Baptist.

The over-all impression is that the San Angelo families studied were in slightly better economic condition than were those in Waco.

These figures give roughly a picture of the families involved in the disaster situations. It is important to emphasize that the two samples display no major differences. Hence, it seems fair to assume that such differences as do appear are to be attributed to differences in the nature or effects of the disasters upon the victims, or to their reactions to them.

Comparative Intensity of the Tornados as Reflected in Property Damage, Injuries, and Fatalities

The disasters were notably different. In San Angelo the tornado had destroyed or damaged the home of every family interviewed; in Waco, the percentage was much lower. Further, and importantly, the Waco tornado caused great destruction in the business area, a fact producing the definitely different economic effect reflected in the data on families in that city.

This greater intensity of the San Angelo tornado as shown by the extent of damage also appears in the statistics on injuries. In Waco, 4.95 per cent of the families had one or more injured members; in San Angelo this statistic was 20.7 per cent.

TABLE 11

Extent of Damage to Homes in Tornado Areas

Extent of Damage	Percentage of Homes	
	Waco	San Angelo
Destroyed	8.8	61.3
Heavily damaged	23.6	18.0
Moderately damaged	23.0	14.7
Slightly damaged	26.9	6.0
Undamaged	17.7	0.0
Total	100.0	100.0

This difference between the intensity of the storms appears most dramatically in the fact that in both cities our interviews uncovered the same number of families (three) of whom a member had been killed in the disaster. But almost twice as many families with twice as many members were included in the Waco sample as in the San Angelo sample. Percentagewise, this difference is still more striking. In San Angelo, our sample of families included 30 per cent of all fatalities; in Waco, only 3 per cent. These data indicate an intensity of the San Angelo storm in the residential area several times as great as that in Waco.

At the time these families were interviewed, approximately seven to nine months after the tornadoes, exactly the same proportion— 53.3 per cent—of those injured in each city were reported as fully

TABLE 12

Extent of Damage to Household Goods

| | Percentage | |
Extent of Damage	Waco	San Angelo
Total destruction	3.9	49.3
Heavy damage	11.4	18.0
Moderate damage	8.2	8.7
Slight damage	19.6	12.7
No damage	56.9	11.3
Total	100.0	100.0
Actual number of cases	283	150

reoovored. No ono was reported as seriously ill from injuries received in the disasters, though some were still convalescent.

Income, Unemployment, and Rehabilitation

The families studied had a median annual income of between $2,500 and $3,000 in both cities, with a somewhat greater range in San Angelo. Data showed predisaster unemployment in almost 10 per cent of the homes, slightly less in San Angelo than in Waco. An-nual income for San Angelo families averaged slightly more than $125 than for those in Waco. There was an observable tendency for Waco family incomes to cluster in the "Below $2,000" category and for a few more to be in the "$6,000 plus" bracket in San Angelo. Father-husbands were the sole wage-earners in both cities in more than half the cases; however, in Waco, family income was supple-mented more often, in about 7 per cent of the cases, by other family members. The mother was twice as likely to be the only earner in Waco as in San Angelo. Income from pensions supported 6 per cent of the Waco families and 8 per cent of those in San Angelo. Families living at this economic level are not likely to be able to withstand serious interruption of their income without suffering.

The greater intensity of the tornado in San Angelo is again reflected in the fact that about 60 per cent of the families there had employment interrupted, as against 30 per cent in Waco, where many more places of employment were forced to suspend business for a time. It seems logical to assume that downtown Waco businesses drew their employees from many parts of the city and that some of

TABLE 13

Injuries to Family Members

Persons Injured	Percentage	
	Waco	San Angelo
Families with:		
Husband injured	3	3
Wife injured	6	16*
Children injured	3	3
Other relatives	1	2
Husband and wife	1	7
Total	14	31
Sample families with injured members .	4.95	20.6
Total persons in sample families injured .	1.5	7.0
Actual number of families with injured member	265	150
Actual number of injured persons in total sample	993	543

* Obviously, the greater rate of injury of wives in San Angelo accounts for the significant difference between the two cities as displayed in this table.

them must have lived in the tornado area. The relatively greater destruction of homes in San Angelo and the higher incidence of death and injury, then, would seem to be one logical factor in explaining the greater unemployment in the San Angelo sample.[1] These expectations are borne out by the respondents' answers to questions on unemployment. In San Angelo, the most common reason for unemployment—cited by 38 per cent of those interviewed—was to rebuild their residence or some other essential structure. In Waco, 16 per

[1] Informants were asked two questions relating to the interruption of employment: What was the cause of loss of work time? How long was employment interrupted? The interruption of employment was calculated from replies to both questions. In San Angelo these two questions gave a difference of approximately 3 percentage points. Which estimate secured the more accurate result is debatable, but the variance falls within estimated limits.

cent of the families reported unemployment as a result of damage to their employers' property.

In Waco, the number of workdays lost was between 7 and 10 for fathers and between 11 and 15 for working mothers; in San Angelo, the median for working mothers is within the same bracket, but that for fathers rises to the 16–30-day category. In San Angelo a significantly larger percentage of persons were voluntarily unemployed in order to aid other victims of the disaster. Although most of the unemployed in both cities were husband-fathers, in Waco there was a

TABLE 14

Sources of Funds for Repair and Reconstruction

Source	Percentage	
	Waco	*San Angelo*
Personal funds	69.5	44.3
Banks	2.1	0.0
Savings and loan associations	3.7	11.5
Construction firms	0.5	1.5
Federal agencies	0.5	5.3
Individuals	0.0	1.5
American Red Cross	14.2	26.7
Other sources	9.4	9.1
Total	99.9	99.9

noticeably higher percentage of mothers unemployed, and in San Angelo, as would be expected from the greater intensity of the storm, more families had two or more members unemployed.

Since rebuilding was an immediate and serious problem of beginning rehabilitation, it is pertinent to see how this was accomplished. As previously indicated, insurance played an important part in providing funds; but less than 10 per cent of the families reported they had sufficient protection to cover their losses. In Waco, 31 per cent of the families said they had enough insurance to cover a major portion of their losses; in San Angelo, 15 per cent made this estimate. The other families in the samples reported they either had no insurance or the amount was seriously inadequate.

How did these people manage to rebuild? The most important source was family savings. In Waco, 70 per cent of the families reported they financed rebuilding and repairs themselves; in San Angelo, this figure dropped to 44 per cent. The next most often-used source was American Red Cross, which gave aid for rebuilding to 14 per cent of the Waco families and to 27 per cent of those in San Angelo. Other sources of funds were banks, savings and loan associations, construction firms, federal agencies, and individual loans, presumably from friends and relatives. In Waco, about one-third of the families appear not to have required aid in financing repairs to their homes. At least they did not report assistance for this purpose. In San Angelo, this was true of only 16 per cent. Waco families indicated that 13 per cent of them received aid ranging from $300 to $500 for rebuilding. In San Angelo, 37 per cent so reported, with the amount of assistance ranging from $1,000 to $2,500.

It is interesting that only about one-third of the families in these cities employed contractors to rebuild their homes. Approximately one-eighth of the families did the work themselves. In San Angelo, almost an additional 20 per cent were aided by friends, but this resource was used by little more than 6 per cent in Waco, reflecting again its more metropolitan character. Workmen were employed to aid in preconstruction by 10 per cent of the San Angelo families and 20 per cent of those in Waco.

Groups Contributing Emergency and Rehabilitative Aid

Although rebuilding a home is one of the most fundamental factors in rehabilitation, especially from the point of view of the family, other things must be accomplished first, beginning with the effort at physical survival in the period immediately following the disaster. It is here that relief organizations give their first help in the long, slow process of resuming normal functioning. In both cities several such sources functioned almost immediately after the moment of impact and continued to be available for several months.

These relief agencies were used freely, but it must be noted that many families did not seek their assistance. In Waco, 76 per cent of the families in our sample reported they received no emergency aid from sources outside their own families, as compared with 28 per cent in San Angelo, where the impact was much more drastic. This, it may be said, is high testimony to the ability of families of somewhat below-average financial status to take care of their own needs under extremely adverse circumstances.

Those who did require aid, however, often needed it in various forms. Customarily, we think of relief agencies as operating immediately and only after a disaster in saving lives, dispensing hot coffee and doughnuts to rescue workers, bandaging wounds, and performing services of this sort. Table 15 indicates the relative importance of such emergency help when compared with various other aids for rehabilitation. Figures in other portions of this report also point up the same relative position of emergency aid. Perhaps this further word of explanation is needed about Table 15: if each family had received only one type of aid, the totals would have been for Waco, 23.7 per cent, and for San Angelo, 72 per cent. The fact that the to-

TABLE 15

Types of Aid Received by Sample Families

| Type of Aid | Percentage Receiving Aid | |
	Waco	San Angelo
Emergency (food, first aid, etc.) . . .	14.1	58.0
Rebuilding homes	13.4	35.3
Replacement of household goods . . .	5.3	36.7
Medical care	1.8	12.0
Re-establishing business*	1.1	1.3
Actual number of families	68	108

* Represents aid only to sample families who lived in the tornado area and whose businesses were damaged. If this figure included all persons in Waco who were aided in re-establishing their businesses, it would be much higher. Needless to say, all the differences in the table, except those in the last line, are highly significant and reflect the much greater impact of the disaster upon the San Angelo families.

tals run much higher is a measure of the extent to which each family received more than one type of aid. While it is true in each case that emergency aid—medical care, food, and clothing—was the type most often sought, it is also true that in Waco almost as many people required help to rebuild their homes as to solve the problems facing them immediately after the tornado.

Those who received aid obtained it from a wide variety of sources.[2] American Red Cross, with its tradition of coming to the rescue of those in distress, was by far the outstanding source, making contributions of some sort, alone or in conjunction with other agencies, to about 21 per cent of the Waco families interviewed and to 47 per cent of those in San Angelo. It should be pointed out that the Red Cross became, in effect, the fiscal agent for the San Angelo Disaster Relief

[2] See Chapter 8, "Donors and Donations," for other data on funds used for relief.

97

Fund; but San Angelo's higher percentage also reflects its greater proportion of families suffering losses too great for them to bear alone. In Waco, 13 per cent of the families received aid from the Red Cross alone; in San Angelo, one-fifth of the sample reported it as their sole source of assistance.

The Salvation Army, with its equally fine tradition of dispensing

TABLE 16

Sources of Aid Received by Families

Source	Percentage	
	Waco	*San Angelo*
American Red Cross only	13.4	20.0
Local disaster-fund only	2.1	9.3
Salvation Army only	1.4	2.7
Church group only	1.1	7.3
Relatives and friends only	0.3	5.3
American Red Cross and Salvation Army .	1.8	12.7
Multiple sources	3.5	14.7
Total	23.6	72.0
No relief funds received	76.3	28.0

Statistical tests rate differences between the two cities as highly significant in all the categories except "American Red Cross only" and "Salvation Army only." Perhaps the universalistic practices of these highly organized institutions are reflected in this evenness of treatment in the two cities.

relief in the immediate wake of disaster, was in action in both cities very shortly after the tornadoes hit and continued operations through the emergency-rescue period. In San Angelo, 30 per cent of the sample families reported help by the Salvation Army; in Waco, 7 per cent. It was the only agency contributing to the needs of 2.7 per cent of the San Angelo families and of 1.4 per cent of those in Waco.

When we checked our own schedules against the files of the Red Cross to determine whether there was any inconsistency, we found that an additional 5 per cent of the San Angelo sample families had received aid through the Red Cross but did not report it. In Waco, 0.7 per cent of the families were similarly confused or withheld the information. Certainly it would have been easy in either city to confuse Red Cross and the other local relief-agencies.

Local disaster-funds were set up in both cities. In Waco, this fund operated separately from other relief programs, largely to supplement the efforts of other agencies. Of the Waco sample, 2 per cent reported aid from this source only. In San Angelo, the situation is confused. Of the families interviewed, 9 per cent reported receiving aid only from the local fund. But the San Angelo fund gave direct relief to families only through the Red Cross. However, it also gave indirect relief by paying taxes on damaged homes and by setting up a lunch program at Lake View School. Whether the 9 per cent who reported aid only from the local fund meant that they had received aid from that fund through the Red Cross, or whether they meant they had received aid in the form of relief from tax payments or by their children's participation in the school lunch program, or whether they were confused as to the source of the aid they had received we could not tell. The most reasonable assumption seems to be that these families received aid from the local fund via Red Cross, but chose to recognize the original source rather than the agent of that source.

Church groups were active in both cities in supplying aid. In Waco, 1 per cent of the sample reported such assistance; in San Angelo, 7 per cent. Friends came to the relief of 5.3 per cent of the San Angelo families, and to 0.3 per cent of those in Waco. Finally, nearly 15 per cent of the San Angelo sample and 3.5 per cent of that in Waco stated they had received aid from more than two sources.

It was noted above that a considerable proportion of the families interviewed did not receive aid from any outside source, being able to meet their losses from their own resources. This raises the question of whether they were forced to assume debt to do so. The answer was "No" in a surprisingly large number of cases. In San Angelo, 35 per cent of the sample families said they did incur debt as a direct result of the tornado; in Waco only 16 per cent did so.

These statistics appear inconsistent with those giving the percentage of houses damaged and the percentage of families receiving aid. No probing was done in this portion of the study; hence, there is no way of knowing whether the figures reflect the situation accurately. It would seem logical that a large proportion of these families must have incurred some debt. It is possible that the problem here is one of semantics, that the respondents gave information only on debts incurred at banks, building and loan associations, or other financial institutions, and did not include loans from friends and relatives. They may also have excluded accounts with furniture stores or lumber yards.

Efficiency Ratings Given Relief Groups by Respondents

When people receive clothing, food, shelter, medical care, and the like, they naturally form opinions about the givers.

We have been warned often during the past two decades that the effects of receiving aid may be of more importance than the aid itself, and that the attitudes engendered by easy getting can constitute a drastic danger to American civilization. At the same time, most of us have been taught that only a churl is not grateful for a helping hand extended when he is overwhelmed by forces beyond his control. This is merely one of many possible examples of conflicting values in our American way of life.

Hence, it seemed pertinent to inquire how the victims of these two disasters felt toward the various groups that had come to their rescue and had aided in their rehabilitation. Each contributing group was listed, and the informant marked those he felt had done an "adequate job in helping the victims of this disaster." Table 17 shows how the informants ranked the various groups with regard to the adequacy of their performance. Their ranking can probably be interpreted as a relative measure of their approval of these groups.

In spite of differences in the communities and in the extent to which these groups participated in the disaster operations, there is a fair amount of agreement in these rankings: in both cities, the military, state and city police, the Salvation Army, and church groups are in the top half of the ranking; other local agencies, relief funds, and governmental agencies other than the military and police fall into the lower portion of the ranking; the National Guard, the local churches, and the city government were given identical rank.

Many factors might be cited in explanation of the rankings. For instance, in Waco, heavy Army equipment was brought in to aid in removing debris and searching for bodies. In both cities, Air Force units were among the first rescue squads on the scene. Another factor contributing to the high ranking given the military may be a subconscious reaction to a well-organized and disciplined group, who by tradition and action demonstrates stability in crisis and functions to assure security. To a lesser degree, this observation applies to the ranking given the performance of state and local police.

In San Angelo, a State Highway Patrol car literally followed the tornado for some forty miles before it devastated the area. Hence the patrolmen there were active within a matter of minutes. Units from the National Guard—another organization recognized for its ability to meet crises—were quickly mobilized and were active in both rescue and protection of property. Local churches opened their doors to refugees. The Red Cross and Salvation Army had mobile units in San Angelo within less than an hour after the storms and were very active in both cities. Local and state government officials took charge of operations, and other local-government personnel ren-

TABLE 17

Ranking by Informants of the Adequacy of Performance of Participating Institutions

| | Rank | |
Institution	*Waco*	*San Angelo*
United States Army	1	6
United States Air Force	2	1*
National Guard	3	3
State and city police	4	1*
Local churches	5	5
Salvation Army	6	4
Municipal government	7	7
State government	8	9
Local relief-fund	9	8
Federal government	10	12
Local agencies not named here	11	10
American Red Cross	12	11

* Tied for first place, each with 90.6 per cent approval.

dered many emergency services. The federal government was slower to get into the picture, though a "task force" from the Dallas regional offices of several federal agencies was in Waco the day following the tornado, and Federal Civil Defense Administration contributed to rehabilitation in large amounts.

Since various local welfare and relief organizations placed their personnel and facilities at the services of the Red Cross and Salvation Army, they did not appear to be as active in disaster work as they actually were. American Red Cross constitutes a special case and is discussed at some length in another portion of this report. Let us say here only that this institution, having dual functions, seems to suffer from a dual personality. It appears first as the Great Mother, giving with a lavish hand during the emergency stage; but later, when it demands strict proof of need before it will aid in long-range rehabilitation, it is transformed in the minds of its beneficiaries into the Wicked Witch.

It should be observed also that the respondents in San Angelo—where a higher proportion asked for and received Red Cross aid—showed a distinct tendency to be more critical of it than did those in Waco. The Salvation Army, the Air Force, the National Guard, and the police forces found high favor, and to approximately the same degree, in both cities. Differences in opinion about the adequacy of the part played by the United States Army in these cities may be explained by the fact that the Army was not active in San Angelo; and perhaps the same fact explains the relatively low opinion of activities of the federal and state governments in both cities. As might be expected, there was a noticeable tendency for groups not known to be active to draw a higher percentage of "Undecided" replies.

These rankings present a fascinating problem for future research. To what extent are they indicative of the actual feelings of these particular persons and to what extent are they reflections of conventional opinions? How pertinent, for instance, as an explanation of the low rank given federal government agencies is the fact that for more than a decade Texas political leaders had expressed stern opposition to "federal interference" in local affairs? This attitude had been particularly true of the newspaper editor and city officials in San Angelo. Since the First World War, American Red Cross has customarily been ranked low in the opinions expressed by many persons, though studies have often demonstrated that little concrete information is used as a basis for such opinions.

A Place of Refuge

Since religion is an important and sanctioned outlet for emotion, data were gathered on the religious activities of the persons and families interviewed.

Of some importance is the fact that the "No church preference" category ran lower in Waco than in San Angelo, giving some indication that Waco is a more church-minded community as measured by the families in these samples. This absence of church interest is shown even more clearly in the fact that almost 20 per cent of the San Angelo sample rated themselves as "Not active" religiously, whereas in Waco only 6 per cent gave this answer.

What effect did the tornadoes have on church activity? Remarkably little, assuming data obtained from the samples are truly representative. About 85 per cent said their religious interest and activity

102

remained the same. About 11 per cent in each city reported that their church activity had increased, while less than 5 per cent reported it had decreased. These changes are so slight that their pertinence is subject to doubt; but the evidence they supply is that perhaps one person in ten was drawn more closely to the church, while somewhat less than half this number found themselves withdrawing from religious affairs to some extent.

Clergymen occupy a unique social position in time of disaster. Usually their training and experience are invaluable to those who have seen their world devastated and who must face a strange and threatening new life. Accustomed to dealing with emotion, ministers find in disaster a great opportunity to be of spiritual service.

The clergyman . . . is present at the great emotional moments of life, at times of greatest happiness and deepest sorrow. . . .

For generations, religious leaders have been working with the human personality, helping people to fight their own individual battles. With kindness and understanding, with insight and skill, the clergy has led people to a better adjustment to life. . . .[3]

The Federal Civil Defense Administration has recognized the importance of the religious elements in society during times of great crisis. Its publication *The Clergy in Civil Defense* contains valuable suggestions for clergymen and religious institutions in disaster situations. Waco afforded both opportunity and test in ample degree.

Respondents were asked whether they were visited by clergymen. Slightly more than half the families reported such visits, and about one in eight reported their pastor had called four times or more. The average number of pastoral calls was 1.4 in Waco and 2.0 in San Angelo. This statistic does not jibe with the evidence that the people of San Angelo had somewhat less interest in organized religion than did those in Waco. But the greater severity of the damage in San Angelo may well account for the greater pastoral concern there. It is, of course, also possible that the people in San Angelo sought such consolation more eagerly; or it could be that the pastors there happened to be more active among their members, or that they lived nearer the stricken area.

As one of the fundamental institutions of our society and as that one primarily charged with the task of maintaining morale and build-

[3] *The Clergy and Mental Health* (New York, National Association for Mental Health, Inc.), pamphlet based on Charles S. Kemp's "The Minister and Mental Health—His Opportunity and Responsibility," *Mental Hygiene*, Vol. 32 (January, 1948), pp. 72–79.

ing hope for the future, the clergy and the churches had definite tasks to perform. They became emergency shelters; they aided in rehabilitation; they carried on their customary services for the benefit of their members. The clergymen offered consolation and solace to the injured and bereaved and, perhaps most significant, attempted to interpret the disaster to their congregations and the public in general in such a manner as to reinforce the prevailing picture of a God of love and justice. They did this by applying the basic Christian values of brotherhood, altruism, self-sacrifice, and help to those in need. All these were of immediate assistance in alleviating the effect of the disaster, as well as in aiding personal rehabilitation and community reorganization.

Churches were not immune to physical damage. Fifteen places of worship reported a total damage of $105,000. In Waco one church was totally destroyed; another was so badly damaged as to be declared unsafe, and this congregation held joint services with another for several weeks until repairs had been made. All the affected churches were inspected by engineers and if they were found to be structurally safe, regular services were held, though in some, windows were out and debris was scattered about the grounds. Two downtown churches, one with damage estimated at $25,000 and the other at more than $10,000, accounted for a considerable portion of the total destruction of church property. The reconstruction of churches was aided in some cases by funds from national organizations of the denomination. Individual congregations often made gifts to aid in the rehabilitation of either the church building or its members. One small congregation raised its own funds for rebuilding by selling the church to the members at $10 per "share."

Religious groups and their buildings were used a great deal during the emergency. The East Waco Church of Christ, which though located in the disaster area had received only minor damage, turned one of its buildings into a relief storeroom, collected food, clothing, and bedding and dispensed them to some two hundred families. The Wesley Methodist Church, though damaged, also served as a relief station, aiding more than five hundred persons with food, clothing and bedding. The St. Francis Mission, located just west of the disaster area, continued its aid work for two weeks after the disaster, housing thirty-three persons and feeding seventy daily.

The First Presbyterian Church, located on the south edge of the battered business district, was not damaged. Shortly after the tornado hit, the church officials opened its doors to the homeless and served food and coffee to the police, National Guard, and the families waiting anxiously across the street at the main receiving station for bodies of the tornado victims. Because of its strategic location and facilities, this church was used as the emergency Red Cross headquarters for ten weeks.

The minister turned over his office to Robert Pierpont [chief of American Red Cross activities] and his assistants who moved into the office of Julian Huffer [Director of Christian Education]. The accounting section of the Red Cross set up equipment in the session room. The choir room became a base of operations for the work of five members of the Red Cross Nursing Service. . . . Sunday-school rooms were arranged for case workers interviewing families who registered for help. A switchboard was set up in the entrance hall to handle the heavy volume of phone calls.[4]

St. Paul's Episcopal Church opened its kitchen on the night of the disaster and served coffee to the police and National Guardsmen. The next day the church was turned into an emergency housing unit, with cots supplied by American Red Cross. More than a hundred meals a day were served for four days and thousands of sandwiches were made in the church kitchen. Police and rescue workers were also fed and housed here. Seventh and James Street Baptist Church, located some distance from the scene of destruction, opened its doors to seventy Latin Americans who were members of one of its missions in east Waco, and who lived at the church for three days.

Within hours after the tornado, donations began to arrive at various churches, and they began to dispense emergency aid immediately. Donations of money were sometimes used to buy food and clothing, but more generally cash gifts were allowed to accumulate until after the emergency period and were then used to assist in the rehabilitation of victims or to repair damaged churches.

The five Church of Christ congregations in Waco organized a relief agency that supplied clothing, food, and furniture, more than $2,000 being contributed for food and clothing alone. Members provided the victims with transportation to and from the various church buildings where supplies were stored.

Cash donations made directly to churches totaled a rather impressive amount. Although some clergymen could only estimate the amount their churches handled and others would not divulge this information, fourteen churches reported contributions of more than $35,000. Several thousand dollars from church groups went directly

[4] *Texas Presbyterian,* Vol. II, No. 6 (June 15, 1953), pp. 8, 9.

into the Waco Disaster Fund, and they also sponsored various special projects. A Church of Christ congregation and a Seventh Day Adventist congregation each erected a new home for one of its members from materials supplied by American Red Cross. The young people's association of the Episcopal Church raised funds for rebuilding dressing rooms at the swimming pool on city property as a memorial to one of their members killed there during the tornado.

The main effect of the tornado on religious services seems to have been to increase the number of meetings, the attendance at these services, and the offerings made at each service. Some decrease in church attendance is normal in Waco at the end of the school year at Baylor University. This occurred, but not to the anticipated degree. Many churches held special services on the Sunday following the disaster. A commemorative Holy Communion was held at St. Alban's Episcopal Church, with the Bishop of Texas assisting; St. Mark's Lutheran Church held a prayer and thanksgiving service; Waco Catholic churches offered special prayers for the dead after masses, and a Requiem High Mass was also held at St. Mary's Church four days after the disaster.

Each of a small sample of ministers indicated a heavy increase in counseling during the emergency period, reporting an average of approximately fifty extra pastoral calls. Clergymen serving congregations with a large proportion of members in the general disaster area had the heaviest loads, of course. Dr. W. W. Melton, pastor of the Columbus Avenue Baptist Church, conducted thirteen funerals during the four days following the disaster. In an interview recorded in the *Waco Times-Herald* for May 17, he stated: "It's been the worst strain I have ever passed through."

One religious group saw the disaster as an occasion for evangelism. Fifteen men and women from the American Soul Clinic visited more than two hundred disaster-affected homes during the weeks immediately following the tornado. They reported "conversion to Christianity on the part of 35 [people]."

A majority of the pastors in the city used the disaster as a theme for sermons on the Sunday following the storm. The local newspaper listed these topics: "Thank Thee, Father," "The Tornado and God," "An Available Hiding Place," "After the Storm, the Still Small Voice," "Let's Rise Up and Rebuild Waco," "Faith for This Hour," "Be of Good Cheer," "Christian Faith and Tragedy," "Storm-Proof Religion," "Meditations at a Ruined Building," and "God Speaking to Waco." A week later these topics were listed: "Safe in the Storms,"

"God's Message for Waco," "The Heavens Do Rule," "God Has Called," "Other Refuge Have I None," "Miracles Can Happen Now," "Hope or Despair?" "Faith for This Hour," and "Fear Not." Some ministers gave a series of sermons on the disaster, continuing for five or six consecutive Sundays.

Most of the sermons were designed to induce the acceptance of the disaster as being within the will of God, though a few saw it as an expression of His displeasure. The general theme of acceptance was expressed in these words: "With the lesson of Job before us, let us carry on our ideals to rebuild the wastes and above all to stand together in unity and dispense loving kindness in the hour of supreme need."

A plea for acceptance with overtones of mental hygiene came from a clergyman who said:

No matter who we are, there is nothing in the world we can do to change the situation. . . . It is not wholesome that we should be borne down by regrets that anything we have done or left undone should have brought this tragedy upon us. Of course, we can do all in our power to avert a like tragedy in the future—but let us not unnecessarily worry over what might have been . . .

Then attention is turned to the inevitable query why does God permit such tragedy . . . and the answer is given. We have a God like Jesus who asked for himself no immunity from the tragedies of life . . . Anchor your faith in the fact of a God who loves you . . .[5]

Another minister pointed out that faith and fear are incompatible and supported his position with a reminder of man's impotence. "When man surrenders to God, then God can do to us as he wishes." He recommended that "people should seek Christ when they can't understand; and trust Him if they can't know."

Perhaps the most unusual theme was sounded by the pastor who said:

Out of this dust, rubble, and wind a greater city shall come in all the physical improvements that connote newer architectural designs . . . and more rigid adherence to later codes affecting buildings. This shall add to our economy. Unquestionably, this will attract thousands more to our city, so that we could easily visualize a city of 200,000 people or more in the next few years. . . . We bow our heads and mourn with those who mourn.

[5] Special message by Bishop Clinton S. Quinn, Episcopal Diocese of Texas, to the people of Waco, as quoted in *Waco Times-Herald*, May 17, 1953.

We lift our heads with courage and faith as we mark the path of opportunities we shall take that presage a greater Waco. God bless us all.[6]

About one month following the disaster, internationally famous evangelist Billy Graham conducted a service in memory of the victims. Graham said the storm shows what God can do "if we do not repent. Out of the storm comes a message of warning to the 50 per cent of Wacoans who do not attend church." He told the survivors to live with hope and to prepare their lives so that they will "again be with those who have left this world." He also observed that the experience had demonstrated anew the value of the church, the Red Cross, the Salvation Army, and other relief agencies, and that it furnished a lesson in unity, because Waco forgot racial prejudices and political differences to work as a team in recovering from the tornado.

In most sermons the disaster was used as the basis of a plea to lead a more Christian life, as is illustrated by one clergyman, who, after assuring his congregation that "calamity is not to be taken as the divine judgment on individuals as such," went on to say that there must be some explanation, some rational reason, for such events:

Every accident, every calamity of a small nature has its cause, whether carelessness or negligence or temper or wrong-headedness. Why is it not logical to assume that large calamities also have their reasons, though they are so big that we cannot trace them? . . . We must hasten to do something about repenting and living fruitfully. The penalty for not doing so may well be additional catastrophe upon calamity until we . . . heed. Let us take up repentance and fruitful living seriously ere God's mercy is exhausted."[7]

Using the disaster to induce persons to lead a more religious life appears also in newspaper advertisements carried by many of the churches. For example, one read: "We consider the *privilege* of assisting those in physical need an opportunity to serve our Lord and Master. . . . We are more eager to break the 'bread of life' to hungry souls and pass the living waters of Christ's gospel to thirsty spirits than in doing anything else in the whole of the world."[8]

The clergy and organized religious groups in Waco realized their

[6] Bishop Joseph Gomez, African Methodist Episcopal Church, as quoted in *Waco Times-Herald*, May 24, 1953.

[7] The Rev. Thomas B. Gallaher, pastor, First Presbyterian Church, Waco (from manuscript of sermon supplied by Mr. Gallaher).

[8] Advertisement appearing in *Waco Times-Herald*, May 23, 1953. Space bought by Church of Christ congregations in Waco.

opportunity to administer physically, spiritually, and emotionally to victims of this disaster, thereby aiding in the rehabilitation of these phases of social living so grievously disrupted by the experience.

Material and Emotional Impact

Finally, what was the over-all effect of these two disasters on the families who experienced them? How did they feel some months later when they were well on the way toward rehabilitation? What is their opinion of how the disasters affected their neighborhoods and their cities, and what will these catastrophes mean for the future of the places in which they live?

In Waco nearly two-thirds of the families thought they were about as well off as they had been before the tornado. In San Angelo approximately one-half the families expressed this feeling. Almost one-fourth of the Waco families felt they were worse off; in San Angelo this proportion was one-third. There is left, then, approximately one-tenth of the Waco families and one-sixth of those in San Angelo who felt they had managed by some means to turn disaster into opportunity and emerged in better condition than they had been in before. These data in somewhat greater detail and in more exact ratios are given in Table 18.

TABLE 18

Family Estimate of Its Over-all Condition, with Reported Emotional Disturbance

Material and Emotional Condition	Percentage	
	Waco	San Angelo
Better off; no emotional upset	4	2
Better off; emotional upset	5	14
Worse off; no emotional upset	9	5
Worse off; emotional upset	16	31
No noticeable change; no emotional upset	30	12
No noticeable change; emotional upset .	36	36
Total	100	100

Emotional damage does not seem to have been a factor in the evaluation these families placed on their own condition, except in one category. The San Angelo families who reported themselves in worse condition also reported having emotional upset about six times as often as they reported having none. But, also, the families reporting themselves in better condition reported a greater prevalence of emotional upset in both cities, though the proportion was greater in San Angelo. It would seem, then, that the data reflect the higher general rate of emotional stress in San Angelo more than anything else.

The picture that emerges when we look at the effects of the tornado on the material lives of the families in San Angelo is one of dire suffering. Their bodies were buffeted; their pocketbooks hard hit.

TABLE 19

Health Conditions in Sample Families

| | Percentage | |
Condition	Waco	San Angelo
Families with member ill before disaster .	11.3	18.0
Families with member ill after disaster .	12.7	14.0
Persons ill before disaster	4.2	5.7
Persons ill after disaster	4.0	5.9

Obviously, much work would be required from them before they could regain their predisaster status. But often more important, we discovered, was the emotional stress under which these people were placed and its effects upon them. We investigated this aspect of the problem in two ways. Several questions designed to get at emotional behavior were included in the schedule used for formal interviewing. Later, intensive interviews were held with a small number of persons and were recorded on tape. These were subjected to very detailed and careful study.

Since the medical profession is now quite certain that many pains and other physiological symptoms are expressions of deep emotional stress, we attempted to get at the less tangible effects on health by asking whether there were ill members of the families before the tornadoes and at the time of interview. The results are not conclusive; indeed, they are somewhat contradictory. In San Angelo, there was a notably higher incidence of illness reported for the period immediately before the storm, 18 per cent of the families reporting that one or more members had been ill at the time, as compared with 11.3 per cent in Waco. At the time of interview, however, the Waco incidence had risen to 12.7 per cent, but the San Angelo figure had decreased to 14 per cent. Calculated on the total number of persons involved, there was a drop in the incidence of illness in Waco of 0.2 per cent, and an increase of the same magnitude in San Angelo.

It seems probable that the statistics on illness before and after the disasters may reflect the medical care given disaster victims and their families which they otherwise would not have obtained. But there is no evidence in the data to support such a hypothesis; it is purely speculative. It is also enticing to speculate that improved water and

TABLE 20

Family Members Reported as Displaying Emotional Stress

Member	Number	
	Waco	*San Angelo*
Husband only	6	6
Wife only	33	21
Child only	7	16
Husband and wife	18	32
Parent and child	10	20
Multiple members	39	120
Total	113	215
Percentage of persons in sample suffering emotional stress	11.4	30.0

sewage systems in San Angelo might be responsible for the change in illness rates, but again there is no evidence to support such speculation. The history of the area may be an important factor; the stricken community formerly was a place of residence for many persons who had been patients in a nearby tuberculosis sanitarium.

The term "illness" in the above discussion has been used to denote easily recognizable physiological symptoms. When we move into the less well-charted emotional area, we find an entirely different picture. Informants were asked, "Have you noticed any emotional stress among family members as a result of the disaster?" We made no attempt to define "emotional stress"—a task at which experts have not had signal success—since what we sought was the respondent's opinion about whether the tornado had serious, but obscure, effects on members of his family. In Waco, 23 per cent of the answers to this question were affirmative; in San Angelo, this figure soars to 72.7 per cent. In addition to the greater intensity of the residential devasta-

111

tion in San Angelo, it is possible that the answers reflect something of the pervasive awareness of the danger of storms in that city, an aspect that we shall note later, as well as the more complete involvement of the sample members in that city.

Support for this hypothesis is found in the fact that whereas in Waco emotional stress was reported as observed only in the parents of half the cases, in San Angelo it was reported for parents and children in almost two-thirds the cases and for parents only in about one-fourth the cases. When the base on which the above statistics are calculated is changed from number of families to number of persons, the results are in the same direction, though the difference is not so great. In Waco, 11.4 per cent of the total persons in the sample were reported as showing emotional stress as a result of the disaster; in San Angelo, 39.0 per cent were. Furthermore, in San Angelo, the emotional effects seem much more prevalent among families than individuals.

Reference was made above to a pervasive awareness of the danger of storms.[9] Respondents were asked, "Have any family members expressed fear at unusual weather conditions since the disaster?" Answers to this question closely parallel those concerning the display of emotional stress. In Waco, 58 per cent of the families reported that one or more members did express such fear; in San Angelo, more than four of each five families—81.3 per cent—reported this reaction. In terms of the number of persons affected, these figures become 31.6 per cent and 48.4 per cent, respectively. Again, that fear of threatening weather was much more pervasive in San Angelo than in Waco reflects the more intense impact of the tornado in that city.

Certainly it would be both unwarranted and unfair to conclude from this evidence that a serious problem of mental health was created in either city. But it seems fair to say that the evidence does suggest that there are emotional resultants which deserve more intensive study and which may be of importance in interpreting some of the actions undertaken and some of the opinions expressed by persons who survived these disasters. Whether these emotional states should be diagnosed as mental illness is a problem for expert opinion.

When the persons interviewed looked beyond themselves to their neighborhoods and their cities and tried to assess the effects of the disasters on a broader scale, there was a distinct shifting of opinion. More than 33 per cent of the Waco respondents thought their neigh-

[9] Detailed data on this aspect of the study appear in Chapter 5 (Table 38 and related discussion).

112

borhoods were better off; "worse off" judgments were voiced by only 5 per cent. This is in distinct contrast to the one-fourth who saw their families as being in worse condition. In San Angelo this shift was even more pronounced, where 62 per cent saw their neighborhoods as better off, while only 16 per cent thought their own families were in better condition. The condition of the neighborhood was said by 16 per cent to be worse, but 33 per cent held this judgment of the condition of their own families.

Looking into the future of their neighborhoods, the respondents were more optimistic. Less than 2 per cent in Waco and slightly less

TABLE 21

Family Members Reported as Showing Fear of Unusual Weather Conditions

Members	Waco		San Angelo	
	Number	Percentage	Number	Percentage
Parents only	117	37.3	51	19.4
Children only	15	4.7	16	6.1
Parents and children	182	58.0	196	74.5
Total	314	100.0	263	100.0
Families with member showing fear of weather		58.0		81.3

It is interesting to note that although the differential impact of fear on the adults in the two cities was great, it apparently was not significantly different with the children.

than 10 per cent in San Angelo foresaw any permanent ill effects, while 52 per cent in Waco and 74 per cent in San Angelo could foresee a neighborhood better than it had been before the tornado.

Their expectations for the future of their cities, as contrasted to their neighborhoods, were most sanguine of all. In Waco, 66 per cent and in San Angelo, 71 per cent thought their city in the future would be better because of the tornado. Only 5 per cent in Waco and 3.4 per cent in San Angelo felt that the net effect would be adverse.

These persons assessed their own situation and that of their family more critically than they did the conditions of their neighbors and their cities. It is, of course, true that they knew more of their own losses—material and sentimental and symbolic. It seems plausible to assume they were judging the condition of others by what they could see—new homes, new cars, new furniture—and ignoring, or being ignorant of, the particularly meaningful items furnishing the emotional stress that might flare into anger at unexpected times, the strained relationships, and all the other nonmaterial factors that are often more important than new wall paper, carpets, or even a new house. But these are factors that could not be probed adequately with the type of research we did. This field of research needs persons highly trained in assessing mental health.

Perhaps the outstanding impression from this portion of the study of the disasters is the marked optimism characteristic of these families and their communities. This could be the most significant finding of the study. Certainly it goes far to explain why these cities have recovered as well and as quickly as they have from the catastrophes. Perhaps it demonstrates once again the vitality of our own particular society and its basic democratic organization.

114

5. The Dispossessed

Since the primary purpose of this study was to discover the effects of tornadoes on families as a unit and on their individual members, we made a concentrated study of postdisaster housing, for nowhere is the difference in the intensity of the impacts better demonstrated than in the statistics relating to this. The material that follows takes no account of the very heavy damage in the downtown district of Waco because not many homes were located there and the few that were, were not typical of the city. Hence, this, as well as all other material relating to families, refers only to those families living within the pathway of the tornadoes when interviewers visited them some seven to nine months later.

Displacement of people is one of the most serious, as well as one of the most immediate, problems in most disaster situations. To understand the residential movement of families in Waco and San Angelo, we had to find answers to many questions. Where did the displaced find temporary housing? How long did they stay in temporary housing? How many times did they move before they were permanently located? Were there significant differences between those families who moved and those who remained in their pretornado homes? Was there any relationship between moving and such factors as the amount of insurance carried, aid received from welfare agencies, the value of the home, the amount of damage suffered, the interruption of employment? Particularly, were those who moved more emotionally affected than those who did not? Were their attitudes toward the agencies active in disaster relief and toward their postdisaster situation, their neighbors, and their communities greatly different from those of people able to remain in their homes?

Most of the data that follow in this chapter have been used comparatively to determine what differences, if any, the tornadoes had upon those who were forced to evacuate their homes as contrasted

115

with those who were able to remain in their homes. The results of the comparisons can be taken also as a further measure of the difference in intensity of the disasters.

Emergency Housing for the Displaced

In San Angelo, not one of the persons interviewed lived in a house that had not been damaged. More than six out of each ten had lived in houses that were totally destroyed. But in Waco, fewer than 10

TABLE 22

Distribution of Sample Families According to Change of Residence

| | Percentage of Families | |
Moved:	Waco	San Angelo
To rented emergency housing	10.2	43.3
To other property owned	0.0	2.7
Temporarily with friends or relatives . .	3.9	26.0
Away from city	2.8	3.3
Into area after disaster	7.1	0.0
Total who moved	24.0	75.3
Did not move	76.0	24.7
	100.0	100.0
Actual number who moved	283	150

With the exception of the "Away from city" line, all differences in this table meet tests of statistical significance. This applies to the line "To other property owned" in spite of the small number of cases. Fisher's Exact Method applied to this line gives $P < .05$.

per cent of the sample had their homes destroyed and better than one in six lived in a house that came through without any damage at all.

In Waco, 76 per cent of the sample families *did not* move from the house in which they were living at the time of the storm; in San Angelo, 75 per cent *did* move as a result of the disaster.

Of those forced out of their homes, about half in each city rented emergency housing. But in San Angelo about 25 per cent of these found refuge in the homes of friends and relatives, while in Waco this was true of only about 15 per cent. This difference may reflect the more urban patterns of the larger city or perhaps it may reflect a greater spirit of helpfulness engendered by the more intense devastation of the Lake View neighborhood in San Angelo. That Waco is subject to somewhat greater mobility is indicated by the fact that 7 per cent of the families interviewed there had not been living in that area at the time of the tornado; no newcomers were found in the San Angelo sample.

Again, a distinct difference appears in the fact that in Waco slightly more than 50 per cent of the families who made temporary moves paid rent on their new quarters, whereas in San Angelo 85 per cent did so. Rents paid averaged about $8.00 per month more in San Angelo than in Waco, in spite of the fact that San Angelo is a smaller city. Those who moved to other property owned by themselves, as some families did, were not counted as having paid rent. Those who lived with friends and relatives usually did so rent-free; only one informant said that his family had paid rent to relatives with whom they were housed.

Data on all families who incurred rent bills as a result of the tornadoes show 43 per cent for San Angelo and 7 per cent for Waco. These figures are another clear indication of the relative effects of the two storms in displacing families in the two cities.

It might seem logical that many families whose homes had been destroyed or damaged so severely that they were forced to move out of them would have preferred to leave the area in which they had suffered so grievously or would have been forced into less desirable sections of the city. The families we interviewed sustain the first of these expectations but not the second.

In Waco, 11 per cent of the sample moved outside the storm area but remained in the city; in San Angelo, 59.3 per cent did so. That is, a little less than half the Waco families who moved found emergency homes beyond the limits of the tornado pathway; in San Angelo, this proportion is about four out of five.

Few families left town in search of temporary housing, only 3 per cent in Waco doing so and 4 per cent in San Angelo. All the others—with the exception of the 18 families in the Waco sample who had not been living in the area at the time of disaster—moved to new homes within the path of the tornadoes.

The evidence is that the displaced families in both cities found new homes of about the same character as those they had been occupying. In San Angelo, 44 per cent and in Waco, 11 per cent reported this to be true. When we recall the much higher percentage of San Angelo families forced to move, we see that these percentages represent about the same proportion of those involved in both cities.

But an interesting difference appears when we examine the percentages of families who moved to better or poorer housing. In Waco, the figures indicate that these displaced families were about three times as likely to go into better housing as into poorer. In San Angelo, the chances were better than two to one they would find themselves in poorer places.

These statistics are somewhat puzzling. Perhaps the best explanation is that Waco, being a larger city, would offer a wider variety of housing from which to choose. And it should be recalled also that the

TABLE 23

Families Remaining in, or Moving from, Devastated Areas

| | Percentage of Families | |
Status	Waco	San Angelo
Remained in area and moved to		
similar housing	2.1	8.7
better housing	0.7	0.0
poorer housing	0.4	2.0
Moved temporarily out to		
similar housing	8.8	35.1
better housing	1.8	8.0
poorer housing	0.4	16.0
Did not move	76.0	26.7
Moved into area after tornado	7.1	0.0
	100.0	100.0

path of the storm in Waco cut across the city in such a fashion as to include most socio-economic levels, whereas in San Angelo the devastation was confined to what may be described impressionistically as a lower-middle-class portion of the community.

The picture changes again when the sample is divided into those who moved out of the stricken areas and those who remained. Of the group remaining in the area in San Angelo, no family found better housing, but in Waco, the chances were two to one that the families remaining did find better houses.

At the time of the interview, these families seemed to have become fairly well adjusted to their new locations, though certainly some of them would be expected to make further moves in accordance with the general pattern of family mobility. In both cities, almost 85 per cent of the families were back at their old addresses, either in the houses they had occupied before the disaster or new ones built on the old sites. Only about 1 per cent were reported as still occupying housing they had gone into as an emergency measure immediately after the disaster.

The effects of the tornadoes on the housing of the families may be gained from a quick glance at Table 24.

TABLE 24

Changes in Housing of Sample Families before and after the Tornadoes

Waco	Percentage	Rent	Value
Renters			
Before	23.3	$31	
After	24.4	30	
Owners			
Before	76.7		$4,509
After	75.6		4,556
San Angelo			
Renters			
Before	12.2	43	
After	13.4	38	
Owners			
Before	87.8		5,882
After	86.6		6,321

It is evident that the disasters made little difference in the housing occupied by these persons. But there is one interesting change. The value of the homes owned by the people in San Angelo rose on an average by more than $500. At the same time, those who rented found cheaper homes when they settled permanently. The increased value of owned homes probably reflects rising costs of construction as much as anything else, while the slightly lower rentals paid most likely were due to the lowered economic status of those who did not own homes.

While the evidence is clear that in both cities rents in the storm areas decreased and the values of houses increased, why and how this contradictory situation developed is not clear.

The net impression is that within little more than half a year the families who had suffered damage to their housing had returned to almost the same conditions which they were in on the afternoon of May 11, when the tornadoes swirled in on them. Most of the changes noted are of too small a degree to be statistically significant; normal mobility and chance error in the technique of selecting the particular families interviewed could account for the differences observed.

The extent of damage to a house would logically be expected to determine whether the occupants moved or not. Actually, this corre-

TABLE 25

Extent of Damage to the House and Moves of the Family

	Percentage of Families Affected			
	Waco		*San Angelo*	
Extent of Damage	*Did Not Move*	*Did Move*	*Did Not Move*	*Did Move*
Destroyed	0	52	14	74
Heavily damaged	24	33	25	16
Partially damaged	28	7	42	6
Slightly damaged	30	8	19	4
Undamaged	18	0	0	0
	100	100	100	100
Actual number of cases	219	46	36	114

lation was not high in San Angelo or in Waco. In San Angelo, 14 per cent of the people reported their homes had been totally destroyed, but also said they did not move. This anomaly can be explained by the fact that several families literally camped out on their property in the ruins of their former homes. Other families purchased or rented housetrailers and moved them onto their property and lived in them while constructing a new home. Still others lived in garages or outhouses on their property until new homes were built.

Figures 1 and 2 (pp. 4, 26) show the location of the residences of the sample families at the time the tornadoes struck. They also show the extent of damage the residences received, according to the opinion of the resident. The spotty nature of the heavy damage in Waco is quite obvious on the map.

Homes very near each other differ greatly in the severity of damage reported. The adequacy of construction would be an obvious explanation of this fact, and would, perhaps, also indicate the relative value of the houses, a well-built house being generally of greater value than a poorly constructed one.

120

In Waco, of the 204 sample families who owned their homes, 170 did not move. The average value placed on these homes by their owners was $5,232; that of the homes whose owners did move was $3,786. This is a highly significant difference.

In San Angelo, the same general difference existed in direction,

TABLE 26

Location of Sample Families When Interviewed

| | Percentage of Families | | | |
| | Waco | | San Angelo | |
Status	Did Not Move	Did Move	Did Not Move	Did Move
Renting at the original location . .	16	9	6	11
Living at original owned site . .	77	76	94	76
Living in house rented for emergency	0	4	0	2
Purchased other housing in the disaster area	3	4	0	7
Renting a different house in the disaster area	4	7	0	4
	100	100	100	100
Total living at original location . .	93	85	100	87

though not in degree. There only 33 of the 128 home-owners did not move. The average value of the homes for this group was $6,359; for the 95 owners who did move, it was $5,686.

If, as some contend, rents are also a partial indication of the adequacy of the construction of a house, further evidence of this exists in the Waco sample. In that city, 48 of the 61 renters did not move. These families were paying an average of $33 per month rent. The 13 who did move paid an average rent of $27. Comparable statistics for San Angelo are not available since too few renters appeared in the sample from that city to make the figures meaningful.

Where did the displaced families find emergency shelter? In San Angelo the area contiguous to the path of the tornado was the first choice for temporary relocation of the displaced families, particularly along the main street from the downtown area into Lake View. The displaced families in Waco found temporary residences in the less severely damaged areas within the general path of the tornado and on its immediate borders.

Comparison of Pretornado and Emergency Housing

In order to understand the ways in which rehabilitation takes place, we gave a great deal of attention to whether temporary housing was better or worse than predisaster housing. For this purpose several indices were available—the amount of rent paid, the estimated value of the house occupied, the number of rooms in the house, the presence or absence of utilities, and, finally, the impression of the general economic level of the neighborhood into which the displaced persons moved.

TABLE 27

Comparison of Pretornado and Emergency Housing

	Percentage of Families	
Rating of Emergency Housing	*Waco Did Move*	*San Angelo Did Move*
Within disaster area		
Similar	2.1	8.7
Higher	0.7	0.0
Lower	0.4	2.0
In nondisaster area		
Similar	8.8	35.7
Higher	1.8	8.0
Lower	0.4	16.0
Moved away from the city	2.7	3.5
	18.0	74.0
Did not move	76.0	26.0
Not living in disaster area at time of tornado	7.0	0.0
Total	101.0*	100.0

* Total percentage exceeds 100 because of rounding off.

Those families who settled at a new location were faced with the task of re-establishing their life-pattern among new neighbors in the new area. This was, of course, a burden not faced by those who did not move.

The fact revealed by Table 27 that 7 per cent of the Waco sample reported they did not move because at the time of the disaster they

were not living in the area indicates a normal mobility that this research did not take into account. Presumably these families moved
into the storm area to secure better housing or suitable housing for
less money than they were paying elsewhere.

We also needed to know how many times the families moved as a
result of the tornadoes and the total distance of their moves. In order
to measure the actual distances involved in the various moves, each
case was plotted separately and the straight-line distance between
residences was measured in miles. In this process, five cases in Waco
and twenty-eight in San Angelo had to be discarded because the information on their schedules was not sufficient to permit plotting.
Table 28 presents the data for the remaining cases.

TABLE 28

Number of Moves, Including Final Location and Average Total Distance
Covered in All Moves

Number of Moves	Average Total Miles		Percentage of Families	
	Waco	San Angelo	Waco	San Angelo
1	2.0	2.7	15	3
2	3.5	3.1	70	68
3	3.2	4.1	13	29
4 or more	4.1	. . .	2	. .
Total average distance covered .	3.2	3.4		
Actual number of moves in sample	41	86		

Some 15 per cent in Waco and 3 per cent in San Angelo made one
move only. The larger proportion of families in each sample moved
twice: to one emergency residence and back. But San Angelo families
evidently had more difficulty in finding satisfactory temporary residences, since 29 per cent moved three times. The average total distance in both cities was most similar.

The longest move was the first. Each subsequent move was more
likely than not to be in the direction of the pretornado home. The
relatively short distances moved suggests two things: a desire to remain as close to the destroyed home as possible and a desire to remain
within the general socio-economic level of the destroyed home. It
may be surprising that the length of the San Angelo moves were as
great as those in the larger city of Waco. However, the less intense

devastation of the Waco area must have left available many more nearby homes for those forced to move, as is indicated by the fact that in Waco only 14 per cent moved out of the damaged area, while

TABLE 29

Average Number of Rooms per Residence for All Families

| | Average Number of Rooms | | | |
| | Waco | | San Angelo | |
Residence Sequence	Did Not Move	Did Move	Did Not Move	Did Move
(1) Pretornado	4.5	4.6	4.7	4.4
(2) Emergency	4.4	4.1	4.1	3.4
(3) Posttornado	5.0	4.3	4.6	4.4
Change between (1) and (3) . .	+0.5	—0.3	—0.1	0.0

in San Angelo 63 per cent did so. Moves to other homes within the tornado path would usually be shorter, of course.

The home is considered the symbol of the family, and buying a home is a major economic investment for a family to make. Therefore it was important to know what changes in the size and adequacy of homes had occurred as a result of the tornado. One cost factor that may be compared between the pretornado, emergency, and post-tornado residences of the sample families is the average number of rooms per house.

As might be expected, the dispossessed families in both cities moved into smaller homes; but not smaller to a significant degree. One surprise comes from the statistics on the size of pre- and postdisaster housing: in Waco, those who were not forced to move managed to add half a room, on the average, to their homes within the few months between the tornado and the time they were interviewed, whereas those who moved resettled in houses one-third room smaller on the average. In San Angelo no such differences were reported. The Waco figures, again, suggest that those families forced to move suffered more heavily than those who managed to remain where they were. It is possible that Red Cross or local disaster-funds granted for the repair of damage may have been stretched to cover an additional room in some cases.

The number of rooms, of course, is no sure indication of the quality of a house. Perhaps a better index of quality is provided by figures on the public utilities used by the householders. Waco shows little change in the type of facilities used in the homes before and after the move. The figures suggest again, however, the real difference between the quality of the residences of those who were forced to move and those who were not. Seemingly, the evacuated residences were rebuilt to near the original condition, without being improved to any great extent.

Before the tornado, a large segment of the population in Lake View relied on septic tanks, shallow wells, and bottled gas instead of public utilities. Shortly after the storm, San Angelo extended water and sewer lines farther into the area and residents utilized these when rebuilding their homes. One other possible factor explaining the increase in the use of gas, water, and sewer lines in San Angelo (a change of 19 per cent was recorded) is that during the emergency period most of the persons who moved out of Lake View went into homes served by these facilities, their moves being predominantly toward the more urbanized portion of the city, where such facilities are supplied regularly.

A second indication of the quality of the homes may be seen in their use of electricity and telephone service. In this comparison the difference found in the homes of our Waco sample indicates that there is a real difference between the economic levels of those who moved and those who did not. The nonmovers used these services more than the movers. In San Angelo, the changes for both groups were similar, with a general decrease in telephone service in emergency housing.

Changes in the value of the original and the reconstructed residence is a third factor indicating changes in the adequacy of housing.

TABLE 30

Variations in Home Values (Owners Only)

| | Average Value per House | | | |
| | Waco | | San Angelo | |
Period	Did Not Move	Did Move	Did Not Move	Did Move
Predisaster	$5,232	$3,786	$6,078	$5,686
Postdisaster	5,165	4,007	6,359	6,294
Change	−0,067	+0,221	+0,281	+0,608

The picture of home reconstruction is quite similar for the two cities. In San Angelo, the average increase in postdisaster home values was greater for the movers. In Waco, those who moved also returned to a somewhat better home, while those who did not seemingly suffered some loss in home value. These figures may indicate more adequate financial assistance given to San Angelo victims.

In general, this detailed comparison of several indices on the quality of housing supports two conclusions: (1) A real difference was found in the level of living of those who were forced from their homes and those who managed to stay put. (2) When they were again resettled, they occupied houses remarkably like those they had before the disaster.

It is interesting that most of the renters in Waco who went through the tornado also chose to remain in the area in spite of their experiences. In Waco, of the 48 renters who did not move immediately after the tornado, 17 per cent later rented other homes within the disaster area and 8 per cent purchased homes in that section. Of those renters forced to evacuate their homes, 25 per cent later bought homes in the area. In San Angelo, only two families who were renting were involved in this aspect of the study; hence, no generalizations can be made concerning them. Of all those who did move, almost 50 per cent returned to their original homesites. More than 33 per cent rented other housing in the disaster area and 18 per cent purchased homes in that area. Such behavior is certainly indicative of a refusal to be frightened out of the area in which homes had been built. This spirit is also found in other attitudes expressed by these people.

The interesting changes in the postdisaster location and condition of the renters suggests the mobility of this segment of the sample populations. In San Angelo, the renters who bought homes placed a higher-than-average value on them; in Waco, the reverse was true. Thus, it seems that in the two communities the renters represent different types with different patterns of value.

Economic Status of the Movers and Nonmovers

Being forced to leave the home because of storm damage is obviously a severe economic blow to any family. In an effort to determine just how severe this blow actually was, we investigated several economic factors. We attempted also to discover whether there were pertinent predisaster differences in the economic status of the families forced to move and those able to remain in their homes.

In Waco, the movers had a significantly lower income, their average annual income being $2,372; those who were able to remain in

126

their homes had $2,985. In San Angelo, the difference between these two classifications was only $13. There, it will be recalled, the stricken area was a highly homogeneous residential section, so that this difference would not be likely to be great.

Another fundamental difference appears when employment is considered. In both Waco and San Angelo, the families who did not move were more likely to depend upon the father only for income from employment. Although almost one-fifth of the families in these two cities had no member at all employed, there appears to be no significant association between this factor and whether they moved or not.

Interrupted employment would naturally be of consequence to families already suffering financial losses. As would be expected, the families not forced to move suffered less loss of employment than those who were. Although of the nonmovers 27 per cent in Waco and 28 per cent in San Angelo reported no loss of time from work, there were 46 per cent in Waco and 59 per cent in San Angelo who did have family income interrupted in this way. It is, of course, to be expected that if such duties as searching for a suitable house, moving in, and taking care of the emotional reactions of other family members were not required, absence from the job would be less. Once more we see the heavier burden falling upon those forced to leave their homes.

It was also important to determine the duration of the interrupted employment. In Waco, the families who moved represented not only a larger proportion of those whose members lost working time, but the average time lost was also longer—emphasizing again the greater misfortune of these victims.

In Waco, 27 per cent of the nonmovers reported job-interruptions of from 7 to 10 working days; of the movers, 40 per cent reported such interruptions as between 16 and 30 working days. The same pattern is repeated in San Angelo: of the nonmovers only 31 per cent reported work-interruptions of from 7 to 10 working days; of the movers, 62 per cent were affected by work-interruption of from 16 to 30 working days.

Thus, loss of income from employment was added to loss of the home.

"Why was the employment interrupted?" Responses to this question illustrate a basic difference between the nature of the Waco and San Angelo disasters. A much larger proportion of San Angelo families stopped work to rebuild their homes. A larger proportion of families in Waco suffered work-interruption because their places of employment were damaged by the storm. It will be recalled that the downtown business area in Waco was the scene of greatest destruc-

TABLE 31

Reasons for Interrupted Employment

| | Percentage of Families Affected | | | |
| | *Waco* | | *San Angelo* | |
Reason	*Did Not Move*	*Did Move*	*Did Not Move*	*Did Move*
Place of employment damaged . .	16	18	3	3
To rebuild residence or other family buildings	3	13	22	42
To participate in rescue and emergency activities . . .	2	0	3	6
Injury suffered during the storm .	1	0	0	3
Illness incurred during disaster period	1	2	0	1
To care for family member injured in disaster	0	2	0	3
Other	4	11	3	4
Total	27	46	31	62
No interrupted employment . . .	73	54	69	38
Actual number	219	46	36	114

χ^2 tests on relationship between moving and interruption of employment give $P < .05$ for Waco; $P < .01$ for San Angelo.

tion and death, whereas very few business firms were affected in San Angelo.

Obviously those families forced to move would have suffered greater economic loss in the destruction of such things as goods, cars, and houses than those who were able to stay put. Indeed, such loss was one of the major reasons for moving. The extent of this difference is interesting and pertinent. In San Angelo, the loss of the movers was about twice as great as that of the nonmovers; in Waco, it was four times as great.

The total of losses for the Waco families was $189,204; for the San Angelo families, $714,678. But the average loss per family in Waco was $760; in San Angelo, $4,764. These data clearly demonstrate the greater and more widespread loss in San Angelo homes, as well as the greater financial loss of those families in both cities who moved during the disaster period.

Insurance must also be considered in discussing the economic losses of affected families. Again, the families who moved are in a less

TABLE 32

Proportion of Those with Loss and Average Loss

| | Waco | | San Angelo | |
| | Did Not | Did | Did Not | Did |
Description	Move	Move	Move	Move
Percentage of families with loss .	72	84	86	96
Average loss per family	$481	$2,024	$2,711	$5,413

favorable position. In San Angelo, 34 per cent of the movers had no insurance whatever; only 20 per cent of the nonmovers were without. The same pattern appears in Waco, where 41 per cent of the movers had no insurance, and 21 per cent of the nonmovers were without.

One of the best indicators of total loss may be the indebtedness acquired because of the storms. In response to a question on this,

TABLE 33

Indebtedness of Disaster-Affected Families

	Percentage of Families			
	Waco		San Angelo	
	Did Not	Did	Did Not	Did
	Move	Move	Move	Move
Families incurring debt to re-establish the home . . .	11	46	23	38

significant differences were uncovered. Table 33 shows the reported indebtedness. Thus, we see the recurring picture of the more severe economic impact of the disasters being upon those families who were forced to move, and of the greater impact upon the San Angelo families than upon those in Waco.

Sources of Financial Aid for Displaced Families

An alternative to incurring debt in the effort to rehabilitate the family was to turn to the American Red Cross, the Salvation Army, or the local disaster-fund. Obviously, those families who moved were much more likely to request and receive such aid, and, as a rule, they

TABLE 34

Sources of Financial Assistance and Percentage of Families Receiving It

| | Percentage of Families | | | |
| | Waco | | San Angelo | |
Aid Received from:	Did Not Move	Did Move	Did Not Move	Did Move
American Red Cross only . . .	9	41	8	24
Salvation Army only	2	0	0	4
Disaster fund only	2	2	8	10
Church group only	1	2	3	6
Friends only	1	0	8	4
Red Cross and Salvation Army . .	0	11	7	16
Multiple sources	1	14	17	19
	16	70	47	83
Received no aid	84	30	53	17

also received greater amounts than did those families not forced to leave their homes. The sources furnishing aid are listed in Table 34. The types and average amounts of such aid are shown in Table 35.

The types and amount of aid received differ to a significant degree.

TABLE 35

Aid by Type, Percentage of Families Receiving It, and Average Amount

| | Waco | | | | San Angelo | | | |
| | Did Not Move | | Did Move | | Did Not Move | | Did Move | |
Type of Aid	%	Amt.	%	Amt.	%	Amt.	%	Amt.
Emergency and long-term aid of food, clothing, housing .	10	$ 15	48	$ 20	33	$ 20	66	$ 25
Rebuilding house* .	10	358	47	1,327	22	1,185	48	1,700
Replacing furnishings	2	50	14	150	17	150	43	200
Medical aid	1	125	3	25	..	...	16	150
Re-establishing business	2	500	3	400	..	...	2	75

* Excludes renters.

130

We separated the types of aid into six categories, following the definitions used by American Red Cross: (1) emergency aid; (2) food, clothing, shelter; (3) aid in re-establishing the house; (4) aid in replacing household goods; (5) assistance for medical care; and (6) occupational supplies and equipment. The data in Table 34 make it clear that there was a tendency for the dispossessed families to be cared for more by Red Cross than by any other source.

Obviously, the percentage of families receiving aid is not so large as that of families in need. Needless to say, the amount of aid re-

TABLE 36

Major Sources of Funds for Restoration and Repair of Homes and Percentage of Families Using Sources

| | Percentage | | | |
| | Waco | | San Angelo | |
Source	Did Not Move	Did Move	Did Not Move	Did Move
Personal resources	69	33	73	34
Bank loan	2	4	0	0
Savings and loan association. . .	1	14	3	16
Loan from federal agency . . .	0	3	9	4
American Red Cross	8	35	12	32
Other	4	11	3	14
No large expense required . . .	16	0	3	0

ceived could not provide complete rehabilitation of the family except in most unusual cases. In particular, re-establishing the home was a major problem. The major sources helping to finance the repairs or rebuilding of the home are shown in Table 36.

When we attempted to elicit the attitudes of the respondents concerning the twelve organizations that offered aid in some way following the disasters, only one significant difference appeared between those who had moved and those who had not. In Waco, the movers were much more favorably inclined toward the American Red Cross and the local disaster-fund than the nonmovers. But this was not true in San Angelo. In both cities, the American Red Cross ranked near the bottom. The San Angelo nonmovers gave it a rank of tenth, while the Waco movers ranked both the Red Cross and the disaster fund seventh in the list of twelve.

The explanation for the apparent discrepancy between those indicating they received Red Cross aid in Table 34 and Table 36 is that Table 36 shows the *major* source of reconstruction funds. The Red Cross probably helped many other families to rebuild their homes, even though their major source of funds was a loan.

Family Evaluation of Its Postdisaster Economic and Emotional Condition

What was these families' own evaluation of their over-all economic position at the time of the interview as compared with the pre-tornado situation? A significantly larger proportion of the movers felt their condition to be worse off than did the nonmovers. Surprisingly enough, the proportion of the movers who also felt themselves to be better off than before was significantly larger than among the nonmovers. Some reasons for this paradoxical and optimistic evaluation by the movers may be: (1) The houses they finally located were more adequate than those they had before. (2) Many of the families had outstanding debts paid off. (3) In San Angelo, city and county taxes were paid for all home-owning families for one year. (4) Many families received clothing and household supplies to meet their needs. Most of the nonmovers considered themselves to be in about the same condition.

Several basic differences between families who moved and those who did not became immediately obvious when we studied their eco-

TABLE 37

Family Evaluation of Its Economic Condition

| | Percentage | | | |
| | Waco | | San Angelo | |
Postdisaster Status	*Did Not Move*	*Did Move*	*Did Not Move*	*Did Move*
Largely unchanged	17	33	69	45
Worse	23	39	29	35
Better	6	28	2	20

nomic characteristics. We felt, however, that the real significance of the differences might run much deeper than was apparent. To determine whether this was so, we compared several fundamental characteristics. No significant difference in the average number of members in the family was found between the two cities or between those who moved and those who did not. San Angelo families appeared to have slightly more members over 65 years of age. Conversely, in Waco, the families were more likely to have children under 15, and those with children were a little more likely to have been forced from their homes. Families broken by death, divorce, or separation were also more likely to have been forced out of their homes.

This suggests that the greater vulnerability of those families forced to move was quite a real thing, with other than just economic factors

TABLE 38

Relation of Emotional Stress to Family Moves

| | Percentage of Families | | | |
| | Waco | | San Angelo | |
Member Evidencing Emotional Stress	Did Not Move	Did Move	Did Not Move	Did Move
Adults	17	22	25	29
Child	3	2	11	11
Parent and child	2	2	6	7
Multiple family members . . .	5	4	19	29
	27	30	61	76
No family member	73	70	39	24

conditioning their situation. The death of an adult family member was the most frequent problem in these cases. It is tempting to speculate that their being forced to move often was a result of their living in poorly constructed, lower-value houses, a fact that in turn is indicative of the more fundamentally insecure status of these families.

As might be expected, a larger proportion of injuries had occurred among the movers than among the nonmovers. Of the latter, only 3 per cent in Waco and 6 per cent in San Angelo had one or more family members injured. Of the movers, 15 per cent in Waco and 25 per cent in San Angelo had some family member injured.

More important, perhaps, than physical injuries are the emotional disturbances that became evident—in some cases, months after the storm. Emotional disturbances were much more prevalent in San Angelo than in Waco, as would be expected. In this city a difference also appears in the reported emotional difficulties in families of movers and nonmovers, though this difference is not large enough to meet statistical tests of significance. There is no appreciable difference of this nature in Waco. The more important statistic in Table 38

133

is that revealing the incidence of emotional stress in three or more members of one family. This incidence is higher among the movers in

TABLE 39

Families with Some Member Expressing Fear at Unusual Weather Conditions

| | Percentage of Families | | | |
| | Waco | | San Angelo | |
Member	Did Not Move	Did Move	Did Not Move	Did Move
Adults	30	37	28	22
Child	6	4	6	12
Parent and child	3	9	8	12
Multiple family members . . .	17	26	30	38
	56	76	72	84
No family member	44	24	28	16

χ^2 test gives $P < .001$ when data from two cities are combined. The indication is strong that fear is a manifestation of the greater emotional impact on those families forced to move.

San Angelo than among the nonmovers and probably reflects the greater emotional impact of the destruction of the home plus the additional strain of adjusting to a new home.

Fear of unusual weather conditions is closely allied with emotional disturbances—in some cases is synonymous. A larger proportion of the families who moved had members who expressed such fears. Differences in each city are significant. Again, it is pertinent

TABLE 40

Welfare Agency Visits to Sample Families

| | Percentage of Families Visited | | | |
| | Waco | | San Angelo | |
Agency	Did Not Move	Did Move	Did Not Move	Did Move
Red Cross only	13	52	8	21
Salvation Army only	3	2	3	17
Red Cross and Salvation Army . .	1	7	14	26
Three or more agencies	5	9	6	5
	22	70	31	69
No visit from any agency worker .	78	30	69	31

that this difference between the movers and the nonmovers appears primarily in the multiple-family-members category.

In conjunction with the rehabilitation of the family, visits by representatives of the various social-welfare and relief organizations may have had considerable influence. Certainly the frequency of such visits is an indication of the real or supposed need for such assistance. Again, the data show more than twice as high a frequency of such visits to those families who moved.

In view of the differences in the experience of movers and nonmovers, it might also be expected that differences in opinion and attitudes would exist, particularly where the family's own condition is

TABLE 41

Family Evaluation of Its General Condition

| | Percentage of Families | | | |
| | Waco | | San Angelo | |
Postdisaster Status	*Did Not Move*	*Did Move*	*Did Not Move*	*Did Move*
Better	30	65	59	62
About the same	65	28	24	22
Worse	5	7	17	16

concerned. An example of this is that when asked whether they thought their family was better off because of the tornado, the larger proportion who seemed to feel that it was came from those who had moved.

The greatest percentage difference occurred in the Waco sample. Evidently, the families there who did not move were much less affected.

Perhaps the most pertinent thing about the attitudes of these families is the high degree of optimism expressed by both those who moved and those who did not. It is somewhat surprising that in both cities the movers were slightly more optimistic than the nonmovers; however, in San Angelo, this difference is so very slight as to be without significance. In Waco, it will be remembered, American Red Cross aid to displaced families often was supplemented by aid from the Waco Disaster Fund, and this fact may explain the very great difference in attitudes between those who moved and those who did not move in that city. The much higher proportion of the San Angelo families with definite opinions as to whether they were better off or worse off is also pertinent in that it is related to the much greater intensity of the storm experienced by these families.

When informants were asked to enlarge their field of consideration to include their neighborhood and the entire city in which they lived,

TABLE 42

Future Condition of the Neighborhood

| | Percentage of Families | | | |
| | Waco | | San Angelo | |
Opinion	Did Not Move	Did Move	Did Not Move	Did Move
Will be better	36	70	74	75
Will remain largely unchanged . .	62	30	19	16
Will be worse	2	0	7	9

it will be noted from Tables 42 and 43 that their optimism increased greatly. Again, it is to be noted that those families forced from their homes actually were more optimistic than those not suffering such displacement. This is more marked when they are considering the city than when they are considering their neighborhood and it is

TABLE 43

Future Condition of the City

| | Percentage of Families | | | |
| | Waco | | San Angelo | |
Opinion	Did Not Move	Did Move	Did Not Move	Did Move
Will be better	63	74	51	77
Will remain largely unchanged . .	30	22	46	19
Will be worse	5	4	3	4

more marked in the case of Waco than San Angelo. Perhaps the best way to measure the optimism of these people is to compare the number of those who believe their family, neighborhood, and city will be better off with the number of those who express the reverse opinion. When this is done, the proportion of those holding the optimistic point of view is overwhelming, the ratio running from about four to one up to fifteen to one or even higher.

It is noteworthy that optimistic attitudes toward the city's future were expressed more often by those who were forced out of their homes than by those who were not. As between the two cities it is interesting that differences between these two classes of family are statistically significant in Waco on the questions as to the future of the family and neighborhood, but not as to the city. The reverse is true of San Angelo attitudes, where the greatest difference is found in opinions as to the future of the city.

The data on dispossession appear to warrant some tentative conclusions.

The moves of families following these tornadoes were positively related to three things: (1) the type of area devastated; (2) the magnitude of the destruction; (3) the adequacy of the construction of a building.

Poorly constructed homes were much more vulnerable to destruction than were other homes, increasing the problem of moving for residents in the lower economic areas and classes.

Families who moved had certain characteristics different from those not forced to move: (1) lower family income, (2) more employment of multiple family members, (3) larger number of children per family, (4) greater probability of a disorganizing experience (death, divorce, separation) in the family history.

Those families who moved suffered greater financial loss, physical injury, and more emotional disturbance. Their disaster-caused problems included:

1) Greater economic loss — four times as large in Waco, twice as large in San Angelo as those families who did not move.

2) Added expenses of moving and establishing the family in temporary and, later, new permanent residences.

3) Greater loss through interruption of employment.

4) Less insurance protection. (This factor was offset somewhat by the aid these families received through the relief agencies.)

5) A larger proportion incurring debt, and the average debt incurred being larger.

6) More family members injured in the disasters.

Thus, we see a general picture of the most vulnerable class of families in these cities and of the greater loss and damage they suffered because of the disasters.

Usually there were two moves: one to an emergency location and the return to the original location. In some cases there were two or more moves to other temporary locations. Owners were more likely to: (1) find an emergency residence as near to the destroyed home as possible; (2) make only one emergency move; and (3) return to the original location.

The areas in which emergency residences were found had these characteristics:

1) They were located in densely populated sections of the cities.

2) They were near the damaged home, either within the disaster area, on its periphery, or along main roads leading into the area.

3) Emergency housing was usually quite similar to the occupant's damaged residence—both in type of facilities and in value. More displaced families located temporarily in poorer housing than in better.

4) If more than one move was made before returning to the original location, each subsequent move tended to bring the family closer to the original location.

5) Those families who did not return to their original site generally located in better houses than the ones they had left. This was particularly true of renters, who usually paid less rent for these newly occupied residences than they had been paying for the old.

In reconstructing the damaged house, improvements were generally in quality rather than in size. On the average, repaired and rebuilt homes had a higher value than they had had before, particularly in cases where the house had been completely destroyed and was rebuilt.

The families who moved constituted the larger proportions of those who felt their neighborhood and city would be better off in the future. These attitudes and opinions are probably related to the family's own evaluation of its position and future.

The movers also constituted the larger proportions of those who disclosed emotional disturbances and fear of weather. A second study disclosed that emotional consequences were clearly evident more than a year after the tornadoes and after most material problems had been worked out with some degree of success. From the evidence in hand, these families found it much easier to solve their economic problems than their emotional ones.

6. The Aged

Oₙₑ ₒ𝐅 𝐭𝐡ₑ 𝐬𝐭𝐚𝐫𝐭𝐥𝐢𝐧𝐠 social phenomena of the past few decades has been the constant increase in the number of aged persons in our population. Sociologists and other students of population have speculated at length about the effect these elder citizens have on our familial, political, and community life. The phenomenon, however, is so recent that not much research has yet been done.

Since persons of more than 65 years of age obviously are unable to take part in many of the activities associated with disaster—rescue work, fleeing from danger, and aiding in the rehabilitation of others—it seemed to us that those families with aged members very likely had reacted in ways distinctly different from those without such members. Hence, we divided data on families according to five family types and made comparisons between these various types.

Type I is the conjugal family, composed of mother, father, and children.Few of these families had been broken by death, divorce, or desertion; and where such break had occurred, it often had been repaired by remarriage. No aged members are found in this type of family.

Type II is the family composed of three generations of related persons, usually grandparents, parents, and children. About one-fourth of these families had been broken, the break being generally in the grandparent generation.

Type III is the family composed of grandparent-generation members plus either parent or grandchild generation. The typical pattern of this type is that of the grandparent-child relationship. The distinguishing characteristic, however, is the absence of one of the generations who normally would be present in a complete family. This is a small family, averaging about three persons. Nearly half of these are persons more than 65 years of age. It must also be noted that the "child" in this situation often refers to a person well over 50 years of age but standing in the relationship of child to one or more aged persons in the family.

Type IV is the family composed of aged persons, usually man and wife, though sometimes of an aged parent and a middle-aged or aged child. Type V is composed of a family "by definition only." In this type, there was a single aged person living alone but maintaining a household. These might be referred to as "residual families."

Obviously, any given family might move from one classification to another at any time. If, for example, a married daughter with children returned to her parent's home to make her permanent residence, a Type V family would automatically become Type II. In such a case, it was believed the new relationships necessary would create new social situations and would result in the building of new behavior patterns. This is almost a sociological axiom and has been developed in several recent studies of family composition. Ivan Belknap and H. J. Friedsam, for example, have pointed out the poor mental health growing out of the grave isolation of the Type IV and, particularly, Type V families considered here.[1]

Since the status of the family is much more dependent on the husband-father than upon the wife-mother, we decided to ascribe the status of the "husband" to the wife, regardless of her actual age. This was largely a matter of expediency, since we discovered that the data arranged in this manner became more meaningful than when the wife was placed in the category indicated by her actual age. For instance, a 62-year-old wife of a 67-year-old man we classed as "aged."

Perhaps the most pertinent fact about the five types to keep in mind is that all of them, except Type I, include one or more aged persons.

Type I (the conjugal family) made up almost 75 per cent of the cases from Waco and San Angelo. Type II (the extended family) comprised 6 per cent; Type III (the broken-extended type), 5 per cent; Type IV (the elderly couple), 10 per cent; and Type V (the single survivor), 6 per cent. With such a high percentage of the families concentrated in the first type, it is evident that statistics referring to the other types must be viewed with a great deal of caution. Types II, III, and V each had 20-odd members; Type IV had 39; Type I had 292 families. Nonetheless, and with this caution, we thought fig-

[1] Ivan Belknap and H. J. Friedsam, "Age and Sex Categories as Sociological Variables in the Mental Disorders of Later Maturity," *American Sociological Review*, Vol. XIV (June, 1949), pp. 367–76.

ures relating to the various types should be presented for the value they may have in suggesting possible, or even probable, differences in the ways in which such varied families react to disaster.

Of the single-survivor families, 85 per cent were women. The conjugal families, as might be expected, had the largest annual income—just short of $3,000—while the Type V families received the smallest, an average of $1,682. More than one-third of the one-aged-person families had no regular income at all, but more than half of them received a pension. None of the aged-type families averaged as much as one wage-earner per family. In the cases of Type V, only 1 in 8 of the families had an earner. Hence, we see aged persons as the most vulnerable economically to the disaster situation. In only one aspect did the Type V families appear to be more adequate. This was in housing, where both the value of the house and number of persons per room were more favorable than for the other types. The social isolation of the old one-person family is indicated by the fact that almost one-third of these persons said they were no longer active in religious affairs.

Reports of losses indicated that the three-generation family suffered most heavily of the types. Just why this should be true is not clear, though perhaps it is connected with the lack of typicality in this type of family. Those families composed entirely or almost entirely of aged persons—Types IV and V—reported the smallest losses. This may be a result of the very low rate of automobile ownership (20 per cent) in these families. Families composed of the elderly couple suffered more injuries, percentagewise, than any of the other types. This again points to their relative vulnerability and the probability that both members of the family were at home at the time of the disaster. The likelihood of women being in the home, especially on a rainy day, also accounts for their high percentage of injuries in all the types, as indeed it does throughout the entire study.

Families of the typical, conjugal type were the most likely to have been forced from their homes, though the difference here is too small to be considered significant. The elderly-couple families were significantly most likely to have been taken into the home of friends or relatives, but the single old person was least likely to have received such aid. It is interesting also that all the families occupied emergency housing of approximately the same size. Differences were very slight, but actually the conjugal families occupied the smallest houses, whereas the one-older-person, residual family occupied a house in the upper size range.

Families composed of husband, wife, and children were the least likely to have received aid from public agencies, whereas those with three generations were the most likely to. These two types also were most often forced to incur debt in repairing their homes or replacing necessary household furnishings. For obvious reasons, those families composed of elderly persons did the least personal labor in reconstructing their homes. This inability to aid one's own rehabilitation would, of course, be very important if a disaster reached such proportions as to make it impossible to supply aid to others. The three-generation families had the highest percentages of those relying on relief funds, being without insurance, incurring debt, and depending on their own labor and that of individually hired craftsmen. This indicates again the greater vulnerability of this type in disaster.

Since many of the destroyed homes were in older portions of the city, it is not surprising that the rebuilt houses were slightly higher in value than those they replaced. It is perhaps pertinent that the three-generation families, who depended most heavily on public-welfare agencies, registered the greatest gain in value of homes occupied. The residual, one-older-person family occupied the smallest post-disaster home, though only very slightly smaller than that occupied by the other types. This slight shift probably is explained by the fact that a somewhat higher percentage of these persons moved into one- or two-room apartments. Also aid granted by the Red Cross for reconstruction was rather strictly tailored to the actual needs of the occupants. There was some evidence also that some of the elderly families supplemented their income by renting rooms or small apartments, and this may explain in part the slight difference between the size of the homes occupied by these families and that of the larger families.

Although the three-generation type family was most likely to have received aid in rebuilding their homes, it was the one-elderly-person family to whom the largest average grant of such aid was made. At the same time, the one-person families were the least likely to have received emergency aid; in fact, the average amount given them was less than half that of the next lowest type. The person composing a Type V family also was least likely to have received aid in replacing household furnishings and when he did, the amount was well toward the bottom of the amounts dispensed. The amount of aid received by this type for medical care was considerably below that received by any of the other types. These differences are, of course, largely explainable in terms of the one-person composition of this type of fam-

142

ily. Type IV families, composed of elderly couples, for example, received the largest average grant for medical care.

Illness was more prevalent among the aged following the disaster, but this is certainly to be expected, for illness is more prevalent among the aged in any situation. However, this health factor may partially explain the statistic that Type IV families showed an average loss of 37 days' employment where employment was interrupted. This is about the same as that of the three-generation family, but considerably higher than that of the typical family. This high average-loss of employment may also indicate the precariousness with which many of the older workmen hold their jobs.

As was true of other arbitrary divisions that we made of the sample population, almost half the families represented in this aspect of the study reported some member as being emotionally distressed, and well over half reported some member as showing undue fear of threatening weather. But, contrary to expectations, the one-elderly-person type reported the lowest incidence of emotional stress and fear of weather. The broken, three-generation family reported the next lowest incidence of such disturbance. In the case of the Type V (residual families), this result may be more a product of the conditions under which the interviews were obtained than a reflection of the actual condition of the families. It must be remembered that this information came from persons reporting the presence or absence of their own emotional stress. It is hardly to be expected that they would not have rationalized to some extent any emotional stress they may have felt and, hence, would tend to report the absence of such feelings. The same reasoning would apply with less force to Type III families, in which most of the informants were elderly persons. Another plausible explanation comes from Robert Bales's[2] analysis of the interaction process. Bales points out that those families in which mutual understanding is deep and in which there is constant communication offer the greatest possibility for the expression of emotional stress. Conversely, isolated and broken families have the least opportunity to discuss emotional problems. Hence, the expression of emotional stress or fear of weather would not be a true indication of the presence of such factors. This reasoning is given support by the fact that the two-person, aged families reveal the greatest degree of emotional impact.

[2] Robert S. Bales, *Interaction Process Analysis* (Cambridge, Mass., Addison-Wesley, Inc., 1950).

The extended three-generation family was the most likely to have increased religious activity following the tornado, but was least likely to have received a visit from a minister, 57 per cent of them reporting no such visits, in contrast to 31 per cent of the one-aged-person family.

The generally optimistic outlook revealed in other tabulations appears in this portion of the study also. However, an anomaly appears

TABLE 44

Differential Factors by Family Types

Factor	Type of Family by Percentage				
	I	II	III	IV	V
No damage to home	10	4	0	8	0
Car destroyed or damaged . . .	25	30	25	13	8
No financial loss	20	10	10	12	24
Family member injured	8	22	19	23	8
Moved in with friends or relatives .	10	9	14	23	8
Depended on relief agency for rebuilding home	15	36	24	25	23
Incurred debt	26	30	19	13	16
Received aid from 3 or more sources	15	30	19	17	8
Emotional stress reported . . .	45	52	24	54	35
Fear of weather reported . . .	70	74	55	67	54
Optimism about future of city . .	68	74	43	79	73

when the attitude of the two-person and one-person aged families is compared. The highest percentage believing that their neighborhoods were better off at the time of interview was in the one-person aged family; the highest percentage believing the neighborhood to be worse off at that time was in the two-person aged family. But when the question shifts to the future, the views expressed also shift. In this case, the highest percentage of those feeling that the neighborhood would be better off because of the tornado was in the two-person aged family, while the highest percentage believing that the tornado had done permanent damage and the neighborhood would be worse off in the future was in the one-person aged family.

Attitudes toward the various agencies active in the disaster relief were most unfavorable in the case of the three-generation, extended family and most favorable in the case of the extended, but broken,

144

family. Families composed only of aged members—Types IV and V —were less favorably inclined toward these agencies than were the conjugal families, but were less negative than the three-generation families. The one-person aged family was much more likely to be critical in its appraisement of the agencies than was the two-person aged family.

This portion of the study suggests that there are significant differences in the reaction of the various types of families to these disasters. Families with aged members were more often in need of financial aid than were the conjugal families. The extended families, particularly those that had been broken, were lacking in insurance protection. Families with aged members also were generally unable to take part in the repair and reconstruction of their homes to the extent of the other families. In sum, the more pronounced effects of the disasters upon families with elderly members show them to be more vulnerable. The conjugal family type recovered more rapidly and completely from the effects and, therefore, attained a greater degree of rehabilitation.

7. Race Differences in Disaster

Every Southern city contains at least two communities, that of the whites and that of the Negroes. Living in close contact, co-operating consciously or unconsciously, eagerly or unwillingly in a common life, these two cultures manage to remain apart and distinctive. To borrow a term from geology, they are on opposite sides of a cultural fault line. On the basis of this assumption, we supposed that these two communities would show significantly different reactions to a major disaster. If the data sustain our feeling, then their different ways of seeing and behaving are of obvious importance in understanding the rehabilitation of a city following a catastrophe such as the Waco tornado.

The families drawn in the Waco sample were 18.7 per cent Negro, in comparison with a 1950 census figure for the city of 16.4 nonwhite. This percentage difference is not significant. Since there were no Negroes living in the devastated portion of San Angelo, none of the data from that city is included in the following section.

Comparative Attitudes of Negroes and Whites

In order to test the existence of any differences between Negro and Caucasian groups, tabulations were made of some of the basic non-disaster information given by all the families participating in this study. We found little difference in the size and make-up of the two groups of families, though the Negro family was slightly larger on the average. In other characteristics, essential differences do appear. The Negro family was more likely to have been broken through death, desertion, or divorce than the white. Also, Negro families were almost twice as likely to have a member who was ill. White-family income was approximately 50 per cent higher. The mean income for the Negro families was $1,950; for white families, $3,037 a year. Both figures are subnormal for the state, which in 1953 reported a per capita family income of $3,196. Less than half as many Negro families as white received pensions. It is evident that the Negro families were in a much more vulnerable economic position at the time of the disaster and hence could meet the emergency much less effectively.

This vulnerability of the Negro family appears to have been physical and biological as well as economic. Although none of the Negro families reported members killed in the disaster, 12 per cent of them did report some member seriously injured. This is in contrast to the 4 per cent of the white families having a similar misfortune. It is most tempting to correlate this difference in the rate of injury with the difference in the value of homes occupied. Whereas the white families placed an average value of $5,432 on their homes, Negroes reported an average of $2,650. The temptation is great to assume that the value of the home is roughly a measure of its adequacy and protective value in a tornado situation; this assumption would go far in explaining that the rate of injury among Negroes was triple that among whites. Other aspects of this study, particularly the movement of families from their homes following the disaster, also strongly favor this hypothesis.

Other results apparently related to the adequacy of housing appear in other statistics. For instance, 19 per cent of the Negro homes were reported destroyed, in comparison to 7 per cent of those occupied by Caucasians. Conversely, only 4 per cent of the Negro homes were reported as undamaged, in contrast to 15 per cent of those of the white families. Negro household furnishings were damaged in 15 per cent of the cases, but in only 1 per cent of the white homes. All this is reflected in the statistic that 34 per cent of the Negro families were forced to move from their damaged residences, in contrast to 14 per cent of the whites.

When the data on all families were divided according to whether the family did or did not move, we found the following conditions more likely to exist among those forced to move: lower family income, employment of more family members, larger number of children, and a greater probability of some disorganizing experience. These families were also found, as would be expected, to have suffered greater financial loss, more physical injury, and greater emotional disturbance. Negro families display, in general, the same characteristics.

The Negroes not only were economically less prepared for such a disaster, but they seemed to have had fewer friends when it came. At least, considerably fewer Negro families moved in with friends or relatives for the emergency period than did white ones. This, more accurately, is a reflection of the poorer housing occupied by Negroes, at least to the extent that it shows their lack of space with which to provide shelter for additional families.

In economic terms, white families reported an average loss of $1,100, while Negroes reported the smaller average of $494. Any

TABLE 45

Differentials in the Impact of a Tornado Disaster upon Two Racial Groups

| Factor | Ethnic Groups by Percentage* | |
	Negro	White
Cases with past history of death, divorce, desertion, separation	38	22
Damaged house	77	78
Household furnishings destroyed	15	1
Forced to move	34	14
Family member injured	12	4
Family member evidencing emotional stress .	17	30
Family member showing fear of unusual weather	85	53
Average value of predisaster home . . .	$2,650	$5,432
Average annual income per family unit . . .	$1,952	$3,037

* Total number of Negro families in this group is 53; in the white group, 230.

economic loss is undoubtedly a severe problem to the marginal family, either Negro or white; however, it is evident that a true measure of the economic impact of the disaster upon a family would be the measure of its ability to bear such loss. This measure might be considered as the amount of income above a minimum necessary for survival. Being nearer that minimum level, Negro families, even with their smaller losses, probably suffered as much as white families, or even more.

Negroes were more likely to have lost employment than whites, by a ratio of four to three, and the average number of workdays lost was slightly larger. Perhaps more pertinent is the fact that twice as many Negroes interrupted their employment to aid in rebuilding a damaged home. Negro families were more likely in a proportion of three to two, to repair their homes themselves or to hire individual craftsmen rather than to employ a contractor. This statistic ties in directly with that showing 33 per cent of the Negroes as able to pay their rebuilding costs from personal funds, whereas more than 50 per cent of the white families reported they had met these costs in this way. Insurance also comes into the picture. About half the white families reported insurance sufficient to cover all their losses, but only about one in five of the Negro families were so protected. Almost half the Negro families reported that they had no insurance at all.

With these facts in mind, it is not surprising that 33 per cent of the Negro sample said that the total cost of repairing their homes had been contributed by a relief agency, as contrasted with 9 per cent of the white families. But in spite of this greater dependence on donations, 50 per cent more Negroes than whites were forced into debt as a result of the disaster.

Nor was this greater dependence upon donated funds restricted to the reconstruction of homes. Almost half the Negro families, as compared to one-fifth of the whites, received some type of aid from a relief agency, American Red Cross being most frequently named benefactor, both by Negro and white families. But a much larger percentage of Negro families received aid only from the Red Cross, whereas

TABLE 46

Percentages of Two Ethnic Groups Receiving Aid and Amount Received

| *Type and Amount* | *Ethnic Groups by Percentage*[*] | |
	Negro	*White*
Receiving aid from any source	47	20
Receiving emergency aid (food, clothing, shelter)	27	12
Receiving aid in reconstruction of damaged residence	31	9
Mean amount of emergency aid received .	$ 39	$ 68
Mean amount received to reconstruct house . .	$807	$750

[*] Total number of Negro families in this group is 53; in the white group, 230.

white families were more likely to have received aid from two or more agencies.

In view of the greater incidence of damage to Negro housing and household furnishings, their greater rate of injury, and the greater debt they incurred, it is surprising that they received a smaller average amount of emergency aid than did the white families.

On the other hand, Negro families received higher average amounts of aid for rebuilding and repairing homes than did the whites. It seems fairly obvious that the general Red Cross policy of aiding only those families unable to help themselves is in large part responsible for this difference. Insurance also plays a part here, since those families having insurance would be eligible only for the amount of their loss above the insurance coverage. General economic well-being also comes in, for those with funds from which they might rebuild were commonly denied aid by the relief agencies.

The fact that white families were more likely to have received aid from several sources than were Negroes deserves comment. Several factors seem to have bearing. Owing to poorer access to channels of communication, the Negroes may safely be assumed to have lacked adequate information about the various sources of aid available. Furthermore, those white families accustomed to dealing with bureaucratic organizations may be expected to have developed better techniques by which these organizations could be manipulated to their advantage. The Southern Negro, living in a relationship of conditional participation in the total culture, never participating fully and usually participating according to prescribed and significantly different norms, could not be expected to avail himself of relief opportunities as effectively as a white person. Another possible explanation is simply racial discrimination. Unfortunately, there are no data available from this study to support any of these hypotheses. Nonetheless, the fact remains that a significantly higher percentage of white families—31 per cent as compared to 10 per cent of the Negro families—were able to obtain aid from more than one agency, and the inference is that their needs were met more fully.

The over-all impression is that economically the Negro group was more vulnerable, suffered more, and finally came out in about the same relative position it had occupied in comparison with the white group before the disaster.

Negro families had a slightly higher incidence of illness following the tornado, but whether this is directly connected with the disaster is problematic, for they had a higher rate before it also.

But if the tornado did not induce illness among them, it certainly induced fear of unusual weather. At the time of the interview, 85 per cent of the Negro families reported that one or more members showed fear at unusual weather conditions. By comparison, 53 per cent of the white families reported the same reaction. This, of course, is indicative of emotional stress, but when the question was asked whether any member of the family evidenced emotional stress, the relationship of the two groups is reversed. Only 17 per cent of the Negro families gave an affirmative answer, whereas 30 per cent of the white families did so. This is the more interesting in that in all other questions pertaining to weather, the group giving a high percentage of "yes" replies to one also gave a high percentage of "yes" replies to the other. It is possible that the question as phrased was not understood by the Negro respondents; or it may be there is a cultural bias against admitting emotional stress. The question raised is intriguing, and it is most unfortunate that the data supply no recognized clue to the answer.

Negroes reacted to the disaster more sharply in changes in their religious practices than did the white families. Although almost 75 per cent of the Negro families reported no change in religious activities, this was true of 87 per cent of the whites. On the other hand, 10 per cent of the Negroes, as compared with 3 per cent of the whites, indicated their postdisaster religious activity decreased sharply. At the same time, 15 per cent of the Negro sample and 10 per cent of the white reported a sharp increase in religious participation; put another way, religious activity following the disaster seemed less likely to remain static among the Negroes than among the whites. However, the number of families in the sample is too small to make such changes significant statistically. Coincidentally, Negro families were less likely to have received visits from clergymen following the disaster, 63 per cent reporting no such visits, as compared with 51 per cent of the white families.

Data on attitudes toward the twelve agencies most active in relief and rescue work revealed an interesting pattern. On the whole, Negroes were more negative in their judgments of these agencies than were the whites; but they tended to be more favorably disposed than the whites toward the American Red Cross, the local disaster fund, and other local social agencies. The greatest differences appear in attitudes expressed about city, state, and federal governments. Toward these, Negro attitudes were distinctly less favorable than those of the white respondents.

For example, 78 per cent of the Negroes, and 60 per cent of the whites, expressed attitudes favorable to American Red Cross. The city government drew favorable responses from 64 per cent of the Negroes—as contrasted to 80 per cent of the whites who said they were pleased with the way the city had met the emergency. But with regard to the federal government, only 47 per cent of the Negroes and 71 per cent of the whites showed favorable attitudes. On questions relating to governmental units, about half the Negroes declined to comment. This was true of about one-fifth of the whites. Evasion is a well-recognized technique of the less powerful.

These data are particularly interesting because it has frequently been assumed that white interviewers would be unlikely to establish sufficient rapport with Negro informants to elicit truthful negative responses toward status-bearing activities or authorities. Certainly this assumption is not borne out in this particular bit of research. Certainly, also, these figures indicate that in this community, at least, there was a fundamental difference in the way this portion of the population regarded these basic institutions.

Finally, when these people looked back over their experiences and into the future, and expressed opinions, it is to be noted that they were most pessimistic about their condition at the time of the interview and most optimistic when asked what they thought of the future. Whereas only 11 per cent of them thought their families were better off than before the disaster, 55 per cent thought their neighborhoods were, and 74 per cent thought their city would be better off in the future because of, or in spite of, the disaster.

Almost 33 per cent of the Negro informants rated their family situation as worse, whereas only 4 per cent of them so judged their neighborhoods, and none at all held this opinion about the future of the city. As compared with the white families, the Negroes were more pessimistic about the conditions of their own families, but more optimistic in considering the state of their neighborhoods and their city. Whether these attitudes were an outgrowth of the amount of aid received or whether they were an expression of the basic faith in the American future is hard to say. But here again, as in other comparisons of this data, one of the striking features is the optimism expressed concerning the future.

The net conclusion is that the Negro families, less able to meet adversity of this sort, were hit much harder than were white families in the same disaster. Comparisons from other divisions of the data have also indicated that those least able to meet severe losses were the ones on whom this burden fell most disastrously. It was the already fundamentally insecure whose small measure of security was most nearly destroyed.

8. Donors and Donations

AMERICAN GENEROSITY is perhaps nowhere shown so dramatically as in spontaneous donations to areas and persons visited by disaster. Foodstuff, clothing, blankets, supplies of all kinds, from drugs to bulldozers, appear in stricken communities as if by magic, and often in such quantities as to constitute a real embarrassment of riches.

Persons, organizations, and groups that do not find it feasible to supply material relief, or that wish to supplement such efforts, often send money. In some cases the sums are so large as to make their expenditure a very real problem, requiring years of careful planning by the committees charged with carrying out the wishes of the donors. This was true in Texas City following the explosion of two ships in the harbor there. A fund of $1,070,582.83 was not finally disbursed until May, 1953, more than six years after the disaster.

Certainly Waco and San Angelo, sorely stricken, presented pictures calculated to activate generosity. News of their plight was flashed over the nation and the world within a matter of hours, in a story of dramatic impact commensurate with the loss of life and property of which it told—tragic death, the high courage of survivors and rescue workers, homeless families, devastated businesses, personal losses of loved ones and of material possessions. News of the disasters and the response in donations and offers of aid in one form or another were almost simultaneous. Unfortunately, only fragments of information about this response survived the hectic days which followed. No one had time, or inclination, to record telephone calls, or to file telegrams, or to list the sandwiches, trucks, rescue workers, repair crews, or blankets that converged on the cities. But some bits of information did survive.

Thousands of letters containing cash or checks arrived during the weeks following the tornadoes. Usually the contents were removed, a notation made of the donor and donation, and the letters thrown into convenient boxes for later attention. Time was never found to give them the attention planned, and most of them were later destroyed. But some of them were located when research on the disasters was undertaken. In Waco, 81 such letters were located and in San Angelo, 58 more, and a number of envelopes in which donations had been received and which bore legible return addresses were also discovered. Finally, 410 addresses were obtained, including those of the 139 letters. These letters and envelopes might be referred to as a "survival sample" from a much larger mass of material. There is no known reason why these particular items should have been saved; indeed, one box of this material was discovered by a member of the research project when he was going through other papers in an office in Waco.

Who Gave; and Why

Obviously, such a tragedy as a severe tornado is a tremendous spur to immediate response. During the two hours between the time Waco received news of the San Angelo disaster and the time of the strike at Waco, a campaign had been launched in Waco to raise funds for the San Angelo victims. Donations began to follow the telegrams of sympathy into both cities on the day following the tornadoes. The distribution of these messages by time offers a rough measurement of the emotional impact brought about by the knowledge of these disasters and of the easing of the tensions this knowledge created.

The number of messages rose rapidly during the first days and then dwindled away, indicating that within one month the urge to aid in this fashion had been satisfied or had been dissipated in some other manner. Those who chose the more rapid and dramatic telegram dropped out of the picture after only four days. Interesting is the rise in the number of letters and envelopes (probably containing letters) received on Wednesday, May 19—one week and one day after the disaster. Though there is no evidence to support the notion, it would seem plausible that these letters were written on the weekend following the tornado.

Several large personal gifts came in almost immediately. On May 15 came the largest single donation—$5,000—and on the next day, another, of $1,000, both personal. On May 23 there was another personal gift of $3,000. But there were few gifts of more than $100 from individuals.

As would be expected, the greatest number of donors were residents of Texas. Of the 410 addresses secured, four-fifths bore a Texas postmark. The remaining 87 came from thirty-one other states and from two foreign countries (see Fig. 9 and Table 47).

More complete records are available as to the total amounts received in donations from all sources and the number of donations. In Waco, records of the Waco Relief Committee show total receipts of $419,542.64 from 3,767 persons, groups, and agencies. Direct donations to American Red Cross for tornado victims amounted to $45,-261.64, and those to the Salvation Army to $30,342, both amounts being supplemented by donations of food, clothing, blankets, and other supplies. In San Angelo, the totals are $266,159.55 to the Disaster Relief Fund, plus $14,076.08 sent directly to American Red Cross, and $8,257.05 to the Salvation Army. The number of donors to the San Angelo fund can only be estimated. Bank deposit slips put the number at about 3,000.

The sums mentioned above do not represent the total made available by voluntary contributions for relief and rehabilitation in these two cities, particularly in Waco. Various churches, business houses, and fraternal organizations received funds directly and dispensed them without reporting their totals or fitting their programs into those of the more formal agencies. How much money was handled in this manner is impossible to estimate with any accuracy; the sum of $50,000 has been mentioned and seems perhaps lower rather than higher than the amount actually involved. The American Red Cross contributed $351,923.35 from its national disaster-fund, in addition to amounts received through local agencies.

Thus it would appear that from $1,185,000 to $1,200,000 was available to help the citizens of the two cities recover part of their losses. Of this amount, approximately $800,000 should be allocated to Waco. Although this amount is small indeed compared to the amount of loss, it looms large as a voluntary and largely unsolicited contribution.

In both cities, committees of local citizens were set up to receive and disburse relief funds. These committees retained all donations coming to them not specifically marked for some other agency, though the San Angelo committee used Red Cross to distribute most of the money it handled.

Our analysis of the funds received by the Waco Disaster Fund by date, amount, and source was made on the basis of lists published in the *Waco Times-Herald* from the date of the disaster through July. This source is not official or complete. Donations as reported in the newspaper total only $363,969.66 as against the official total reported by the Waco Disaster Fund of $419,542.64. Since there is no reason

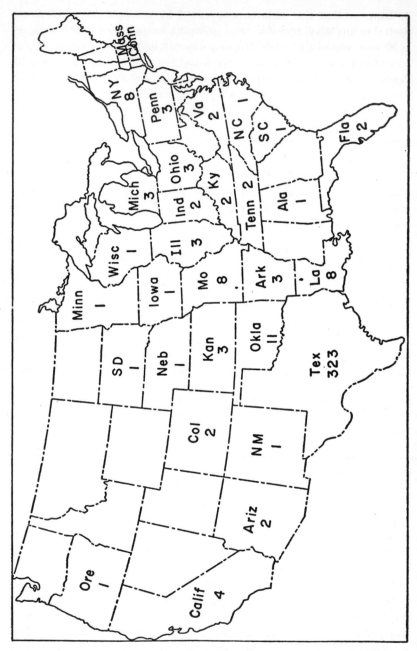

Fig. 9. Number of donations in sample by states.

to suppose that the donations reported by the newspaper were selected in any way, and since the amount accounted for in this manner is 87 per cent of the total, it seems safe to assume that our analysis is essentially correct. But the newspaper sample accounts for only 61 per cent of the total number of donors reported by the Fund. Thus,

TABLE 47

Geographic Distribution of 410 Donations

From:	Waco	San Angelo	Church*	From:	Waco	San Angelo	Church*
Alabama	1	0	0	New Mexico	1	0	0
Arizona	0	2	0	New York	5	3	0
Arkansas	1	2	0	North Carolina	0	1	0
California	3	1	0	Ohio	3	0	0
Colorado	1	1	0	Oklahoma	4	7	0
Connecticut	0	1	0	Oregon	1	0	0
Florida	1	1	0	Pennsylvania	0	2	1
Illinois	0	3	0	South Carolina	1	0	0
Indiana	1	1	0	South Dakota	1	0	0
Iowa	0	1	0	Tennessee	0	1	1
Kansas	2	1	0	Texas	118	161	44
Kentucky	1	0	1	Virginia	1	1	0
Louisiana	5	3	0	Wisconsin	1	0	0
Massachusetts	1	0	0	Dominican			
Michigan	1	2	0	Republic	0	1	0
Minnesota	0	1	0	India	1	0	0
Missouri	5	3	0				
Nebraska	1	0	0	Total	163	200	47
New Jersey	2	0	0	Grand total		410	

* Donations sent directly to churches to be distributed by the churches.

it is evident that the average donation reported in the newspaper is higher than that for all donations received, being $158.39 for the newspaper list as compared to $111.37 as computed from figures supplied by the Fund.

We divided the sources of donations into three classes: personal, collectivity, and agency. We classed as "personal" those contributions where the indication was that a single person, acting as such, had made the donation. "Collectivity" gifts were those made by formal or informal groups, such as one from the employees of a large firm, a collection taken on the streets of a town, or one coming from several

TABLE 48

Donations as Listed in the *Waco Times-Herald*, May–July, 1953

Date*	Personal		Collectivity		Agency		Total	
	No.	Sum	No.	Sum	No.	Sum	No.	Sum
May 15	7	$ 5,044.00	2	$ 946.50	12	$25,500.00	21	$31,490.50
May 16	30	1,820.00	2	38.46	11	9,465.00	43	11,323.96
May 17	205	5,846.00	17	5,068.81	51	11,777.65	273	22,692.46
May 18	84	554.25	..	......	14	160.00	98	714.25
May 19	83	1,225.50	10	1,854.75	15	17,615.00	108	20,695.25
May 20	163	2,989.00	10	4,782.15	45	12,630.00	218	20,401.15
May 22	125	1,763.50	10	6,108.67	31	4,775.00	166	12,647.17
May 23	115	4,947.20	19	3,537.98	69	23,719.18	203	32,204.36
May 24	58	1,298.95	10	2,427.87	21	11,877.00	89	15,603.82
May 26	52	709.50	13	1,320.23	17	3,233.91	82	5,263.64
May 27	69	754.00	2	17.00	8	2,905.00	79	3,676.00
May 28	18	646.00	8	1,442.13	9	6,414.51	35	8,502.64
May 29	51	1,044.50	18	1,370.98	33	6,541.57	102	8,957.05
May 31	126	1,737.25	24	3,705.74	70	4,614.50	220	10,057.49
June 3	54	1,535.35	24	7,125.32	31	1,960.75	109	10,621.42
June 5	51	456.55	11	3,253.53	12	787.00	74	4,497.08
June 7	11	167.00	9	40,481.84	17	1,891.50	37	42,540.34
June 10	18	596.52	5	5,067.38	3	230.00	26	5,893.90
June 11	41	1,200.70	16	2,784.99	16	6,179.95	73	10,165.64
June 12	2	10.00	2	168.00	1	200.00	5	378.00
June 14	14	154.50	6	532.91	15	7,800.00	35	8,487.41

Date	Personal No. Gifts	Personal Total	Collectivity No. Gifts	Collectivity Total	Agency No. Gifts	Agency Total	Total No. Gifts	Total
June 15	1	5.00	:	......	1	100.00	2	105.00
June 17	:	......	1	5,455.20	:	......	1	5,455.20
June 19	5	19.00	8	582.33	8	2,695.00	21	3,296.33
June 21	3	20.00	7	28,982.02	4	5,250.00	14	34,252.02
June 24	1	5.00	1	3,229.00	1	50.00	3	3,284.00
June 26	2	31.50	6	484.19	:	......	8	515.69
June 28	10	50.05	4	20,028.00	13	130.00	27	20,208.05
July 2	9	45.00	9	1,473.88	33	528.50	51	2,047.38
July 5	18	197.00	11	1,806.85	7	775.00	36	2,778.85
July 8	2	30.00	2	34.01	2	87.11	6	151.12
July 19	11	154.03	6	538.70	6	490.00	23	1,182.73
July 26	:	......	6	3,675.76	4	204.00	10	3,879.76
Totals	1,439	$35,056.85	279	$158,325.18	530	$170,587.63	2,298	$363,969.66

* Dates not included are dates on which the newspaper carried no donor lists.

TABLE 49

Donations by Months (Waco)

Date	Personal No. Gifts	Personal Total	Personal Average	Collectivity No. Gifts	Collectivity Total	Collectivity Average	Agency No. Gifts	Agency Total	Agency Average
May	1,186	$30,379.65	$ 25.62	145	$ 32,621.27	$ 224.97	406	$141,228.82	$347.85
June	213	4,251.17	19.95	100	118,174.71	1,181.75	122	27,274.20	223.56
July	40	426.03	10.65	34	7,529.20	221.45	52	2,084.61	40.09

159

persons who had lumped their contributions together. Also included here were funds obtained from newspaper or radio drives. The "agency" category was for funds received from businessmen on behalf of their firms, from industries, and from organizations, such as civic clubs or other formally organized groups, which were given as contributions of the organization as distinguished from its members.

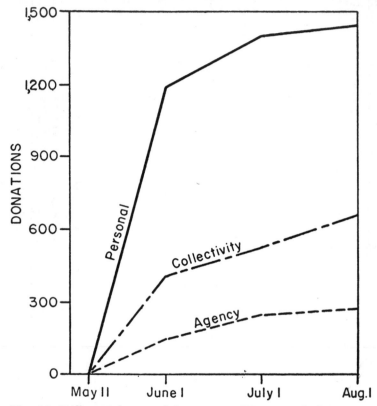

Fig. 10. Differential rates of donations in Waco sample by source.

Table 48 shows the day-by-day distribution of donations listed in the *Waco Times-Herald*. Here again it may be observed that the number of donations and the amounts they represented rose rapidly right after the disaster and declined drastically by the end of July. But is should be noted that the collectivities and agencies were slower to send in donations and that these donations continued to arrive in large numbers after the personal gifts had declined. This, it would seem, is the result of having to secure concerted or formal action be-

160

fore donations could be made. But it is interesting that the agencies acted more rapidly than did the collectivities, in spite of the formal acquiescence presumably required. More than 400 of the total of 580 organizations made their gifts between May 11 and June 1, while among the collectivities only 145 of the 279 donations were reported in this period. Individuals made 1,186 of their 1,439 gifts during the remaining nineteen days of May. The time pattern for organizations approximates that of individuals much more closely than that of the collectivities.

The amount of donations from collectivities was much higher than that from organizations or individuals, averaging $567.47 The agency average was $294.12, and that for persons, $24.36. Personal gifts ranged from $5,000 to 10 cents, with decided clustering at multiples of $5 and $10. The gift of $5,000 in the personal category boosted this average from $20.90 to $24.36. Without it, the average drops from $21.42 in May to $19.96 in June and to $10.65 in July.

Lists of donors and stories of unusual donations carried by the newspapers during the weeks following the disasters give a picture of the variety of sources and some insight into how individuals, business firms, and other institutions were moved by these tragedies. From the *Waco Times-Herald* these sample listings have been culled for illustrative purposes:

People of Greater Kansas City (through radio station KUDI.)	$2,500.00
Citizens of McGregor, Texas	1,227.55
Senior High School Student Council, Denton, Texas	6.50
DeWitt C. Bolinger, Philadelphia	20.00
Rocket Fuel Division, Phillips Petroleum Company	616.50
Bricklayers, Masons, and Plasterers Union 33, Fort Worth	25.00
Fourth-grade Class, Edison School, Waterloo, Iowa	1.75
Veterans of Foreign Wars (national office)	5,000.00
Citizens of Meridian, Texas	740.50
Zale Jewelry Company	500.00
Pabst Brewing Company	2,000.00
Mrs. R. J. Fields	2.00
Waco Home Show	1,624.61
Glenwood Methodist Church, Gilmer, Texas	10.00
Glass Bottle Blowers Association of the United States and Canada, Philadelphia, Pennsylvania	500.00
Presbyterian Daily Vacation Bible School, Adamsville, Texas	7.25
Dr. and Mrs. W. M. Brook, Lampasas, Texas	50.00
Uhland Women's Guild, San Marcos, Texas	20.00
Carl Bitter, Keyport, New Jersey	5.00

Anonymous	2.00
Home Demonstration Club, Moody, Texas	5.00
Employees of Texas Transport Company, Amarillo, Texas . .	40.50
M. Clifford Truitt, San Francisco, California	100.00
A friend, Tyler, Texas	10.00
Dallas Dachshund Club, Dallas, Texas	10.00
Kindergarten, Central Christian Church, Waco, Texas . . .	8.00
Southwestern Bell Telephone Company, Mineral Wells, Texas .	152.30
Two men in Red Oak, Texas	2.00
Waco Anglers Club	100.00
Gulf Oil Corporation	4,140.00

The first bale of the 1953 cotton crop was auctioned at the New York Cotton Exchange, and the proceeds divided between the Waco Disaster Fund and the national Crippled Children's Society. Texas State Optical Company gave all of the proceeds of one day's business at its Waco store, and 25 per cent of proceeds at twenty-seven other stores, to the Waco Disaster Fund. An offering taken at the convention of the Diocese of Southern Ohio of the Episcopal Church was donated to the tornado victims.

The May twenty-fourth donors included the following organizations: Lions clubs, American Legion posts, a junior chamber of commerce, a junior student council, Explorer Scouts, Rebekah Lodge, I.O.O.F. Lodge, postal employees, Veterans Administration Hospital employees, State Home for Ladies, Business and Professional Women's clubs, Rotary clubs, A. F. & A. M. lodges, Kiwanis clubs, and garden clubs.

A pastor moving to Waco from Lamesa during the week following the tornado arrived with a van of supplies. The trucker moving his household goods had announced that he had a small amount of space and would be glad to use it to take to Waco any material people wanted to send to the tornado victims. The response was so hearty that an extra van was required.

A postal money order brought $15 from the men of Detachment A, 552nd Engineer Base Depot, stationed at Taegu, Korea. The Rotary Club of Wimborne Minster, Dorset, England, in the area of devastating floods the previous year, adopted resolutions of sympathy. In Austin, some three hundred entertainers staged five shows in various parts of the city and then combined in a radio-television broadcast with appeals for funds. All money received was sent to Waco for relief.

One of the Waco disaster-committee leaders summed up this aspect of the situation:

> The wonderful part was the co-operation. . . . We had calls offering aid from nearly every state in the nation. I'll never forget one man who called from Eugene, Oregon, though I didn't know where the call was from. He said he had several trucks and bulldozers. . . . I asked him how soon he could get here. He said about five days. I asked where in the world he was calling from and when he told me I like to have fell over. I told him that was too much to expect. He told me he would start a collection for Waco instead, and he did. He sent over a thousand dollars.

Letters accompanying donations usually, but not always, expressed some motive or gave some insight into the impulse that had prompted the gift. In running through the available letters, certain themes were found. These we categorized into eight "motifs," not mutually exclusive; in fact, a letter would often contain two or three. These categories were used as a descriptive device to indicate something of the motivation of the writers. Excerpts from letters illustrate the basis for our division:

Theme 1: *Religion.* "Our prayers are with the great people of Waco in this hour of need and our hope and prayer is that these terrible disasters God is sending us all will draw everyone closer to Him."

Theme 2: *"Mite."* "I know it seems awfully small as the need is so great, but I just wanted to do my small part."

Theme 3: *Sympathy.* "Many of us viewed on television the disaster caused by the tornado which has stricken your town. We wish to express our deepest sympathy in regard to your recent loss of life and property."

Theme 4: *Experience with disaster.* "It was just a little more than twenty-three years ago that the tornado struck —————— where I was pastor of the local Methodist Church."

Theme 5: *Identification with the stricken community.* "During 1942 when I was an aviation cadet at the Waco Army Air Base the people of Waco made our stay a memorable one."

Theme 6: *Offer of physical aid.* "I am a poor Negro man forty years old. Is there anything I can do to help the city of Waco? I will do my part. I am a painter and a concrete finisher. Anything I can do, pay or no pay."

Theme 7: *Restriction of use of donation.* "The —————— group would like for you to use this $10 for the Waco disaster, but *do not* turn it over to any organization, please."

Theme 8: *Curiosity.* "It was just in 1928 we toured through Waco, and if my memory serves me right Waco had a skyscraper of some twenty stories. I have seen no mention of it at all in the reports on tornadoes. It has simply aroused my curiosity to the extent of writing these lines."

TABLE 50

Percentage Distribution by Nature of Source of Themes Expressed in Letters Accompanying Donations (May 12–June 26, 1953)

| Theme | Source of Letter by Percentage | | |
	Personal	Agencies and Collectivities	Church Sample
Religion	21	12	38
"Mite"	25	24	19
Sympathy	20	35	33
Similar experience	2	5	0
Identification	10	4	5
Physical aid	4	4	0
Restriction on use	2	8	0
Curiosity	6	4	0
Other*	10	4	5

* Includes such themes as kinship with person living in the disaster city, personal friendship with a resident, queries concerning employment or business opportunities growing out of the disaster, request for publication of name of writer, etc.

From these materials it seems that the dominant motives behind donations in a disaster situation are religion and a nonspecific feeling of sympathy. Notable also is the high percentage in each group who deprecated, or apologized for, the smallness of their donation.

Worthy of note is the role mass-communication agencies play in securing gifts. An old tradition with newspapers, it appears that radio and television stations have also adopted it. Several newspapers and radio stations opened campaigns for relief funds almost immediately after the tornadoes struck. The *Journal-Gazette* of Mattoon, Illinois, where a tornado struck about twenty years previously, was the first newspaper to send in a donation. Although no accurate accounts were kept the amount sent was estimated by the newspaper at "something over $500." The *Wichita Daily Times* and the *Wichita Falls*

Record News collected a total of $3,053.66, which was divided between the two cities as indicated by donors. The *Dallas Morning News* secured a total of $108,062.30; the *Austin American-Statesman* collected between $7,000 and $8,000; and an Amarillo radio station sent $3,092.99. Several other newspapers and radio stations were reported to have raised funds, but the amounts are not available.

Only a small fraction of the donors placed any restriction on the use of their gifts. In both cities, the disbursing committees were composed of local citizens, partly in an effort to assure donors that local persons thoroughly familiar with local needs would make distribution of the donations rather than allowing them to be handled by "outsiders" unfamiliar with the obligations of the particular committees. This action reduced the donations to the national relief organizations, such as American Red Cross, by an amount it is impossible to estimate since any donation not specifically earmarked was retained by the local committee. For this reason, the amounts contributed to these organizations in this particular situation cannot be taken as typical of the response to, or attitude toward, such national institutions.

The way in which support was given these communities in their severe crisis is a direct reflection of the values of American culture, with its Judaeo-Christian ethic and its tradition of the frontier. Americans have always been noted for their readiness to aid those in distress, whether a person who has suffered loss or a nation seen as the victim of overwhelming oppression. Our long history of supplying funds to victims of flood, famine, or other disasters testifies to this. From our frontier experiences we have developed other co-operative patterns of helpfulness to those in need. Building new homes for those burned out, cultivating crops for those ill at critical periods, the volunteer fire departments still existing in small towns—these are concrete expressions of this general behavior-pattern. Experiences in Waco and San Angelo attest that this pattern is still very much alive and very powerful. Perhaps no better expression of this spirit could be found than is embodied in the following letter:

MATADOR, TEXAS
June 11, 1953

DEAR SIR:
Enclosed you will find a check in the amount of $101. It is a token of our citizenship's sympathy in your recent disaster. We are aware the amount is not impressive, but it is from the hearts of the people. We are a ranching country in the throes of the most severe drought in our entire history. Our

cattle are dying of starvation, our farmers are looking at barren fields, we have no oil or other industry, and our entire county's population is less than 4,000. Our contribution, therefore, is the widow's mite, but it is made in the spirit of Texan neighborliness. In the event you wish to give credit for securing the amount, kindly include the Matador Lions Club, Mr. ———, cashier of the First State Bank, Mr. ———, manager of the West Texas Gin, and the *Matador Tribune*, of which I am publisher.

Disbursement of Relief Funds

If the response of the American public to the plight of Waco and San Angelo was magnificent in the amount of money donated and in the spirit of helpfulness it displayed, the need for such assistance was equally great. But receiving such sums imposed severe problems of equitable distribution on the local committees and relief agencies charged with meeting the needs of the tornado victims—insofar as the donations would permit.

One of the first community actions in each city was to set up a local disaster-committee to solicit, receive, and distribute the funds which began to pour in immediately after news of the catastrophes was flashed over the world. In both cities these committees were composed of highly respected and trusted businessmen. It is noticeable that in this emergency the professionals who are commonly entrusted with the relief of suffering were not placed in top positions, though they were retained as consultants and workers under the authority of the committees.

The disbursement of relief funds called for, first of all, establishing policies and creating machinery. Here American Red Cross, with its history of decades of disaster-relief work, was utilized—in one case directly as the agent for local funds and in the other as a source of advice on local arrangements. In both cities the local committees followed the Red Cross pattern fairly closely.

The Red Cross and Salvation Army went into action immediately in both cities to meet the emergency needs of the victims and also those of volunteer workers and military forces engaged in rescue work. Red Cross remained after the emergency period to become a major resource for the rehabilitation of families. Other professional welfare workers and agencies placed themselves under the direction of the Red Cross and Salvation Army rather than setting up separate disaster programs of their own, relying upon the experience of these agencies and relinquishing much of the credit for the work they performed.

How did the four major agencies—the two local committees, the Red Cross, and the Salvation Army—dispose of the funds? The answers are taken largely from the records of the agencies themselves.

The account of the San Angelo Disaster Relief Fund was closed on February 13, 1954, and final accounting was made on March 5, 1954.

The San Angelo businessmen who made up the committee early came to the conclusion that it would be wisest to ask American Red Cross to handle rehabilitation. Accordingly, an agreement was made

TABLE 51

Disbursements by San Angelo Disaster Fund

To	Amount
American Red Cross	$204,716.37
Lake View Independent School District Cafeteria Fund . .	32,610.12
City of San Angelo	2,368.07
Tax Collector, Lake View Independent School District . .	11,846.10
Tax Collector, City of San Angelo	10,655.63
Tax Collector, Tom Green County	3,963.26
	$266,159.55

Source: Records of San Angelo Disaster Committee.

whereby Red Cross workers interviewed persons and families who wished to submit requests for aid. The cases were then presented to the committee at weekly meetings, and a check for the total amount approved was given to the Red Cross, which in turn disbursed these funds to families, contractors, hospitals, physicians, and others who had performed services. This policy was adopted in an effort to escape pressures which it was felt would be brought against committee members on the grounds of personal friendship, business connections, or other relationships. Indeed, so fearful of pressure was the committee that its membership was kept secret, insofar as this was possible, and the chairman was selected partly because he had no local business interests.

The final audit of the fund shows that American Red Cross handled $204,716.37 in the manner described above. This amount is in addition to slightly more than $60,000 supplied by the Red Cross from its national treasury and $14,076.08 contributed directly for relief in San Angelo during the period immediately following the tornado. None of the money allocated to the Red Cross for rehabilitation was used to pay its salaries or overhead expense, that being one of the conditions under which it became disbursing agent for the Fund.

The $32,000-odd given to the Lake View Cafeteria Fund was the residue after other disbursements had been made. The committee decided that no better use could be found for the remaining funds than to furnish free meals to children of families who had incurred losses in the disaster and to whom the charge for school lunches might represent a serious burden. In the spring of 1954 this fund was being used at the rate of $1,650 per month, according to the superintendent of the Lake View schools. It was estimated then that it was sufficient for two years. The payment to the city of San Angelo was to cover the cost of additional labor used in clearing debris and doing general cleanup work immediately following the disaster.

The funds used to pay taxes to the school district, the city, and the county deserve more lengthy comment. Both the city and the county were operating on a deficit basis at the time of the tornado and neither could well afford what seemed an inevitable loss of tax revenue. On the other hand, the victims, it was felt, should not be asked to carry this burden in addition to others they could not escape. But another and perhaps more important argument was advanced in favor of having these payments come from relief funds. Lake View was an area that had grown up on the edge of the city nearest the state tuberculosis hospital, about twenty miles away. Many of the residents who built the first homes in the area had been patients in this hospital and had settled in the Lake View area to be near friends and physicians in the institution. Water could be obtained at very shallow depths (there had formerly been a lake covering part of the area) and at small cost, a circumstance resulting in the refusal of many of the residents to secure—and pay for—water from the city plant. And since the area was outside the corporate limits until 1950, there was no way to force them to do so.

Many of the houses had been constructed on the cheapest possible plan and were of minimum size. Later additions had given something of a hodgepodge effect to some of them. Although it would not be correct to describe Lake View as a fringe slum area, it certainly was not the most attractive residential section of the city.

As often happens in such circumstances, friction had grown up between the older portions of the city and this new addition. In 1949 a vote on consolidation of the Lake View schools with those of San Angelo had lost by about two to one. Two years later, the Lake View area had been taken into the municipality of San Angelo over its vigorous vocal protest, though the residents of the area had no vote in this election. Civic leaders were conscious of this antagonism and were eager to make a gesture that might lessen it.

Still another factor was operative. Civic leaders were also eager to see improvements made in the area. They felt that if loans were made easily available, many homeowners in the area would construct better homes than they had owned before the tornado. Banks would handle such loans only if there were no unpaid tax claims against the property. Hence, supplying funds for the payment of taxes on homes that had been destroyed served several purposes. (It may be added at once that this planning worked as predicted and that the area did become the site of better housing than before the disaster. And one other result should be recorded. Immediately after the tornado, the city extended water and sewage lines through the area, making it feasible to abandon the use of shallow wells and septic tanks. There is a temptation to say that here disaster was converted into opportunity.)

Because an ample supply of vacant houses and apartments was available and because many San Angelenos opened their homes to disaster victims, no emergency housing was provided. Immediately after the storm, a call was issued for all homeless persons and school children separated from their families to gather at the city gymnasium, and a few persons spent the first night there. Later, a considerable sum was used to pay rent for families whose homes were destroyed or damaged so badly they could not be used, and to buy food for them.

Working under a Red Cross staff member, 37 social workers handled inquiries coming from forty-four states concerning the welfare of 1,342 families in the area. The social workers were volunteers from the city department of public welfare, the local family-service agency, and other sources. Other volunteers sorted and distributed the clothing which poured in from all parts of the nation—an estimated three-and-a-half boxcars of it. Nurses, recruited locally and brought into San Angelo from Abilene, Fort Worth, and Dallas to the local hospitals, were paid by Red Cross. Physicians and hospitals declined to charge for emergency care of the injured.

Later, Red Cross workers, volunteer and professional, investigated the rehabilitation needs of displaced families, aided them in making plans for their recovery, dealt with contractors engaged to rebuild or repair homes, referred victims to physicians where need was recognized, and provided counsel when problems arose. Counseling ex-

169

tended beyond the period for which records were kept on disaster operation, and the total of the costs is not, therefore, included in the accounting above.

The Salvation Army, upholding its fine tradition, was also active in both cities immediately after the disasters. In San Angelo it furnished a station wagon to bring children from the school and the surrounding area to the community gymnasium. A kitchen was set up in the school cafeteria, and a mobile canteen circulated through the area where rescue squads were at work, dispensing an estimated two

TABLE 52

Expenditures in Waco and San Angelo by American Red Cross for Emergency Relief and Rehabilitation

Category of Relief	Waco Persons Assisted	Cost	San Angelo Persons Assisted	Cost
Emergency	8,000	$ 23,649	1,500	$ 5,930

Rehabilitation	Families Assisted	Costs	Families Assisted	Costs
Food, clothing, and maintenance	679	$ 26,807	162	$ 10,550
Building and repair	289	190,063	126	173,915
Household furnishings	368	39,923	185	46,163
Medical and nursing service	115	39,350	45	10,700
Occupational supplies, equipment	36	9,800	27	2,800
Total individual family care	978*	$305,943	285*	$244,148
Total relief cost		$329,592		$250,078†
Service Costs				
Family service (all expenses incurred in development of cases)		$ 36,800		$ 15,765
Administration (salaries, maintenance, supplies, etc.)		15,699		13,202
Total cost		$382,091		$279,045

* Many families were assisted in more than one category; this is a *net* total of families served.

† Of this figure, $204,716 was supplied by the San Angelo Disaster Relief Committee.

Source: Records of the American Red Cross.

thousand cups of hot coffee and about the same number of meals during the first twenty-four hours after the tornado. Within three days, more than seven thousand meals were served by this agency. It also distributed clothing and furniture to victims who applied at either of its two warehouses and, at a cost of $1,200, gave Bibles to more than 200 families. It spent some $2,000 on new clothing and shoes. The total amount spent by this agency on the disaster was reported as $8,257.05, the amount secured from donations. To this should be added, of course, the value of materials received and distributed by the agency.

In Waco, Red Cross activity was commensurate with the greater loss there. Here the local committee chose to handle its own funds so that it might supplement grants made by Red Cross or give relief to persons excluded under Red Cross policy. Hence, the figures on expenditures by Red Cross in the two cities are not comparable.

The first Red Cross action was to establish canteens to aid in feeding the hundreds of rescue workers. Staff members from the local chapter, joined by others from Dallas, Fort Worth, and Houston, began the task of listing the dead and injured and of answering as many as they could of the nearly eight thousand inquiries which came in. Schoolteachers, staff members from the city Department of Welfare, the nearby Veterans Administration Hospital, churches, and other community agencies volunteered their services. Indeed, so many volunteers appeared that not all of them could be used. Most of the interviewing of families seeking aid was done by volunteers. They also operated canteens, and served as clerks, typists, and receptionists. Red Cross set up three emergency shelters, staffed by volunteers. As rapidly as possible the victims were moved into homes, temporary or permanent; in family groups or with others. The expense of food and rent was paid by Red Cross after applications for aid had been made.

As in San Angelo, nurses were recruited and their salaries were paid by Red Cross. Again, as in San Angelo, physicians made no charge for their emergency services.

Overhead expenses incurred by Red Cross in administering aid in the two cities amounted to $81,200. These expenses included all the costs of developing and handling applications for aid; dealing with contractors who rebuilt and repaired homes, and with others who supplied foodstuffs and other supplies to the families served; salaries of workers employed, maintenance of offices, and postemergency medical care.

171

The Salvation Army reported (*Waco Times-Herald,* May 11, 1954) it had records of 4,754 grocery orders issued in Waco in May, 1953. Records also showed issue of 76,150 garments and 36,862 pieces of bedding, including 562 mattresses and 355 pillows. "At least 250" pieces of furniture were distributed. "People, you see, brought the stuff to us. We distributed it at once. There wasn't time to keep books," it was explained. Salvation Army workers came to help from Dallas, Houston, Fort Worth, Austin, San Antonio, Texarkana, Paris, Corsicana, Beaumont, and Orange. Baylor students and welfare workers from agencies in the city also aided.

Although Red Cross, as well as similar organizations, is commonly pictured in action during the emergency phase of a disaster as en-

TABLE 53

Estimated Disbursements, Waco Disaster Relief Fund

Item	Amount
Business restoration	$200,000
Rebuilding and repair of homes	100,000
Medical and funeral expenses and maintenance of survivors and dependents of survivors	50,000
Replacement of tools, equipment, and supplies	30,000

Source: Personal communication from Harlon Fentress, chairman, Waco Disaster Relief Fund.

couraging rescue workers, passing out cigarettes and sandwiches, operating emergency shelters, aiding overtaxed hospital staffs, a glance at the figures on expenditures by Red Cross in Table 52 will show how incomplete is this popular conception of what the function of this organization really is.

The great bulk of Red Cross expenditure—95.6 per cent—came after the emergency, and was used less dramatically for rehabilitation through the months when families were working toward regaining their self-sufficiency. A sandwich or a cigarette looms large in the mind of a rescue worker or a victim of disaster. It is vitally important. But in comparison with the need for continuing care and counsel, for food, clothing, and rent, for household furnishings, and houses in which to put those furnishings, for medical bills, supplies, and nursing care, cigarettes and sandwiches cost little, may be dispensed by untrained workers, and fade into unimportance during the lifetime of the recipients. Much more important is the long pull up from the devastation and despair inflicted by the disaster to the resumption of normal living in normal surroundings. It is here that rehabilitation work by trained workers becomes essential; and it is very expensive.

One aspect of rehabilitation is often overlooked. In Waco, 36 families, and in San Angelo, 27, were given aid toward resuming their former occupations. Such aid included buying new sewing machines for women who had earned part of their income as seamstresses, purchasing trucks, or financing instruments necessary for professional workers. This particular aspect amounted to $12,600 of the total $550,600 granted by Red Cross for rehabilitation in the two cities.

In June, 1956, the Waco Disaster Relief Fund had not made a detailed accounting of the funds it had handled. But the total amount received was set at $419,542.64, and the number of cases handled at 691. Figures used in Table 53 are estimates, probably very nearly accurate, supplied by officers of the Fund.

These amounts indicate a disbursement of $380,000 during the year following the disaster. At that time it was announced that all cases involving property loss had been finally disposed of and that only cases of an emergency nature involving tornado victims would be considered in the future.

The balance of approximately $40,000 in the Fund was to be used to aid families whose earner had been killed in the disaster and who were unable to support themselves, and for the education of children orphaned by the tornado who needed assistance. In the spring of 1956, it was estimated that the remaining money would last through 1961 or 1962 and that by that time all the qualified children would have been given the opportunity of a tuition-free college education.

Though operating independently, the Waco Disaster Fund patterned its procedures closely on those of American Red Cross. Forms and criteria of the national organization were adapted for use by the local committee, so that there was a minimum of confusion when Red Cross disaster-workers withdrew and the local committee took over. However, the criteria were modified to the extent that grants which could not be made under national Red Cross policy could be made from local funds when the aid was essential. For example, Red Cross policy did not allow the rebuilding of businesses that employed more than three persons; the Waco Disaster Fund considered such aid legitimate and made grants to some such applicants where need was shown. Similarly, many craftsmen and small operators of stores and shops were aided in resuming their businesses. Several properties on which applicants depended for their income, as rent houses, were restored through grants from the Fund, and some widows were aided in buying homes that would also be used partly to supplement their income. Some mortgages on homes were paid off when it was shown that the applicant was unable to do this because of tornado losses and was in serious need. The criteria used were based on shown need and the absence of other resources, plus actual tornado loss. Of the 691 requests made to the Fund, 127 were denied.

When the earner in a family had been killed, leaving the family unable to care for itself, subsistence grants were made on the basis of the earnings of the person killed or in an amount sufficient to meet the minimum needs of his survivors. Businessmen who had supplied tools, vehicles, or other equipment for use in rescue operations and who could show that the loss constituted an undue burden on them were given aid.

The emphasis on the restoration of business is evident. This category of grants is twice that of the next largest—rebuilding and repair of homes. Two factors explain this: The tornado swept through the central business district, creating a great need for aid in re-establishing businesses. And the policies adopted by the Waco Disaster Fund seem to have made possible more aid to businesses than is common. It should be emphasized that any grant for restoration of a business was merely a supplement to the proprietor's own resources. These policies were very much more liberal than those of American Red Cross, the chief dispenser of rehabilitative aid following disasters. This liberality was made possible by the large number and amounts of donations received in this specific disaster, the horror of which deeply touched the American public. Hence, this is something of a special case; it is impossible to say whether funds on this scale would ordinarily be available for assistance to disaster victims.

Work of the committee was performed by a paid staff consisting of a building contractor, who supervised construction grants; case workers, who investigated and presented requests; a secretary; officials of the Council for Social Welfare and the United Fund for part-time duty; an unpaid advisory committee composed of a lawyer, a merchant, an insurance executive, and a building contractor. Unpaid volunteers from local and state welfare agencies were used extensively during the early months of the rehabilitation program.

On the anniversary of the disaster, the chairman of the Fund issued a statement announcing the closing of activities and praising the American Red Cross for its own work and for its aid in the operation of the local Fund. He voiced the general policy of the Fund when he said: "We tried to administer this fund with the same spirit of impartial generosity in which it was given, making as certain as possible that all real needs were met and that no money was wasted."

Insight into the kind of problems facing those persons undertaking to aid in rehabilitation of tornado victims and the way some of these problems were met is given in the following summaries excerpted from the minutes of the Fund. It must be emphasized that these excerpts are *illustrative only*. They have been selected to reveal the types and variety of requests made and for the evidence they yield on the factors considered important by this committee. All identifying information has been deleted.

Request for window shades and curtains which applicant forgot to request when she applied to American Red Cross for rebuilding of home. Award of $32 approved.

Request for funds to rebuild house and replace furniture. Request withdrawn by applicant's wife, who said American Red Cross had made a satisfactory award. She said applicant is senile and came to Waco Disaster Fund office without her knowledge.

Request for dentures and dental work in amount of $200 to $300. Applicant had tornado damages but has resources sufficient to meet losses. Application denied.

Request for three-year delinquent taxes. American Red Cross cannot complete building plan until taxes are paid. Award of $52.92 approved.

Request for assistance in meeting cost of rebuilding church parsonage. Skilled labor required in installing plumbing and wiring. Award of $1,744.21 approved.

Request for replacement of truck and tools used in business and destroyed in tornado. Award—purchase of car on dealer's bill up to $500. Loss-of-tools request deferred pending more information.

Request for assistance in furnishing apartment for applicant's use so that she may receive income from rental of part of her home. Request also for maintenance until she becomes eligible for Social Security. Applicant lost her arm in disaster and was assisted generously by American Red Cross. Award not to exceed $4,500 to meet cost of furniture and maintenance approved. Plan of maintenance grant to meet the level of lost income ($37.50 per week) to be completed with assistance from U. C. [United Charities] office.

A committee member reported that he had been contacted by the ———— Church relative to the availability of $2,000 for disaster relief. This fund is the balance from an accumulation of gifts sent in by churches of this denomination throughout the United States. The committee wishes some plan to be formulated with the ———— Church whereby this fund can be utilized in conjunction with the Waco Disaster Fund.

———— Company. Request for assistance in repair of stock and equipment. This request is to supplement $15,000 RFC loan. Award of $3,500 approved.

Request for assistance in rebuilding seven-room home. Mr. ———— employed and is arrested t.b. patient. He received $1,400 insurance settlement. An award of $1,536 approved in order to decrease amount of RFC loan.

———— Church. Request for assistance in rebuilding church destroyed by tornado. Committee agreed to pay difference between the insurance value of $6,000 and the amount of insurance collected, which was $2,801.20. An award of $3,198.80 approved.

Request for assistance in re-establishing dry cleaning plant. Applicant plans to purchase equipment and rent the building in which plant is located. An award of $7,600 approved.

———— Restaurant. Request for reimbursement of money spent in providing sandwiches and other food used in rescue operations and authorized by American Red Cross. Award of $825.49 approved.

Request for assistance in making repairs to foundation of home and to porch steps. Husband in Veterans Administration Hospital since 1929. American Red Cross made award of $100 and Veterans Administration allowed $125 on repairs. Award of $125 to complete repairs approved.

A Note on Attitudes toward American Red Cross[1]

In view of the large amounts of money and tremendous energy expended by volunteers and professionals in the American Red Cross, the interesting and pertinent question arises as to why many persons look with suspicion and hostility at this institution. Red Cross ranked eleventh and twelfth in a list of twelve agencies active in these disasters, when placed according to percentages of persons saying they thought these agencies had done an adequate job. Other data present the number of families served and the amounts of money spent and show that a high percentage of the distressed families did request and receive aid through this agency.

In San Angelo and in Waco reports quickly spread that Red Cross had not done many things it should have done and had done many things it should not have done. In San Angelo these rumors were so widespread and so persistent that a daily radio program was inaugurated to explain what actually was being done. A veterans' organization became so agitated that it called the chairman of the local dis-

[1] Perhaps it needs to be emphasized that this is an impressionistic essay based on some years of experience working with the Home Service division of a relatively small chapter, plus observation of attitudes displayed toward the institution in these disasters.

aster-relief fund committee and threatened to withdraw its support because, it charged, the Red Cross was engaged in unethical practices. When the chairman offered explanations and took a group to Red Cross operation centers where they could see for themselves that the charges were without foundation, the incident was settled.

Most of the charges were trivial, in one sense. It was said that the Red Cross was charging ten cents per cup for coffee and twenty-five cents each for sandwiches which had been donated by residents of the city; that donated clothing was being sorted and the better garments were being shipped to New York for resale. Investigation established that no charge was being made for food of any sort. Clothing was being sorted, it was explained, so that garments suitable for winter wear might be placed in warehouses until the onset of cold weather. "It doesn't make sense to give overcoats to people who do not have even a suitcase to put them in, when the temperature is in the 80's, does it?" the chairman asked the complainers. Nothing was being shipped away.

But in another sense, such charges are far from trivial. They drastically affect the reputation and, therefore, the performance, of an institution with a long record of relief in disaster situations. Furthermore, these rumors persist. In San Angelo, more than a year after the disaster, an apparently intelligent minor municipal employee assured that the Red Cross, "took a cool $150,000 out of this town on that tornado deal."

Informal discussion suggests several partial answers to this problem. Perhaps they should be presented tentatively, since they have been arrived at by logic and impression, rather than through research.

Perhaps Red Cross has oversold itself as a disaster-relief agency. This important function of the organization is consistently played up in its publicity to a far greater degree than are other services it renders, services that cost much more money. Through this effort to imprint on the public mind that "when disaster strikes, Red Cross is there," the idea is perhaps created that Red Cross will repair all the damage and heal all the wounds, no matter how great the disaster. Such expectations can lead only to frustration.

Perhaps Red Cross is not folksy enough. Several persons in Waco and San Angelo expressed resentment at the "spit and polish" appearance of the Red Cross workers, with their semimilitary uniforms of expensive materials, carefully pressed and worn with an air. Caustic comment was also made on the display of the emblem of the organization and the care taken to make it not only visible but striking. Further, we were told, one had to seek out the Red Cross for service, while the Salvation Army—comparison, covert or overt, of the two is impossible to avoid—went directly to where the men were working and served them there, on a warm, personal, neighborly basis.

Perhaps these complaints are due in part to the organizational structure of the Red Cross. Its officials and volunteer workers seem given to reminding others that Red Cross was set up by an act of Congress and was given certain duties it must perform. Because of this, and because of its traditional ties with the military, the agency has taken on something of the attitude of authority which is acceptable coming from the armed forces but resented when displayed by a civilian institution. Perhaps because of its organizational pattern, Red Cross does not get as close to other agencies as might be desirable. Red Cross does have local chapters with local boards of directors and committee members, as do other agencies. If it is objected that Red Cross has national and regional headquarters, it seems but fair to point out that so do most other welfare agencies. But in other agencies there seems to be less insistence on clearing with higher authority and less imposing of national policies on local units. It could be there is merely less public awareness of the structure of the other institutions.

Perhaps there is a tendency on the part of Red Cross officials and workers to assume the directing of activities in disaster situations to a degree that arouses the antagonism and resentment of local public officials and other organizations. Red Cross workers, particularly those who have been brought in on such occasions, are likely to have had extensive experience in disaster work. They well may feel that they know from this experience much better than the local workers what needs to be done and how it needs to be done. Probably they usually are right in this opinion. But local workers feel that they know the local situation and the people better than any "stranger" can. They are also likely to feel that they have been relegated to positions of relative unimportance, their skills and their agencies ignored when they should be given high recognition. There is here something of the conflict between the "professional" and the "amateur." And there is much to be said on both sides. This local attitude is especially likely to become overt in the matter of disbursing funds. The local worker, or agency, is likely to suggest departing from strict adherence to policy when policy does not best serve the known needs of particular families or persons. The professional worker, on the other hand, is likely to work in an impersonal manner and to insist that the rules be applied as written, holding that departure from stated policy is usually an expression of favoritism.[2] This, in turn, may lead to the opinion that the professional Red Cross worker is a heartless bureaucrat whose milk of human kindness is in scant supply.

All these factors may give to some Red Cross workers an aloofness which is sometimes considered haughtiness and which may be the basis for a remark attributed to a Waco official that the greatest trouble with Red Cross is that it has "too many workers who make people damned mad."

But there is a final and more fundamental reason for the public-opinion position in which Red Cross finds itself.

In an emergency, Red Cross appears immediately with warm food and hot coffee—dispensed without cost to those asking—and with clothing, bedding, housing, and medical care—and these, too, are dispensed without cost. These are vitally necessary, in the literal sense, and are accepted gratefully by those who are not already suspicious of the agency. In this situation Red Cross appears as the Great Mother, giving her loving care and her sustenance without stint and without regard to the worthiness of her children in need.

When the emergency has passed and the long, hard road back to rehabilitation is begun, Red Cross appears in a different role. Of the families to whom she gave food, clothing, shelter, and care just a few days before, she now asks seemingly innumerable and often embarrassing questions. She wants to know how much money the family has in the bank and whether there is any objection to signing a form giving her authority to check with the banker on the truthfulness of the statement made. She wants to know how much the family owes, and to whom. She checks on these figures, also. She wants to know whether the family *really* needs as much space as its old, destroyed house had, and why it would not be better to cut off this room or that from the reconstruction plans under consideration. (Red Cross will, of course, handle negotiations with, and make payments to, the contractor who repairs or rebuilds the home.) All the while the Red

---

[2] When Robert C. Edson, national director of Disaster Services for American Red Cross, was asked to comment on this observation, he wrote: "Quite the reverse is true in Red Cross experience. . . . More often than not, it is the non-professional worker who, because of inadequate understanding and basic insecurity in her own competence, places insistence on 'rules.'" (Personal communication, February 5, 1957.)

Cross worker in her crisp uniform is filling in forms as she asks questions. And gradually the uniformed worker is transmuted from Great Mother to Wicked Witch, and is cursed accordingly.

This situation develops, of course, because of Red Cross policy that no one shall be helped in rehabilitation unless he can clearly demonstrate his need and his inability to meet that need from his own resources. Red Cross is not an insurance company ready to meet all the losses of disaster. It believes that the American public would be incensed if it undertook such a task. Further, from a practical point of view, Red Cross officials are certain that the public would never give the agency enough money to repay the total losses of disasters. Rather, they argue, Red Cross policy is in line with fundamental American ideology by insisting that everyone help himself as much and as long as he can before asking for aid to supplement his own insufficient efforts.

This Red Cross policy of insisting that families and persons who have resources use them before receiving assistance, or use them in conjunction with assistance from the organization, is often interpreted by disaster-affected people as putting a penalty on thrift and foresight. It is argued that the person who has been improvident and therefore has no funds with which to rebuild his home or provide for his family is given everything he needs; whereas the person who has established a savings account, or paid insurance premiums for years, or otherwise sacrificed in order to be able to meet emergencies receives none of the benefits of public generosity when he is in need. That the shiftless and lazy benefit while the frugal and prudent pay the costs is, of course, the argument advanced against many fields of social welfare. In San Angelo stories were told with great indignation of the refusal of Red Cross to aid a family when it was learned that insurance would repair the losses, while, "that family down the street, who never saved anything, got a fine brand new house for nothing."

Furthermore, persons suffering from the shock and frustration of a catastrophe utterly beyond their control and clearly incurred through no fault of their own are not likely to look at matters in a calm, reasonable, and rational manner. They feel that since they did nothing to incur such misfortune, then someone else must have, and they want to get back at whoever did it. Since they cannot get at the real cause, they are likely to substitute anyone else who seems to be in a position of authority and who is unfamiliar to them. Red Cross workers are quite likely to be on the scene and be assigned this role of scapegoat. The Red Cross was not alone in having this unpleasant role thrust upon it; in varying degrees, other institutions and agencies were faced with the same problem, more pronounced in Waco than in San Angelo.

Nor is this to argue that Red Cross is blameless. If the foregoing analysis has any merit, it must be obvious that there are things which Red Cross could do to improve the opinions people so often hold of it in disaster situations.

9. Channels of Contact

Society has its very being in communication. Without communication social action is impossible, and in a disaster situation social institutions and systems cannot operate without maintaining or re-establishing communication facilities.

Authorities in Waco expressed strongly their conviction that the two most immediate and troublesome problems following the devastation of their city were lack of communications and control of traffic.

Facilities for communication were never totally lacking in either San Angelo or Waco, but in Waco there was an almost total breakdown of mechanical facilities in the period immediately following the tornado, the time when such facilities were most desperately needed, of course. Their absence added greatly to the handicaps under which city officials and other institutional functionaries labored, and was responsible in no small measure for the period of confusion and inaction in that city.

But at the same time, the inadequate functioning of communication facilities in Waco may have been something of a blessing in disguise during this period. Although many persons crowded into the devastated area almost immediately after the disaster, many others did not know anything unusual had happened until the morning after. Had the information been broadcast immediately, it is almost certain that many more persons would have rushed to the area and that the resulting traffic jam would have been even worse than it was. Less than a year previously, when a report of an industrial accident had been broadcast, streets became jammed with persons trying to get to the scene. As heavy rain followed the tornado, the failure of radio and telephone service was attributed to this, possibly preventing some panic as well as greater congestion of streets and highways. Nonetheless, traffic jams did occur.

At the same time, jammed switchboards at the Waco telephone exchange and power failure that rendered the commercial radio stations impotent for a time, plus the general excitement, resulted in a situation in which runners were used to carry messages from one important center to another for about three hours. It was almost midnight before the key Waco officials finally got together to assess the activities already under way on a more or less spontaneous basis, and to plan how rescue efforts might be co-ordinated for greater efficiency. During that period, social organization in the stricken city was operating at a minimum, with persons spontaneously acting more in terms of training and habit than from direction in this new and drastically changed situation—where habits were not always best suited to deal with the crises.

Telephones

During the war, the district and regional telephone offices had formed elaborate plans for emergency situations. These had fallen into desuetude but were revived to some extent in the disaster. Two emergency generators located in the basement of the Waco telephone building were started about 5:00 P.M. and were kept in operation for the next nine days.

The first indication the telephone company had of the disaster came when the switchboard suddenly "lit up." This jam set off alarms, and repairmen scrambled for head sets to check the trouble. Since the telephone building is completely air-conditioned and is about four blocks from the area of devastation, noises had not penetrated. A man ran in and told of the collapse of a large building. The manager immediately grabbed a test set and tapped the lines to the radio stations to ask them to broadcast an appeal for people not to use their telephones, but both stations were already off the air.

Two telephone officials then took a mobile telephone car into the disaster area, parked it in front of the First National Bank, and put a special operator on the switchboard in the telephone building to handle their calls. This was a communications center for the first three hours, and this action probably had much to do with the bank's becoming disaster-operation headquarters. Orders from rescue workers were given to the telephone car, which in turn sent them on to the proper destination. A company repairman who happened to be in the area tapped two other lines and led them into the bank. Calls went out to telephone workers, and by 9:00 P.M. every post in the system was manned. Normally 12 persons work on the night shift, but 75 were put on duty. Both local disaster-officials and the telephone relay operators said that the "yellow pages" of classified advertising in the telephone directory were valuable in locating equipment and supplies.

After the two radio stations were again in operation, telephone calls were relayed alternately to them and they broadcast all requests for supplies. A telephone number was frequently announced as that officially designated for those who had authority to accept, or to call for, equipment. One operator was assigned to accept these calls, record what was offered, and give directions about what to do with the equipment accepted. After the requested supply was filled, she declined other offers with thanks. This procedure cut down a great deal on duplication and speeded up the rescue process.

By 7:30 P.M. a long line of people had appeared at the telephone office to place long-distance calls. This queue continued, with from 60 to 70 people in it, until four o'clock the next morning. The long-distance dial system was designed to handle 100 calls simultaneously, but incoming calls were so numerous that outgoing calls had to be delayed as much as six hours. Many of the incoming calls were from relatives of Baylor University students. So great was the jam, the manager of the Waco office asked the National Broadcasting Company in New York to broadcast an appeal to the nation that calls to Waco be restricted to real emergency messages. On Tuesday alone, operators completed 3,873 outgoing long-distance calls. The Dallas office of Southwestern Bell system reported that the Waco tornado caused "the greatest long-distance call jam in Texas history."

More than 6,300 telephones in Waco (20 per cent of the total) were knocked out, and 44 of the 100 long-distance circuits were damaged. Calls went out to Dallas and surrounding cities immediately for extra help, and the next day 31 repairmen, 4 long-distance engineers, and 30 operators from Fort Worth and Dallas were working in Waco. Later, company employees came from other cities to help in the restoration work. The supervisor of operators said of the emergency help: "They worked side by side with our girls as if they'd been here always." This competence was generally true of the other trained emergency workers also, and specifically supports LaPiere's comment on the interchangeability of the worker trained to perform a definite job in a bureaucratic structure.[1] It also points up one of the

[1] For an elaboration of this idea, see the discussion of corporations, p. 41.

strengths of such systems, and offers one foundation for planning to minimize disaster effects.

By the morning following the tornado, 50,000 feet of wire was on hand to lay in alleys and streets, plus 6,000 pounds of wire for the repair of long-distance circuits. Reconstruction work started at this time. The *Waco Times-Herald* for May 13 reported:

> Scores of crews of telephone repairmen from half a dozen Texas towns were in Waco Wednesday working to bring the city's storm-battered lines and cables back into service.
>
> District Manager Justin Hoy . . . reported 285 company plant men busy repairing dozens of cables broken by falling trees and flying debris. A total of 117 telephone repair and construction trucks, 50 of them from other towns, were in the city Wednesday morning. . . .

Thursday, May 14, saw a peak in the long-distance calls—5,550—approximately 1,000 more than had been handled on Wednesday. The next day more than 4,000 local telephones had been returned to service, and by Sunday all the long-distance circuits had been restored, and 5,352 local lines had been repaired.

Between about 5:00 P.M. Monday, the day of the disaster, through 5:00 P.M. Friday, the company handled 22,420 long-distance calls. The normal load for a similar period is approximately 45 per cent less than this. One week after the tornado, only 475 cases of telephone trouble still existed outside the downtown disaster area, and repairs within the area were being handled as rapidly as requests were received. The loss of equipment, plus the added costs of operation, totaled more than $100,000, according to officials of Southwestern Bell Telephone Company at Waco.

In no medium of communication was San Angelo affected nearly so drastically as was Waco, owing largely to the difference in size and nature of the area hit. In Waco, the greatest devastation was in the central business district; in San Angelo, it was on the periphery of the city. Furthermore, in San Angelo, the telephone company had received warning of the possibility of a tornado, and had crews ready to respond, with the result that within ten minutes workmen were in devastated Lake View. However, they postponed their primary job of restoring damaged telephone lines temporarily to help with the more urgent one of rescue work.

Actual damage to the San Angelo system was about half as large, in dollars, as that in Waco, but almost one-third of the telephones in the city were unusable for a time. Some 35 to 40 field employees of the telephone company were rushed to the devastated area, and all other available personnel were called to handle the deluge of calls at the central office and to keep equipment operating under the severe overload. Lines to offices of public officials, fire stations, the police station, and hospitals were kept open for emergency use. A special crew of 11 operators was set up to explain why only emergency calls could be cleared. Local calls increased by about 40 per cent; long-distance calls almost doubled.

Repair crews in Lake View ceased their rescue work as soon as the National Guard appeared and began providing emergency service. A cable approximately one mile long was laid to the school gymnasium, which then was used, along with a fire station equipped with radiotelephones, as headquarters for work in the area. Two repair crews were brought from nearby towns in New Mexico, and, except in the devastated area, service was returned to normal within two weeks.

The company manager pointed out that though many of the employees had homes in the area hardest hit, not one of them asked to be relieved to attend relatives or friends reported injured. Persons in high positions gladly employed skills they had learned in the past but had not used for some time.

Telegraph

In Waco the central telegraph office was located in the business area hit by the tornado. Power lines supplying this office were destroyed and were not replaced for four days. All tie-lines and circuits were also damaged beyond immediate repair.

The office manager quickly decided to establish Morse circuits in order to utilize power from distant sources. With this circuit operating, a message was sent to the Dallas office requesting portable generators, which arrived by train at 3:00 A.M. Within two hours after the disaster hit, seven sending- and five receiving-circuits had been put into operation. Code operators are scarce, but the manager located 2 amateurs who volunteered to help; 4 operators arrived from Dallas Tuesday morning; 19 repairmen and operators arrived later in the day from other Texas towns, and by Wednesday, 31 outside workers were on the job. So many messages began to flow that three branch offices were opened. On Tuesday, May 12, the office handled nearly 15,000 messages. (The usual daily Monday–Friday average is about 1,000 messages.)

Two vital problems were encountered: how to receive the messages from senders in Waco and get them on their way, and how to deliver incoming messages to Waco addresses. The problem of sending messages was partially solved by the use of Morse circuits. When streets leading to the main office were roped off, suboffices were established from which telegrams were picked up, conveyed by messenger to the central office, and wired from there. On May 13, more than 1,000 messages were picked up from the substations.

Nearly 37,000 messages were handled in nine days, though regular telephone circuits into the central office were not opened until the fourth day after the disaster. When the volume began to increase so sharply, the manager realized his normal delivery service could not handle it. Again, his decision was quickly made: he hired taxicabs to take over the job. They delivered more than 5,000 messages in three days, at a cost of 30 cents per message. But the backlog of undelivered messages grew so great that the manager then turned to the special-delivery postal service, which handled telegrams for 23 cents each. By the following Sunday, regular messengers were able to handle the job again.

Approximately 16,000 messages were delivered in Waco during the first five days of the disaster. During normal operations, from 2 to 3 per cent of messages are not deliverable, but in this five-day period, only fifteen complaints were received. The manager points out that this was possible only because of the "wonderful co-operation" of the citizens who "went out of their way to help each other." The cost of this extra operation, plus repair to facilities, came to more than $20,000, officials of the company reported.

Telegraph service in San Angelo increased by only about 20 per cent above normal. The local office was able to close at midnight following the tornado in the early afternoon. The problem of delivering messages in the devastated area was met by using an emergency mail-delivery station.

Noncommercial Radio Operations

"Ham" radio station operators have built an enviable reputation for service in disasters. In the Waco situation they augmented this reputation.

Within an hour after the tornado struck, these amateurs had set up and were operating a mobile unit at the City Hall. Two hours later more powerful equipment was moved in to supplement the first unit, and members of the Amateur Radio Club of Waco were exceedingly busy—not only in handling messages but in helping to install emergency power-and-light equipment. Five short-wave stations for transmission to distant points were operated. Within an hour and a half after the impact, messages were being transmitted for persons in Waco to relatives and friends all over the United States. Two centers were established where members of the club accepted telephoned messages for relay. An arrangement was made with the Military Affiliate Radio System (MARS) at nearby Connally Air Force Base by which overseas messages were relayed through that facility. Although exact figures were not recorded, estimates are that the amateurs handled some 2,000 messages during the first three days following the disaster, and that when the operation officially ended on May 22, they had handled about 4,000 messages.

Although Connally Air Force Base responded to the call for aid from Waco with men and supplies almost immediately, no telephone communication between the base and the city existed for some hours. As soon as power was available, messages were sent and received by the Military Affiliate Radio System unit at the military base, in cooperation with amateur operators in downtown locations. The amateurs then contacted the officials and others to whom messages were directed, often by runner. Military officers in the devastated area used this system to request additional men, equipment, and supplies.

MARS also made contact with other military installations to pass on information of the disaster and made initial contact with the American Red Cross headquarters in Washington to report on the extent of the damage. MARS also served as a news source. One amateur operator in California tuned in on the military channel and tape-recorded the broadcasts of news, which he then turned over to a local radio station for rebroadcasting.

Since MARS is limited to the military and is semiofficial, most of its service in the Waco disaster was in getting messages to, or receiving them from, military personnel. This service began about 6:00 P.M. on the afternoon of the tornado and continued for four days on a twenty-four-hour-day basis. During this time some 2,000 messages were transmitted, military officials estimated. These messages went to all the states in the nation and to many military posts in foreign countries. The speed with which some of these messages were delivered is illustrated by the fact that a soldier in Germany received a message that his father had been killed in the tornado two hours after it was sent.

By using radio and teletype facilities, the Texas State Department of Public Safety office in San Angelo was able to handle the necessary communications without aid from amateur radio stations. This office immediately got in touch with the state police office in Austin and with the office of the Governor, and within three and a half hours had handled about 100 messages, mostly official. An average of about 200 radio messages and 75 teletype messages were handled each day for the next five days, many of them personal messages to relatives and friends of disaster victims.

Prior to the impact of the tornado, two highway patrolmen had kept the funnel in sight and radioed its progress constantly to the Department of Public Safety. This office had in turn established connection with the local newspaper office's private branch exchange and, through it, with the essential agencies of the city. The operator at the Department of Public Safety estimated that at least 30 persons were informed of the approach of the storm. One merchant telephoned the department that he was watching the funnel.

Immediately after the storm struck, calls went out to all highway patrolmen, state police officers, and highway department officials in the district. Within three hours 35 cars and trucks had arrived in answer to this summons.

Commercial Radio

Without doubt radio is the medium of mass communication best suited, logically, to emergency use. With receiving sets in approximately 98 per cent of the nation's homes, it is theoretically possible to convey warnings or other messages to a vast majority of the population in a minimum of time by commercial radio. However, experiences in Waco and San Angelo do not fully justify this expectation. Because of power failure, neither the two radio stations in Waco nor the two in San Angelo were operable following the tornadoes for from about three hours and thirty minutes to five hours and thirty minutes, the hours when they were needed most drastically.

This does not mean that the stations were of no value during this period. While their own transmitters were silent, these stations were feeding information and instructions to other stations with which they had established telephone contact. Their most dramatic service was in Waco, where mobile units were used as communications centers in the heart of the devastated business area.

An official of Waco station KWTX happened to be in an office building in the area devastated by the tornado. He returned to the station, made assignments to the staff, and dispatched a mobile unit with a loud-speaker to the business area. This unit, in operation within approximately an hour after the impact, was used by the mayor, the chief of police, the fire chief, and the sheriff to issue orders and to direct rescue operations. However, the fact that the audible range of this equipment was not more than two blocks greatly limited its usefulness. Military equipment was moved in and assumed this task the next afternoon.

By means of battery sets, both Waco stations immediately began to gather information on tape recordings for a later broadcast. Meanwhile, station WACO established telephone contact with a radio station in Fort Worth about 6:00 P.M. and gave a ten-minute interview which was broadcast immediately. Telephone interviews were later given to other stations. Of greatest local benefit was a call to station KTEM in nearby Temple, requesting that the National Guard unit there be alerted and that appeals be broadcast for persons not to drive to or through Waco. The Temple station has a frequency between those of the Waco stations; hence, it was thought that persons trying to tune in either of the local stations and finding them silent would most likely pick up the Temple signal and be reached over that station.

By 10:00 P.M. on the day of the disaster, WACO was tied in with a national chain of some forty stations through the American Broadcasting Company and the Texas State Network. Station KWED in Seguin, near San Antonio, Texas, relayed WACO broadcasts to about fourteen additional Texas stations. After resuming broadcasting through its own facilities, this station failed to actuate its directional equipment, and for the three nights following the tornado it broadcast on open antennae, thereby greatly increasing the territory over which it could be heard. One letter received said that the writer had news of the disaster from this station over a car radio as he was driving in Kansas.

Both Waco stations and those in San Angelo devoted much of their time to personal messages "to relieve the anxiety among relatives." Some 57,000 such messages were handled by WACO during the week following the disaster, it was estimated.

An interesting pattern of tertiary communication grew out of this practice. Several radio stations recorded these messages on tape and later rebroadcast those addressed to persons within their range. Cases were also reported of persons who heard friends, or relatives of friends, mentioned and then relayed the messages by telephone to the persons for whom they were intended. One such instance involved a telephone call from a city in Oklahoma to another in California.

But the task of immediate importance undertaken by the radio stations was that of relaying messages, appealing for supplies, locating unusual equipment, and sending intracity messages between officials and heads of the vital institutions. Officials in the downtown area used both stations for such service, on something approaching an alternate schedule. This service continued even after other channels of communication became easily available. For instance, on the Sunday following the tornado, so many sight-seers crowded into the city that the work of clearing debris was badly hampered, and traffic was so snarled that only with the greatest difficulty could any movement take place. The police used a radio station to plead with drivers to avoid the downtown area except in case of dire emergency and to warn persons outside the city to stay away.

No attempts were made to maintain regular broadcast schedules, though one station included advertising in its broadcasting. Regular advertising schedules were resumed on Thursday, after the last body had been located, but "light" commercials, advertising for intoxicants, and singing commercials were not used until the week following. Much of the advertising immediately after the disaster concerned the opening of temporary places of business, dates for reopening, and similar announcements.

Each station broadcast pleas for donations and other aid. In Waco, the stations also accepted food, clothing, and other supplies for transfer to disbursing agencies. On the day following the disaster when the head of a civic organization in a nearby city found no ready response to pleas for a truckload of emergency supplies to be sent to Waco, he appealed to a Waco station to do a special broadcast aimed at his city. This was done and the supplies were on their way two hours later.

The two Waco stations seem to have held different conceptions of their function in the disaster. Station WACO turned its attention to disseminating the disaster news to the outside world through newscasts and through transmitting personal messages. KWTX adopted a more localized view, describing the destruction, the rescue work, and similar subjects for the local audience. For example, it sent a plane over the city the morning following the tornado, from which one of its staff described the destruction of the various parts of the city. Both stations co-operated closely with city officials and civic leaders in getting information and instructions to the citizens.

Tornadoes over Texas

Radio workers agreed from their experience in these disasters that much more organization is essential than was evident. Not only were civic officials and leaders seemingly unaware of the potentialities of radio in such a situation, but the radio workers themselves were not well prepared. An instructor in radio at Baylor University was curtly told by an emergency operator he was not needed when he volunteered to help at one of the stations. A volunteer announcer re-read the entire list of known dead each time a name was added, needlessly lacerating the emotions of survivors.

Radio reporters had to be very circumspect in interviewing on the scene of the disaster. Gruesome and revolting details, sometimes given with excessive profanity, made such on-the-spot broadcasting precarious; for this reason tape recordings were made and later broadcast.

From the evidence it seems clear that the radio stations in these cities performed exceedingly important, even vital, services to their communities and the outside world in these emergencies. Through their ability to transmit messages to as many persons as were tuned in, they did much to compensate for the partial breakdown of other forms of communication, and they did much to bring to an end the short period of dazed inactivity before social organization reasserted itself and began to function effectively in the new and strange situation in which the city found itself.

The Postal Service

In San Angelo, the central post office was out of the tornado pathway and suffered no physical damage or interruption of service. In Waco, the central post office was on the edge of the devastated area. Windows were blown out, about half the tiles from the roof were lost, and the power supply was interrupted. Employees resorted to candles, kerosene lamps, and lanterns in order to handle the mail.

The primary effect of the tornado upon the postal service in both cities was to increase tremendously the volume of mail, particularly special-delivery letters. In Waco, the number of messengers assigned to this task rose to 36 on the third day. However, many of these messages were telegrams mailed by the local office of Western Union for delivery by the post office. On the fourth day following the disaster, the postmaster asked the local radio stations to read names and addresses of special-delivery mail which could not be delivered so that the addressees might come to the post office for it.

Regular delivery was not interrupted except in the central devastated area, where there was usually no one to receive mail. Delivery of parcel post was impossible, of course; and since the worst hit area was the central business district—where no businesses were open for four days—the storage of this mail created the most serious problem for the post office.

If society exists in communication, then perhaps a measure of the threat to continued social functioning is the extent of the damage to the communications system of a city in disaster; and a measure of the rehabilitative ability of the social system may be the speed with which communication between the vitally important agencies and functionaries regains its essential efficiency.

10. The Newspaper Tells the Story

I f RADIO AND OTHER nearly instantaneous media of communication are vital to the reorientation of the social organization in the period immediately following a disaster, the newspaper seems to play its most important role in the long-run rehabilitation of a stricken community.

Radio has only a front page. Because of the nature of this medium, details of events cannot feasibly be presented. Further, with its focus on the immediate, it is not to be expected that radio would devote as much attention to planning, consideration, and debating as does a newspaper.

Taking these statements as hypotheses, we made a detailed study of the treatment of the tornado by the *Waco Times-Herald*. Because of limited funds and staff, no attempt was made to analyze the content of the other newspaper in Waco, or that of either of the two newspapers in San Angelo. Since in Waco both newspapers are published by the same corporation, we felt that what was true of the one paper analyzed would also be true, within narrow limits, of the second.

The content of the newspaper was first broken down into its three major divisions: news or reading material; photographs; and advertisements. Each of these was further classified into material which had to do with the disaster and that which had no obvious connection with it. Each item was classified as local or nonlocal. Finally, disaster-related reading material and photographs were divided into 13 categories descriptive of general content and each was measured in column inches. The material processed covered a period of thirteen months—May 1, 1953, to June 1, 1954. We felt that by the end of that period the effects of the disaster had been so assimilated that no further influence would be ascertainable.

For the first ten days of May, 1953 (before the tornado struck)

194

the *Waco Times-Herald* carried much more nonlocal than local news, the nonlocal category accounting for about 20 per cent of the total space in each issue and local for about 12 per cent. For the two days following the tornado, 18 per cent of total space was devoted to disaster news. Other local news was subordinated, though not absent. On the first day on which space was given the disaster—May 12—7 per cent of the space was devoted to other local news. This category received only 2 per cent on May 14. But from this point, nondisaster local news began to occupy more space, and by the end of the month in which the tornado occurred it was back up to 13 per cent. Meanwhile, space given to disaster-connected news rapidly declined; in the last two editions for May, it took up only 2 and 3 per cent of total space.

Sunday editions of this newspaper normally carry a greater percentage of local news than do weekday editions. But for the month of the catastrophe, the Sunday edition carried a higher percentage of nondisaster news but not of disaster news. This probably was true because a considerable portion of the local news appearing in Sunday editions is what is known as "time" copy; that is, it is written when convenient and held until there is occasion for its use. In this case, the news was considered so important that it was published as it developed, not held until Sunday.

The use of photographs follows closely the pattern of news treatment with the important exception that the Sunday editions in May used many disaster pictures. In the first Sunday edition after the tornado, such pictures occupied 11 per cent of the total space; a week later, 5 per cent; on the last Sunday of the month no disaster photographs were used. There was the same relationship between the two categories of local photography as in local news coverage. On the Sunday following the tornado, little nondisaster art work was used, but on the following Sunday equal amounts of space were devoted to pictures in the disaster and nondisaster categories; by the end of the month there was about the usual total amount of local material, all nondisaster.

By June 1—less than three weeks after perhaps the most important occurrence in the history of the city—news of that event had been relegated to relatively insignificant space in the newspaper. On no day in June was more than 3 per cent of its space devoted to the tragedy, and on only two days was it that high. In fact, during June, on only five days did news of the tornado and its consequences take up more than 1 per cent of the space. In July, even less space was

TABLE 54

Contents of *Waco Times-Herald* by Percentage of Total Space per Edition for May, 1953

	News Local Dst.*	News Local Ndst.†	News Nonlocal Dst.	News Nonlocal Ndst.	Photographs Local Dst.	Photographs Local Ndst.	Photographs Nonlocal Dst.	Photographs Nonlocal Ndst.	Advertising Local Dst.	Advertising Local Ndst.	Advertising Nonlocal Dst.	Advertising Nonlocal Ndst.
Day												
1	..	13	..	23	..	2	..	3	..	41	..	1
2	..	13	1	29	..	3	..	1	..	21	..	1
3	..	16	..	8	..	8	..	4	..	54	..	1
4	..	11	..	24	..	2	..	1	..	34	..	6
5	..	11	..	24	..	1	..	2	..	36	..	10
6	..	11	..	17	..	3	..	3	..	51	..	4
7	..	7	..	15	..	1	..	2	..	56	..	10
8	..	12	..	20	..	2	..	1	..	45	..	3
9	..	14	..	26	..	2	..	1	..	23	..	..
10	..	15	..	14	..	10	..	4	..	47	..	1
11	..	8	1	20	..	2	1	2	..	32	..	17
12	18	7	1	16	15	..	..	..	2	12	..	10
13	18	3	..	22	6	..	..	1	9	13	..	8
14	13	2	..	13	7	..	..	..	8	32	..	13
15	16	3	..	21	10	..	..	1	24	4	..	5
16	15	4	..	25	7	..	..	1	13	11	..	1
17	13	7	1	15	11	1	..	2	25	12	..	1
18	14	4	1	20	3	1	..	..	13	23	..	10
19	14	5	..	15	5	..	..	..	31	11	..	4
20	10	5	..	15	3	..	..	2	17	26	..	10
21	8	7	..	21	2	1	..	3	20	36	..	3
22	9	7	..	16	2	1	..	1	15	29	..	5
23	8	9	1	14	1	1	..	1	11	20	..	..
24	6	14	..	11	5	5	..	2	17	28	..	1
25	5	8	..	26	1	..	..	3	2	24	..	11
26	5	9	..	17	..	1	..	1	11	20	..	17
27	10	8	..	20	2	2	..	..	15	19	..	8
28	3	8	..	14	..	2	..	1	7	57	..	9
29	5	9	..	19	..	2	..	1	11	31	..	4
30	1	13	..	26	..	2	..	..	3	23	..	1
31	2	13	..	11	..	6	..	4	32	22	..	1

* Dst. = Disaster
† Ndst. = Nondisaster

given to it; on one day only was more than 1 per cent of the space devoted to this subject.

Through June and July, nondisaster local news resumed its rank, occupying from 7 to 16 per cent of all space available. Nonlocal news also resumed its former position of dominance. In short, the newspaper returned to normal, or almost so, within three weeks.

What has been said of news coverage by reading matter applied with greater emphasis to the use of photography. Although the use of this medium for conveying news decreased rapidly after the first week, some photographs were used in each edition throughout May. But the papers for the first Sunday in June, and for fifteen other days in this month, carried no disaster pictures. In July, such pictures appeared in nine editions only.

The Sunday edition of most newspapers customarily makes greater use of photographs than do weekday editions. This was true of the Waco newspaper. It has been noted already that by the end of May, nondisaster local pictures were taking up to 7 per cent of the total space. The trend increased through June and July, reaching 12 per cent on July 26, when no disaster-associated pictures were used. Thus, it appears that in the judgment of the editors the picturization of other local news and events outranked the tornado in importance.

However, this may not be a true explanation of the statistics presented. "Society" news is important in most newspapers in towns of this size—too large for most persons to know directly about entertainment, parties, weddings, et cetera, and not large enough for interest in such news to be restricted to small groups. Moreover, organizations such as churches, the chamber of commerce, and clubs feel it is their due for the newspaper to carry photographs of their functions and changes of personnel. These pictures are almost standing assignments for the photographic crew; indeed, many of them are supplied by persons or organizations themselves. Hence, most editors would agree that they get into print at the exclusion of other pictures of more interest and importance.

The diminution of space devoted to the disaster was both rapid and drastic. During the twenty days of May after the tornado, this newspaper devoted more than 6,600 column inches to the tragedy and its effects. During the next month, this amount decreased to less than 1,300; in July, it went to 678 inches. Space devoted to the disaster in subsequent months became less and less, but did not entirely disappear within the year, as shown by Figure 11.

From the measurements of space devoted to the impact of a great

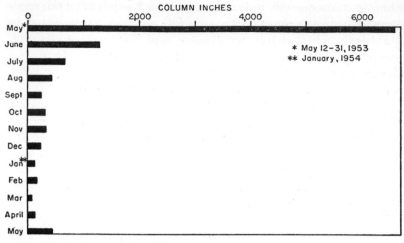

Fig. 11. Column inches of disaster news in *Waco Times-Herald*.

disaster on a small metropolitan area, it is to be concluded that one of the chief media for disseminating information found comparatively little of importance or interest in this tragic event to present to its readers after the first three weeks. This is not to say that this newspaper had lost interest in the disaster. It is to say that the interest

TABLE 55

Category and Rank, by Inches, of Disaster-Related News in *Waco Times-Herald*, May 12–July 31, 1953

Category	May	Rank	June	Rank	July	Rank	Total	Rank
Aid received	1,658	1	642	1	216	1	2,517	1
Human interest . . .	1,599	2	98	4	77	2	1,774	2
Governmental activity .	621	3	117	3	43	5	780	3
Injuries and deaths . .	604	4	5	12	14	10	623	4
Public information . .	441	5	70	5	20	9	531	5
Rebuilding plans . . .	287	8	134	2	65	3	487	6
Physical destruction . .	430	6	..	13	6	11	436	7
Rescue activity . . .	314	7	20	9	..	12	333	8
Miscellaneous . . .	97	12	67	6	42	6	279	9
Salvage, cleanup . . .	233	9	12	11	..	12	245	10
Business effects . . .	136	10	41	8	39	7	216	11
Religious activity . .	122	11	64	7	22	8	208	12
Physical rebuilding . .	61	13	17	10	63	4	141	13

198

which remained—and it certainly was high—did not find correspondingly high expression through this medium, as measured by space devoted to it.

Content

But perhaps more important than the total amount of coverage given to this event and stories related to it are the kinds of news gathered concerning it. For purposes of analysis, thirteen categories of news and photographic material were set up. Table 55 shows how these categories ranked in order of the number of column inches in the first three months of this analysis.

Time is obviously the important factor in this distribution. Imme-

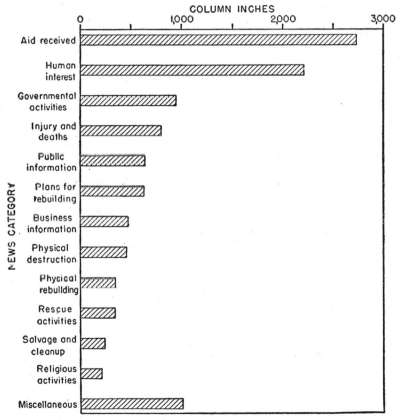

Fig. 12. Space devoted to categories of disaster news in *Waco Times-Herald* for year following tornado.

diately after the impact, there were two focuses of attention: the aid received to ease the blow suffered by the community and to speed recovery, and the interest in the human beings who had suffered

TABLE 56

Category and Rank, by Inches, of Disaster News in *Waco Times-Herald*, May 12, 1953–May 31, 1954

Category	Rank	Column Inches
Aid received	1	2,735.75
Human interest	2	2,218.0
Miscellaneous	3	1,010.5
Governmental activities	4	938.5
Injury and death	5	795.5
Public information	6	638.75
Plans for rebuilding	7	626.5
Business information	8	469.25
Physical destruction	9	460.5
Physical rebuilding	10	345.0
Rescue activities	11	344.5
Salvage, cleanup	12	240.75
Religious activities	13	215.75
Total		11,088.25

extraordinarily in unexpected ways and had lived to tell of their experiences and of their struggles to rebuild their lives.

News about physical destruction, rescue activities, the cleanup of debris, and salvage was soon exhausted.

Plans for rebuilding had to wait until complete information on losses had been gathered and arrangements made for action. These often involved several persons and institutions, particularly in the business area. Governmental activity began with the impact but it could not be completed for many months. Churches received news space for their activities in meeting the emergency, and later for their task of rebuilding their properties and of aiding members to rebuild their lives, in addition to their commemorative services for the dead and of their use of the tornado to point out the need for greater religious participation.

It will be noted that reports of rehabilitation decreased rather than increased as time went by. Since it is certain that these activities did continue, the lessening of the space given to their reporting seems explainable most accurately in terms of a lessened interest in the disaster as a whole.

When news related to the tornado is tabulated by areas of interest over the longer period, from May 11, 1953, to June 1, 1954, changes appear, but the general picture remains much the same. During that period, there was a total of 11,069.25 inches of reading material with direct bearing on the tragedy and efforts at rehabilitation. Of this total, 2,735.75 inches had to do with aid received. This is by far the largest of the thirteen categories; in second place are human-interest stories, with 2,205 column-inches.

However, these statistics may not accurately present the picture of news treatment of the disaster. If the news of actual rebuilding and of plans for rebuilding are combined, a total of 971.5 inches is reached and this new category takes third rank. If to this is added the space alloted to aid received and governmental activity, most of which was of a rehabilitative nature, then 3,645.75 inches, or 32.9 per cent of the total space given to the disaster, is related to efforts to repair the damage and to resume normal functioning. In addition, many of the stories in other categories have some reference to rehabilitation and would add to the total of constructive news treatment.

In two months and twenty days, beginning with the day following the tornado, the newspaper published a total of almost 8,000 column inches of news material directly concerned with this event and its consequences. Of this total, 2,517 inches or 29 per cent, were devoted to one subject: aid received.

Though aid and human interest drew most attention, this is not to say that other categories of news were neglected unduly. What goes into a newspaper depends, day by day, on two factors: (1) what has happened, and (2) how important, pertinent, or interesting what has happened may be. The first is outside the control of the editorial staff; the second is a matter of judgment which must be exercised by the entire staff, from reporter through make-up editor, as they decide what to write, how to write it, and how to display it.

It is an axiom of journalism that few stories are so entertaining and so important that they will hold reader interest for more than a week —or at most become a "nine-day wonder." It should be remembered that the newspaper had told and retold the story of the tornado many times in those first few weeks. What remained to be told was the struggle back toward normal community, family, and personal life. But plans were in the process of being made, and decisions

TABLE 57

Distribution by Column Inches of Categories of Disaster News as Published in *Waco Times-Herald*, May 12, 1953, to May 31, 1954

Month	Aid Rec'd, All Sources	Physical Destruction	Physical Re-building	Human Interest, Opinions	Injuries, Deaths	Rebuild-ing Plans	Rescue, Support	Gov't Actions, All Levels	Other	Business Infor-mation	Public Infor-mation	Salvage, Cleanup	Religious News	Total
May	1,658	433	61	1,598	603	287	313	609	96	136	441	233	122	6,590
June	643	...	17	106	5	134	19	117	66	42	70	12	63	1,294
July	216	6	63	66	24	68	...	43	118	39	16	...	12	671
Aug.	63	...	17	102	4	54	8	67	86	8	22	...	...	431
Sept.	52	...	65	42	19	17	...	7	39	...	1	...	...	242
Oct.	20	6	28	13	12	...	...	22	92	90	32	...	...	315
Nov.	11	18	48	36	36	21	...	...	38	79	29	...	13	329
Dec.	6	...	...	25	52	11	...	...	137	...	...	...	4	235
Jan.	...	...	20	46	...	...	3	9	13	...	36	...	...	127
Feb.	...	...	26	43	3	7	...	...	92	...	1	...	...	172
March	...	1	...	18	14	...	...	19	9	8	19	...	...	88
April	...	...	...	13	...	5	...	...	71	31	4	...	...	124
May	66	...	...	97	31	22	...	33	153	36	12	...	1	451
Total	2,735	464	345	2,205	803	626	343	926	1,010	469	683	245	215	11,069

were being forged within organizations and families and among persons; many of these, perhaps, were not of a nature which their makers wished to make public, or in which the public as a whole would have had great interest.

The routine business of living is never so exciting or so interesting as the unexpected, the break in the routine, though it may be far more important. But since routine does not excite, and because it is often felt unwise to make deliberations public until some decision has been reached, the ordinary business of life does not get into the news columns of newspapers in proportion to its importance.

Photographic coverage diminished more rapidly, in terms of space occupied, than did news. This form of reporting was also more concentrated in a few categories by the very nature of the medium. Pictures of physical destruction, of rescue activities, and those accompanying stories of persons with unusual experiences—human-interest stuff—were immediately available, and were used in profusion. On the day following the disaster 425.75 column inches were devoted to news photographs in these three categories. Such pictures continued to be used in large numbers for approximately one week, but before the end of the month those showing destruction and rescue work ceased to appear. None in either of these categories were used in June or July.

Human-interest pictures, however, continued to appeal and were used frequently through June. By July, even this theme was becoming less interesting, from the photographic point of view, and only two such pictures were used. The great amount of space used to tell of donations and other forms of aid has been commented on already in the discussion of news stories. This same emphasis appears in the use of pictures. The first photographs of this sort appeared on May 15, and such pictures were used with great frequency through May and June. But by July, this source of material also had been nearly exhausted. Only one such photograph appeared in that month.

As the photographic presentation of the horror aspects of the tragedy lessened, there was a relative, though not actual, increase in the portrayal of rehabilitative work. In May, of a total of more than 3,000 inches of pictures related to the tornado, slightly more than 90 were devoted to pictures of rebuilding, or plans for rebuilding. During June, these two categories drew a total of slightly more than 80 in a total of approximately 550 inches. In July, two editions carried a total of 218 inches of such pictures in a total of 402.

It is hard to escape the conclusion that the lens, like the pencil, was

TABLE 58

Paid Circulation of *Waco Times-Herald,* May, 1953

Day	City	Out of Waco	Total
1	16,077	10,498	26,575
2	15,307	10,296	26,603
3	24,555	19,283	43,838*
4	16,134	10,480	26,614
5	16,136	10,455	25,591
6	16,105	10,452	26,557
7	15,884	10,414	26,298
8	15,759	10,420	26,179
9	15,535	10,233	25,768
10	24,349	19,192	43,541*
11	15,428	10,432	25,860
12	22,521	19,804	42,325
13	23,356	19,515	42,871
14	21,117	17,621	38,738
15	20,097	14,436	34,533
16	17,760	12,007	29,767
17	26,454	22,184	48,638*
18	16,242	10,753	26,995
19	17,265	10,570	27,835
20	16,973	10,624	27,597
21	16,874	10,702	27,576
22	16,547	10,729	27,276
23	15,863	10,524	26,387
24	24,867	19,385	44,252*
25	16,450	10,734	27,184
26	16,259	10,748	27,007
27	16,227	10,779	27,006
28	15,790	10,774	26,564
29	15,537	10,759	26,296
30	15,695	10,545	26,240
31	24,297	19,316	43,613*

* On Sunday the *Times-Herald* is combined with the *News-Tribune.*
Source: Figures supplied by *Waco Times-Herald.*

most freely used to record those events and activities which had high emotional appeal in preference to those which were less interesting but might have more truly told the story of how a city reorganizes itself after a major disruption of its life pattern.

The effect of the disaster on newspaper circulation is apparent from Table 58. There was an almost immediate jump of more than 50 per cent in the circulation of the afternoon edition. But this increase rapidly disappeared, and by the end of May, 1953, circulation had resumed its normal pattern. During the next three months there was no apparent effect on circulation figures, and since the time lapse would be great enough that no changes after that period could be ascribed to the tornado with any degree of certainty, it seemed unrewarding to continue this phase of the study.

It will be observed also that the increase in circulation immediately following the tornado was about equally divided between circulation within Waco and outside the city. This seems to indicate that this newspaper assumed the function of informing the public, in Waco and elsewhere, of the situation, i.e., that there was no highly specialized local function, in terms of geographic area, performed by the newspaper.

This newspaper faithfully served the interests of its community by devoting generously its space to important information about the reconstruction of facilities, reporting governmental activities designed to aid in rehabilitation, and in passing on information of value to its readers in making plans for their own rehabilitation. In addition, it gave news of the physical destruction, injury and death, and the grim tasks of rescue and salvage made necessary by the catastrophe. Thus, this newspaper functioned in areas of importance to its community, discharging the tasks expected of it. How well those functions were performed or how some other newspaper might have done these things, it is not possible to say. Comparable studies seem to be nonexistent.

11. Repeat Performance

"LIGHTNING NEVER STRIKES TWICE in the same place" is an ancient bit of folklore which every now and then is proved false. A case in point is the city of San Angelo, or, more specifically, the northwestern portion known as Lake View.

On June 7, 1954, just thirteen months after the devastating tornado had swept through this area, a very heavy hail-, wind-, and rain-storm hit the same area, smashing windows and doors, battering holes in roofs, and flooding the streets with more than six inches of water.

Just preceding this storm, two tornado funnels were seen to the west of the neighborhood. Boats and docks on a nearby lake were smashed, but the tornadoes did not hit the thickly settled area of the city. Wind velocity in Lake View reached 65 miles per hour. Only two injuries were reported, and no deaths resulted. But "lightning" had struck—almost— twice in the same place.

The major insurance agency handling damage claims estimated that more than 8,000 individual claims would be filed as a result of this second storm. The estimated total loss was $2,400,000, roughly an average of $300 per claim.

Obviously, this second San Angelo catastrophe, as it was promptly labeled by insurance adjusters, called for more study. Here was an unexpected opportunity to observe a community under extremely adverse circumstances so closely following a major disaster that it had not fully recovered from the first blow.

Although our study of the tornado of a year before was not complete and in spite of the fact that a new study might seriously tax the co-operative spirit of the people of Lake View and the officials of San Angelo, this second catastrophe presented a research opportunity of such promise it could not be ignored. "Operation Repeat" was designed to investigate what effects this second storm had had

206

upon Lake View residents and also to uncover any relationships that might exist between their experiences in the tornado and their reactions to the second storm.

Using a new schedule, three experienced interviewers reinterviewed 114 of the original 150 families. In 7 cases new families occupied houses at the addresses of families formerly interviewed. Several persons who had been previously interviewed by schedule were also given intensive, focused interviews in an effort to get more deeply into their emotional reactions than would have been possible by the use of a schedule only. No attempt was made to trace down and interview those families who had moved out of the district between the two studies.

Since the two samples did vary in size, we felt it necessary to see whether any great variations were apparent between them. No significant differences were found. A slight increase in the number of families having children was noted, and, perhaps more pertinent, the percentage owning cars had also increased. However, neither change was large enough to meet a statistical test for significance. The increased ownership of cars is suggestive of an improved economic status, though the possession of an automobile under the long-drawn-out installment buying available is a dubious index of prosperity.

But if no changes in the material situation of the families in the two samples were indicated by the statistical checks used, persons in position to know were quick to point out other changes in families, in persons, and in the neighborhood as a whole that had come about as a result of the tornado.

The Lake View School superintendent, for example, explained that the people in Lake View had been very "storm-conscious" following the tornado. Several had dust storms and one tornado warning had caused many parents to come to the school to ask that their children be excused from classes. During the intervening months, little overt interest had been shown in discussing the tornado except on its anniversary, May 11, 1954, when the disaster appears to have been the main topic of conversation. No memorial service was held, however, "because we did not want to continue the memory of the disaster for the children."

The students' reactions, as observed at school, indicated several effects. Disciplinary problems almost disappeared during the school year following the tornado. One teacher commented that she had never known children who obeyed so promptly and so implicity as those in the Lake View School. However, she added, the children did become very nervous when the weather became threatening, and, if more than one child from a single family was in school, the siblings were likely to insist on seeing each other or being together.

A Youth for Christ movement was developed in the school by a student who was also an ordained minister. Although the attempt to develop such a movement had been going on for several years, it was only in 1953/54 that it really caught on. More than 200 students (out of a student body of 1,700) participated in the movement, and during the last week of school in May, 1954, revival meetings were held in the school auditorium each night with large attendance. Other data on religious activities following the storms are presented later in this chapter and in Chapters 1 and 3 of this report.

As stated earlier, free lunches were provided through the aid of the San Angelo Disaster Fund for the children of disaster-affected families if the family so requested. These lunches were handled so as not to embarrass the children, and an average of 275 students a day received them. The tax collections for the school system were also the best on record, with 100 per cent payment. In many cases, taxes were also paid by the Disaster Fund. The school board had ordered a re-evaluation of property in the Lake View area in July, 1954, increasing the tax base by more than $150,000. Enrollment increased during the 1953/54 school year by 120 pupils, considerably above the expectations. The superintendent reasoned from this that not many families had moved from Lake View, whereas many new families had moved in. Transfers from the city system had also increased enrollment. The hailstorm of June 7, 1954, "scared everyone to death," according to the superintendent. More than one hundred windows in the school were smashed, but no students were in the building at this time.

So far as the city government was concerned, the hailstorm was only a minor matter. About 10:00 P.M. (the storm hit about 6:00 P.M.) a city employee telephoned the mayor to come see the vast quantity of water standing in the Lake View area. The mayor felt the condition indicated a "poor job" of providing for drainage following the tornado. Streets and drainage openings which the city had constructed in Lake View after the tornado "violated normal drainage and produced the problem." No citizen made any request to the city for assistance following the hailstorm.

Both radio stations and the television station were forced off the air by power failure during this second storm. None of these stations had provided for emergency power, though the same thing had happened following the tornado. The manager of one of the stations said that "any time the weather looks bad, between thirty-five and fifty people will phone in for a 'personal' weather report—even though the station broadcasts a request for its listeners not to phone in." Just before the second storm, about one hundred calls were received. It was this station's policy to "play down" the second storm and minimize the damage. On the day following this storm, only one program was presented which had not been regularly scheduled. This program featured several local insurance men who gave information about how to file for insurance claims on storm damage.

The local press also intentionally played down the hailstorm, though both editions on the following day carried several pictures of broken windows, damaged roofs, destroyed gardens, and standing water.

From the standpoint of these persons in authority, the period between the two storms was one of achievement; it marked a return to the *status quo ante,* and the second storm was little more than a severe weather phenomenon.

In view of the large amount of damage and the much greater number of persons involved than in the tornado, the attitude of city officials and the press is a bit difficult to understand. It seems to rest primarily on the fact that there was no loss of life and no mass-evacuation problem; hence, no immediate or dramatic action was demanded. There is here the strong suggestion that disaster is defined in terms of physical suffering. This attitude may indicate that the tornado experience had given these persons something of an adjustment to disaster—such as was observed in bombed European cities, though, of course, on a much smaller scale.

A psychiatrist practicing in the city suggested that the tornado had intensified "endemic fear," the expression of which was avoided by minimizing the impact of the second storm. He cited the prevalence of storm cellars and their increase since the tornado of 1953 in support of this belief. He also pointed out that patients who come to him often expressed anxiety when they were taken into a consultation room with no windows—ventilation and cooling being provided mechanically. "How do you get out of here if a storm comes?" is a common question, in some form, from these patients.

At the same time, this physician reported that he had only one patient who showed definite effects of the tornado; and this woman had been under his care for another condition that existed before the tornado. Social-welfare workers said that they knew of none of their clients who were receiving special treatment for "nervous conditions" clearly resulting from either of the storms. Druggists reported only a slight rise in the sale of sedatives following either storm.

But all these informants insisted that placing oneself under a physician's care for "nervousness" or taking sedatives for such a condition are foreign to the culture of the community and thus their absence offers no measure of the incidence of such conditions. "These people simply will not go to a doctor when they are upset; they feel it is a confession of weakness and that the person ought to conquer such illness by exerting will power" was the tenor of their comments. Some evidence to support this feeling was derived from our study.

The physical appearance of Lake View was appreciably more pleasing at the time of the second storm than it had been at the first. Its newly constructed water and sewer lines had displaced the tanks and privies. Streets had been extended and improved. The results of grants for reconstruction and rehabilitation were everywhere evident. Here and there a few abandoned foundations served as ugly reminders of the earlier tragedy, but the new homes and improved streets gave the area a fresh, clean, prosperous look that was noticeably lacking a year and a month before. Such disaster effects as remained—and many were later discovered—were in the personalities of the residents and in the adjustment patterns of families and larger groups. These effects are not visible to the casual observer.

At the time of the second interview all respondents were asked to evaluate the degree of rehabilitation they had been able to attain

TABLE 59

Family Report of Tornado-Induced Problems Remaining at Time of Second Storm

Type of Problem	Percentage*
Financial	13
Emotional	31
Emotional and financial	24
Emotional, financial, and health	4
Total	72
Had no remaining disaster-induced problem	28

* Percentages in this table and subsequent tables in this chapter are based on 114 cases.

210

between the time of the tornado and the hailstorm. Their estimates are condensed in Table 59.

Clearly the problem of rehabilitation involved much more than making financial arrangements and reconstructing houses. These tasks had been largely accomplished; but there remained other difficulties centered in the emotional life of these families. Problems of physical health were relatively unimportant. But of more pertinence, Table 59 reveals that approximately six of each ten of these families were aware of some emotional stress originating in the tornado and persisting for more than a year.

Even so, the figures on emotional problems show a remarkable difference when compared with those collected in the first interviews. At that time 73 per cent of the families had reported some member suffering from emotional stress thought to be associated with the tornado; and 81 per cent of the families had reported that some member showed undue fear of threatening weather. The conclusion seems apparent that the emotional problems of this group were a major factor in their rehabilitation and that such problems remained a matter of concern for a relatively long period.

What effect the reported reluctance to seek medical aid for nervous conditions may have had in this persistence of emotional disturbance is unknown, but likely it was a factor of importance. It may be, too, as a physician with extensive experience in treating mildly neurotic cases pointed out, that such manifestations often do not show up until some weeks, or months, after the precipitating incident.

Perhaps the most tangible evidence of the fear produced by the tornado lies in the fact that one-third of the families had constructed storm cellars in the year between catastrophes. Storm cellars are by no means unknown in the area, but prior to the tornado, less than 10 per cent of the homes in Lake View had them.

When the second storm struck, the respondents' reactions ranged from no admitted difference—claimed by 3 per cent—to "just became physically ill." One-fifth said they were "very uneasy"; one in eight said they were "very nervous and afraid." About 10 per cent said they felt "completely helpless" during the storm. Several thought the second storm was another tornado which would repeat the terrible damage they had experienced a year before. One person commented, "Since the tornado, the worst always happens to me."

In these reactions to this second storm, we observe evidence that the hailstorm reinforced the lasting emotional effects of the tornado.

TABLE 60

How Did You First Learn of the Possibility of a Storm?

Warned by:	Percentage
Radio	11
Television	3
Newspaper	2
Word of mouth	9
Total warned	25
Had no advance warning	75

Preparation for the Storm

Warnings that local weather conditions were extremely unsettled and might result in tornadoes or "severe storms" had been issued frequently during the twenty-four hours preceding the hailstorm. Since these warnings had been carried by the local newspapers, radio, and television stations, it might easily be assumed that everyone within the city must have been aware of the approaching danger. This is an erroneous assumption, as Table 60 shows.

The evidence is strong that some system of warning other than the customary media of mass communication was needed, and that radio and word of mouth were the most effective media. This need becomes even more apparent in view of the fact that almost half of those who did have warning had received it less than an hour before the storm struck. One person reported having been warned for more than eighteen hours, indicating that such information was available but not widespread.

With three-fourths of the persons involved having no warning of their danger, it was inevitable that the actions they took to protect their lives and property were not rationally planned except insofar as they had plans for such exigencies in general. What difference this lack of warning made is not known. What is known, in general terms, is the sorts of action taken in this emergency.

According to the responses, recognition of the imminence of the storm called forth reactions ranging from near-panic ("Fled in automobile") to a seeming lack of fear ("Went about usual tasks"). Of course, the reported instances of "going ahead with routine" may be grossly misleading. Many persons purposely pursue routine when they feel themselves in danger. This is a recognized means of decreasing the attention given to the danger. Sitting and watching may also be a means of keeping as well informed as possible of an approaching threat. Less equivocal are such actions as getting into a storm cellar or making preparations within the house to meet the situation. The fact that 30 per cent of the respondents sought safety in a storm cellar is witness of the high value placed on these refuges in San Angelo, as well as of the fear the storm created.

The emotional impact of the recognized danger is revealed in responses such as "Got a blanket and put it over my arm"; "Went to the church [a minister]"; "Put the children to bed"; and "Tried to stay calm."

Anxiety also motivated many of those who knew of the approaching storm to contact other persons and pass on the warning. By actual count, the 25 per cent of the sample with knowledge of the warning contacted 96 persons, or an average of 4 each, 11 per cent using the telephone and 14 per cent passing on the information personally. Whom did they contact? Family members only were contacted by 13 per cent of the sample; 10 per cent contacted friends only; 2 per cent contacted both family and friends.

There were three distinct periods of activity associated with the hailstorm: actions when the storm was first actually seen or heard; actions during the period the storm lasted; and actions immediately following the storm.

When it was realized that a storm was about to strike, approximately the same number went to storm cellars as remained in their homes, making whatever preparations they thought might be effective. A few took time to telephone relatives. Only 4 per cent reported they went about their usual activities, though another 12 per cent said they simply "sat and watched it." A few drove away from the area. One case of this type of behavior was reported by the *San Angelo Standard Times* on the day following the catastrophe:

HAIL AND RAIN IN LAKE VIEW STIR GRIM TORNADO MEMORY

Shortly before the thunderstorm hit, a family of three was preparing to eat supper at 2028 N. Magdalen St. Mr. and Mrs. Fred Taylor, eight-month-old son Chris, and guests, Miss Joyce Rogers and Lige Majkszak, heard the wind whistling in the eaves of the house.

Taylor walked outside the house and called the family to survey the weather. They had plenty cause—their home, formerly at E. 34th St., was wiped out in the Lake View tornado.

"We were just about to eat," he said. "But after we looked at that cloud

—it looked like it was in a funnel shape—we decided to leave. You see," Taylor explained, "we were wiped out in the tornado last year."

But the Taylor family had no storm cellar. One had been planned at the new home, but had not been started.

"We just piled in my car and started driving away from that cloud," the twenty-seven-year-old printer said.

Taylor said he drove out to the south edge of San Angelo before he heard over the car radio that no tornado was expected. Coming home, the family was hit by the hailstorm at the intersection of 5th St. and Oakes St. They drove under a warehouse roof to wait out the storm.

When they finally arrived home, they found holes in the roof, furniture soaked with rain and windows knocked out of a housetrailer which caught the brunt of the blowing storm.

"My roof had holes in it at least five inches in diameter and my new garden was ploughed under—completely ruined," he said.

A fairly complete picture of the actions of another victim is given in another news story from the same source:

USE BASEMENT TO AVOID BIG HAILSTONES

Mrs. W. C. Brewer, whose house had been rebuilt at 307 E. 41st St., after the tornado of last year destroyed it, thought she and her husband got off lightly in the hailstorm of Monday night. The roof to the house and garage was damaged and shrubs and flowers were lost to the hail. Probably $350 will cover the replacement cost.

With a basement under the house, Mrs. Brewer placed her daughter and granddaughter there until the storm passed. She also phoned her husband at work in Pecos and told him there was small damage and little loss, but he came in to take a look at 10:00 p.m., and then returned to work at Pecos.

. . . .

In the storm of last year, Mrs. Brewer and her daughter took refuge in a clothes closet. It was all that was left after the tornado passed.

During the storm most of those who had not gone to storm cellars were busy mopping up water, plugging up smashed windows with curtains or anything else that could be stuffed into the holes, turning off electricity, or doing whatever seemed to offer protection. A few reported they had gone out into the hailstorm to seek safety in storm cellars. Others took refuge in closets in their homes. Several reported they spent the time praying for themselves and for others.

Immediately after the storm the greatest number—22 per cent—began repairing damage. The next largest category—13 per cent—said the first thing they did was try to get in touch with relatives or friends. This is an important statistic in that it indicates that social contact in such an emergency serves as a means of reassurance. Such a contact is also a means of getting help in determining what the new situation means, and assigning a meaning to a situation is an essential prelude to rational action.

Evidence of the seriousness of the emotional impact of this second storm is found in the fact that 8 per cent of the sample remained in a storm cellar for "several hours" after the storm. A few persons reported they stayed below throughout the night. One person said that during the storm he "broke out in a rash and became ill," a not uncommon occurrence among persons with severe emotional disturbance. But, again, a reluctance to admit emotional upset may be read into the statements of some persons that they had watched television during the storm. A storm of this magnitude would almost certainly distort the television picture. Moreover, the local television station was off the air because of power failure during the storm. Hence, the validity of these reports is somewhat dubious.

Although the storm lasted for about half an hour, with strong winds and battering hail, only two persons were reported injured and only ten members from six families as having become ill because of it. One-fifth of the families said they had two or more members who were emotionally upset, and a slightly larger percentage reported one person so affected. Less than half the families reported no member upset by fear of the weather. In 19 per cent of the homes, one member expressed great fear of weather; two or more members did so in twice as many families.

About one-third of the families with elderly members said they presented special problems of physical illness, extreme nervousness, or deep pessimism and lethargy which upset other family members. In well over half the families with members below fifteen years of age, parents reported that the children had become much more afraid of bad weather as a result of the two storms. However, most of the persons interviewed were neither children nor elders, and there may have been a tendency to project the emotional reactions of the respondents themselves to these other family members. This appeared clearly in several instances which will be cited in Chapters 12, 13, and 14.

Economic problems created by the storm were of two types: those resulting from damaged property, and those resulting from loss of employment. Interruption of the employment of some member was reported by one family in each eight, with an average loss of 4.5 days. This time was lost to help in repairing the residence, to recover from illness, or to care for some member who was ill.

Following the tornado of the year before, approximately 60 per cent of the respondents reported that employment of some family member had been interrupted as a consequence. In comparison with the loss of employment from the first storm, loss due to the hailstorm appears small; yet it amounts to a total of more than 500 working days, a considerable burden for these 114 families.

Financial loss as a result of this storm was reported by 60 per cent of the sample, with an average loss of $545. This average is somewhat distorted by one loss of $5,600, the estimated damage to a partly finished new residence. If this one figure is not included in the calculation, the mean drops to $344. More than one-fourth of the sample (29 per cent) stated they had to incur debt in order to repair their house, furnishings, and/or car.

Only 12 per cent reported insufficient insurance coverage on household furnishings. This is in drastic contrast to the situation following the tornado, when only 15 per cent said they had sufficient insurance to cover their losses. These figures probably reflect the increase in the number of families carrying storm insurance. Even so, the loss must have placed a heavy burden on these families of below-average economic status.

But these families themselves did not admit to being unduly burdened. In fact, almost 70 per cent said the hailstorm had not imposed any new burdens on them. Of those who admitted to new burdens, about two-thirds said they were economic. When it is remembered that these same informants had said in answer to other questions that many of them had incurred emotional upsets, it is evident that emotional difficulties were not considered "burdens" in the sense that economic ones were. But this reluctance to admit difficulties goes even deeper.

In answer to a different question, 60 per cent of these people said that they had incurred financial loss, and for 29 per cent of them the loss meant their having to assume an average debt of $132. But when they were asked after a short lapse of time in the same interview whether this experience had imposed any new burdens on them, more than two-thirds said "No." Clearly there is a serious discrepancy between these two sets of answers. Clearly, also, this is not the result of misunderstanding on the part of the respondents; rather, it is a matter of the light in which the facts are seen, and felt, by the respondents.

From the point of view of an outsider an average debt of $132 looks like a burden; by these people it is not so considered; it has a different meaning, and the meaning is what was secured by their responses. There is no way of being sure exactly what was in the minds of these people when they gave these divergent replies—the interview was not designed to get at this factor. But a guess is that they saw "burden" as referring to something, particularly financial, that would seriously handicap the ongoing of their family life. At the same time, it seems, they saw the debts incurred and the loss of time from work as unfortunate, perhaps, but not sufficiently handicapping to be called a "burden."

Put another way, these statistics strongly attest to a spirit of self-reliance and the ability to "take it"—to meet adversity and keep going without admitting hurt—on the part of these people.

It cannot be reported, however, that the hailstorm made no difference in the living patterns or attitudes of these people. Their answers to several questions made this apparent.

The hailstorm evidently convinced 13 per cent of the sample that Lake View is not a desirable place to live, for they were planning to move away as soon as convenient. An additional 2 per cent stated they had been planning to move since the tornado. Of this combined 15 per cent, 7 per cent wanted to move to a different area in San Angelo, 2 per cent wanted to move outside San Angelo's city limits, and the remaining 6 per cent wanted to move away from the San Angelo area entirely. Assuming the correctness of the statements of 2 per cent of the second sample that they had wanted to move from the Lake View area since their experience with the tornado, the increase in the number of those whose change of mind was coincident with the second storm may be taken as a rough measure of its effect on their attitudes toward their portion of the city. It may be pertinent, too, that many of these families wanted to leave the city entirely, i.e., to escape by physical flight a situation seen as dangerous. Further demonstration of the serious emotional impact of this second storm is seen in Table 61.

The storm itself was the worst part of the experience for the largest number of persons, but other replies give more significance to the meaning of this event. If we combine the five categories designed to reveal fear, we find that 39 per cent of the respondents indicate a basically emotional response. It is notable, too, that only 13 per cent centered their concern on loss of property, particularly in view of the severe financial losses sustained in the tornado little more than a year before. But perhaps the most important statistic in Table 61 is that 10 per cent claimed not to have been "greatly bothered" by the storm. Since it is almost axiomatic that persons dislike to admit to fears (and

TABLE 61

What Was the Worst Part of the Whole Experience for You?

Factor	Percentage
Hail, rain, wind, noise	32
Loss of property	13
Emotional disturbance and feeling of frustration	10
Fear of possible results	9
Worry over family members	7
Fear of tornado	7
Long duration of storm	6
Not greatly bothered	10
Other answers	6

these persons had had some time to regain composure), even this small percentage is probably higher than was actually correct.

No such reticence appears in their response to a question as to the effect of the storm on children. Only about one-third professed to believe there would be no harmful results. More than one-half were fairly specific about the disturbances they thought had already been caused. These parents thought their children would be emotionally upset and would be more fearful, particularly of storms. Half a dozen simply said the effect would be "awful."

The people in Lake View had received considerable financial assistance through public donations during the tornado rehabilitation period. In an effort to ascertain one effect of this generosity, we asked whether they had offered or would offer a donation to the victims of the hailstorm. Seven per cent said that they had already helped some of the victims; 58 per cent answered, "No, but would if were able to"; 31 per cent replied, "No, and would not"; 3 per cent did not reply. Of the total, 65 per cent suggested that the Red Cross, Salvation Army, Disaster Fund, or some other agency should help the victims.

The actions of these persons in the storm area in giving aid to sufferers and their attitudes about what organized relief agencies should do are interesting. Very few had done anything to aid the 60-odd families in their neighborhood who had lost an average of more than $300 each. Many expressed a willingness to help if they "were able to"; but almost one-third put themselves on record as being unwilling to. We are dealing here with a very prized value—the obligation to help one's neighbor. Hence, it may be assumed that some of those

TABLE 62

Why Do You Think This Storm Hit Lake View?

Opinion	Percentage
Lord's will or punishment	21
In pathway of storm	7
Atom bombs	5
Fatalistic acceptance	4
Natural causes	16
No explanation	47

who said they had not given aid but would be glad to if they were able were rationalizing about their ability to help. This impression is strengthened by the fact that about two-thirds of the sample thought some official agency, such as Red Cross, Salvation Army, or a local disaster-fund, ought to give aid in this situation.

Two possible answers to the question posed by these attitudes come to mind. In the previous storm more than 70 per cent of the sample had received aid from some official agency. This may have created the feeling that when a disaster strikes, it is the duty of these agencies to proffer aid, an attitude naturally resulting from the arguments advanced by such agencies when soliciting contributions. At the same time, it should be pointed out that Lake View is a relatively low-income area and that the hailstorm caused financial loss to well over half the sample. It is evident that the level of personal aid, at least monetary aid, must be expected to be low. In line with the local feeling that the second storm was "just bad weather" rather than a major disaster, no public appeal for funds was made, and the absence of this stimulus would also depress the numbers who would ordinarily volunteer aid.

Another interesting facet of the reactions to the storm is revealed in the statistic that 88 per cent of the sample said that they had included the victims in their prayers. This may have been felt to be an acceptable substitute for more concrete aid.

219

Believing that if we could understand the meaning that the victims had assigned to these disasters it would go far toward explaining their reactions to them, we asked a series of questions designed to get at their conceptions. The results are contained in the next three tables.

Some explanation for an occurrence of such magnitude is sorely needed, especially by those who suffer from it. Thus it should not be surprising that only about half the Lake View respondents were willing to admit that they were unable to offer a satisfying interpretation of this particular storm.

But more pertinent, perhaps, are the "reasons" offered. Of these, the greatest number, by far, were couched in religious terms—the storm was God's will, His punishment for sins committed, or some other motive attributed to Him. The belief in a divinity actively interested in, and interfering with, terrestrial affairs is evident.

Two other explanations were offered by a large enough segment to be pertinent. One is the quasi-scientific explanation that this particular neighborhood lies in a particularly vulnerable position for such meteorological phenomena, and, therefore, it may be expected to be struck more often than other areas. A taxi-driver asserted that for twenty years every storm which had struck the San Angelo area had hit the Lake View section of the city.

The third explanation, the atom bomb, would seem to fall between the two mentioned above: it is quasi-scientific in that it invokes known phenomena of great destructive power; it is semisuperstitious in that it invokes this power with no explanation of the mechanism by which the specific effect is obtained. This is an extreme instance of the "correlation fallacy" in which any two events that have occurred at approximately the same position in either time or space are, therefore, considered to be causally connected.[1] Nonetheless, this "explanation" was given frequently enough to demonstrate that it is embedded in folk thinking and is, therefore, a factor which must be taken into account.

Whether such a disaster would be rationalized in similar terms by persons of a different socio-economic status and in another regional culture is an interesting field for speculation. One may wonder, for instance, whether the religious explanation offered by these

---

[1] Since this event there has arisen some respectable, if not always empirically scientific, speculation that perhaps massive nuclear explosions have changed weather patterns. See, for example, Irving Bengelsdorf's "Can the Atom Change the Weather?" *Saturday Review*, July 7, 1956.

informants would be duplicated in areas where other types of church organizations are more prevalent, or whether this tendency to see disaster as an expression of the will of a God of Wrath is a basic part of religious ideology.

TABLE 63

Do You Think Lake View Will Suffer Other Storms in the Future?

Opinion	Percentage
More storms	42
Other tornadoes	21
Small storms	15
No more storms	7
Undecided	15

The pervading acceptance of the storms as a natural part of life is brought out strikingly by the statistic that approximately four out of five expected such catastrophes, of varying degrees of severity, to occur in the future. If those who expressed uncertainty are split in proportion to those answering the question affirmatively and negatively, then this proportion rises to more than 90 per cent. Actually only 7

TABLE 64

Why Do You Think So Many Disastrous Storms Are Hitting in the United States?

Opinion	Percentage
Lesson or punishment by God	31
Result of bombs	18
Natural cycle; will abate	11
End of drought	4
Not actually more frequency but more awareness	5
No idea	25
"One of those things"	4

per cent were willing to say they did not believe such an event was likely to occur again.

Again we find religious and scientific attitudes, alone and in combination, in suggestions given by the respondents about how to escape the eventuality of future catastrophes. Only 8 per cent thought it possible to prevent severe storms, but these persons expressed beliefs falling into the three categories used above by such statements as: "By being better people"; "By humbling ourselves and living in the Right Light"; "Use planes to chart their course and warn people"; "Stop setting off A- and H-bombs."

Further probing revealed that the three major categories of "explanation" remained constant. But unexpected was the widespread belief that more storms of disastrous intensity may be expected (Table 63). Perhaps there was a suggestion to this effect in the wording of the question. However, it is certainly pertinent that only 5 per cent (Table 64) took the occasion to deny that there are actually more such storms now than formerly. If to this are added the percentages of those who offered no explanation, we still have only about one-third of the people indicating any disagreement with this idea; and of these, those who shrugged off the matter as "just one of those things" would seem to agree that the statement is correct. Particularly relevant are the increased percentages of those who assign direct action by the Deity and the explosion of nuclear weapons as reasons for the increase they believe has occurred. Whereas only 21 per cent saw divine intervention directing this particular storm to Lake View, 31 per cent saw God's will or punishment as responsible for a general increase in such storms. Similarly, those who laid the blame at the door of the military nuclear program increased by 13 per cent.

These figures might be used to set up a hypothesis that as a phenomenon under consideration becomes more generalized and more distant, it is more likely to be rationalized in terms of some vaguely believed in, but not demonstrated, cause. Since the "will of God" and "science" are the two most often-used such general explanations, it is not surprising that they should be given in this instance.

The vague generality of the belief that disastrous storms are largely either a willed act of Jehovah or the result of nuclear explosions is also revealed in responses to the question: "Do you know of anyone who has any special thing to say or do to protect him against tornadoes, storms, etc.?" To this query almost three-fourths (73 per cent) replied "No." It would appear that these persons either did not deeply believe in the explanations previously offered, or they felt themselves powerless to influence the action of either God or the military. But one woman displayed a copy of a letter written in English which she assured us had been written by Christ while He was on earth and which had been found in a cave in the Holy Land about a decade ago. During both storms, she had placed herself as close to this precious document as she could and attributed her lack of injury to this proximity.

Of the 27 per cent who said they did know of ways of protection against storms, the great majority—19 per cent—cited religious beliefs, particularly their belief in the efficacy of prayer. The rest placed their faith in a good storm cellar or the combination of a good storm cellar and a strong religious faith.

In an attempt to determine what effect the passing of time and the second disaster had on the attitudes of these families toward the agencies most active in helping them at the time of the tornado, questions on this topic were repeated in the second schedule. Each response toward each of nine organizations was then classified according to the original opinion and the direction of the change, if any. Table 65 gives the results.

About one-third of these people changed their minds about the agencies with whom they and their neighbors had dealt following the tornado. These changes were almost two to one in the favorable direction, indicating once more that as events recede in time, mem-

TABLE 65

Changes in Attitudes toward Nine Agencies

Agency	Favorable	Unfavorable	No Change	Not Ascertained
American Red Cross . .	26	12	71	5
Local disaster-fund .	28	22	50	5
Local churches	15	5	90	4
Other relief agencies . .	40	12	57	5
U.S. Air Force	5	10	95	4
National Guard . . .	8	12	87	7
City government . . .	29	14	63	8
State government . . .	32	17	54	11
Federal government . .	29	14	64	7
Total	212	118	640	56
Percentage				
Direction of change . .	21	11	62	6

ory of them is likely to mellow—or that the unpleasant tends to drop out of our recollections.

But not all the agencies looked better after the lapse of a few months. This is notably true of the two military units active in this situation, though the shift is not great enough to be significant. Further, these units ranked so very high on the first interview that the

TABLE 66

Differentials in the Ranking of Attitudes toward Nine Agencies

Agency	Rank at First Interview	Rank at Second Interview
United States Air Force	1	2
National Guard	2	3
Local churches	3	1
Municipal government	4	4
Disaster Relief Fund	5	7
State government	6	6
Other relief agencies	7	5
American Red Cross	8	8
Federal government	9	9

only change possible was in a negative direction. All the other agencies or institutions were regarded more favorably and in most cases in significant degree.

It must also be noted that the majority of these persons (62 per cent) did not change their opinions, suggesting that a stable evaluation had been reached early in the disaster experience. But again, the greatest number of changes registered was from an "undecided" to a "favorable" opinion—true of 15 per cent—whereas the opposite shift from "undecided" to "negative" occurred in only 3 per cent of the cases.

The nine agencies were ranked according to the highest frequency of positive evaluation. The results are shown in Table 66. Shifts over the months seem to be unimportant, though perhaps it is pertinent to note that the local churches moved up from third to first place, and that the Disaster Relief Fund moved down two places.

Since none of these agencies except the American Red Cross took an active role in aiding the victims of the hailstorm, their changes in attitude toward the other agencies seem to be an outgrowth of the effects of time, mostly affected perhaps by the fact that the hailstorm experience reinforced their memory of the roles played by these agencies after the tornado.

As the changes in attitude were predominantly positive, it is entirely possible that during the months between the two catastrophes the activities of an agency may have been such as to create the new opinion, or reasons for the victims' dissatisfaction at the time of the first interview may have been forgotten.

A second attempt to determine changes in evaluations and attitudes is concerned with the respondents' postdisaster opinion of conditions in their neighborhood and city, three direct questions being duplicated in the two schedules. Each question could be answered "Better off," "Remain largely unchanged," or "Worse off than before." Table 67 presents the responses to these questions as obtained by the

TABLE 67

Changes in Evaluation of Neighborhood and City between Interviews

Evaluation	Better	Worse	No Change	Not Ascertained
Neighborhood now is .	18	23	61	12
Neighborhood will be .	15	23	60	16
City will be	14	32	54	14
Total	47	78	179	42
Percentage				
Direction of change . .	13	24	52	12

When this table was dichotomized into those who believed in a better future and those who did not, as applied to their neighborhoods and cities, χ^2 tests indicated significance at the .05 level or above, for the "Neighborhood now" and the "City will be" categories. At the same level of confidence, net changes in the attitudes were significant only for the "City will be" category.

two interviews. The largest percentage of responses (51 per cent) indicated an optimistic evaluation of the present and future condition of the neighborhood and the city. Only 6 per cent expressed pessimism.

But if the changes toward a more optimistic point of view are compared with those indicating a shift to a more pessimistic outlook, it appears that the early hopefulness revealed by the first interview had been dampened considerably by the time these people expressed their opinions the second time. Twenty-four per cent modified their opinions toward a more pessimistic point of view, while only 13 per cent expressed greater optimism at the second interview.

The largest change in evaluation between the two response periods occurred in the original "Better off" responses that became "Remain largely unchanged" at the second judgment. Although 36 per cent did change their evaluations, only 10 per cent definitely changed to a "Better off" evaluation. It seems fairly safe to say that the experiences of rehabilitation plus those of the second disastrous storm had taken their toll of the faith in the future which was so marked a characteristic of these families after the tornado. Nonetheless, it must also be emphasized that on the whole their attitude remained one of optimism. More than half of these people still believed their city and their neighborhood were better off since the tornado and hailstorm; almost a third were not decided; and the remainder either thought the net effect was bad or did not answer this question.

This optimistic tone about the present and the future condition of the area follows the pattern set in the study of the tornado. As in that study, it can be noted that as the object under consideration moves away from the respondent in time or space, optimism increases. This also indicates once more the generally, rather than specifically, optimistic spirit of these people under adverse circumstances.

To recapitulate, prior to the second storm, the rehabilitation of disaster-wrecked Lake View seemed to have been progressing well. The neighborhood had taken on a different look, with new and reconstructed homes and a modernized school. Taxes had been paid for the victims, a free-lunch system was established for the school children of disaster-affected families, and school enrollment was above the expected.

Changes in attitudes of the sample members toward most of the agencies that had been active following the tornado were also positive. The emotional impact and certain financial problems created by the tornado were still present, however, for a relatively large percentage of the families. These emotional and financial problems were important conditioning factors affecting the reaction to the June storm of 1954.

The widespread fear of weather conditions, the shift of opinions concerning the future of the neighborhood and the city toward a more pessimistic tone, and the conviction of the majority of persons in the neighborhood that the children had been badly upset by the storm all point to lasting emotional effects of these two catastrophes.

One of the most interesting aspects of the respondents' activities during the interim between the two storms is that a large percentage of them constructed storm cellars. This is one positive indication of the recognition of a common danger with a rational effort made to meet it satisfactorily.

This great increase in the number of families who had homes equipped with storm cellars is, perhaps, the best tangible evidence of the emotional reactions precipitated in this neighborhood by these storms. But other evidence of this emotional effect appears throughout the study and indicates that such conditions are often of much longer duration and are more intractable than might be expected. The evidence indicates that these effects are more difficult to deal with than are physical or financial ones.

A further effort to get at the emotional injuries sustained by these persons was made through a series of intensive interviews. We asked a selected number to tell in their own words of their experiences and feelings associated with the catastrophes. This material is the basis for the succeeding three chapters.

12. The Blow of the Wind

As our analysis of the data secured from the first interviews proceeded, it became more and more apparent that there were emotional overtones which were not being uncovered by the research instrument used, that we needed some other means of getting a deeper understanding of the feelings, and resultant actions, of persons involved in these disasters.

Hence, when San Angelo was struck by a catastrophic wind- and hailstorm just slightly more than a year after having been devastated by a tornado, we seized the opportunity to explore more fully the

NOTE.—It may be noted that many of the quotations from disaster victims contained in this report also appear in Martha Wolfenstein's *Disaster: A Psychological Essay* (Glencoe, Ill., The Free Press, 1957). Interviews from which these quotations were taken were made as part of the Waco–San Angelo Disaster Study under the direction of the author of *Tornadoes over Texas*. Their source is acknowledged by Dr. Wolfenstein in her book.

Intensive interviewing was part of a restudy in San Angelo following a second disaster within little more than a year. Funds for this part of the project were supplied in part by the Committee on Disaster Studies of the National Academy of Sciences–National Research Council, and in part by the Hogg Foundation for Mental Health, of the University of Texas. Several of the interviews were made by Miss Jeannette F. Rayner, of the Committee staff, during a visit as consultant to this phase of the study.

The Committee requested transcripts of the interviews so that they might be read by Dr. Wolfenstein, who was then serving as a consultant to the Committee, in line with its policy of promoting exchange of information from disaster research and of looking at primary data from different theoretical points of view.

Unfortunately, the Committee failed to consult with the director of the research project before approving the use of the interview material by Dr. Wolfenstein in her book. It was not until his own book was in press that the director of the project was aware of the prior publication of this material.

The documents were returned after being used by Dr. Wolfenstein and are, of course, now available to any qualified researcher who may wish to use them.

It is deeply regretted that the customary prerogative of the researcher to be the first to present his data in published form was contravened in this instance. The Committee has expressed its regret for embarrassment which may have been caused by this error.

228

emotional consequences of both storms. In addition, a second such study would give a perspective to the entire study of the families in this city impossible to obtain through a single interview.

Four graduate students in psychology at the University of Texas interviewed those victims of both storms whose words and reactions are recorded in this and the two succeeding chapters. Some interviewing was also done by Jeannette Rayner, of the staff of the Committee on Disaster Research, and by the Director of the Waco–San Angelo Disaster Study. The names of these persons reputed to be suffering intense emotional reactions were obtained from school officials, welfare workers, neighbors, and others in the immediate area.

The interviewers were instructed to follow up any leads that might develop as the interviews progressed, but not to attempt to structure the interview other than to keep the conversation directly related to the storms and their effects on the person being interviewed and members of his family. In other words, the interviews were designed to explore the extent of the problems raised rather than to find answers to any definitely stated hypotheses.

This was done for two reasons. We felt that an exploratory delineation of the field would be more valuable than the testing of a stated hypothesis. Furthermore, since only Miss Rayner could claim competence in such interviewing, it was feared that any attempt at probing for specific materials would be poorly done, could not be expected to attain acceptable standards from the point of view of professionals, and might result in emotional harm to the persons interviewed. It was because of this last consideration that interviewers were instructed to change the trend of conversation or to break off the interview when the informant showed signs of great emotional stress.

Twenty-two interviews were recorded on tape. A tape recorder was set up in the home of the informant, and he and the interviewer then engaged in desultory talk long enough to allow the respondent to become somewhat accustomed to the machine. Often, a bit of conversation was recorded and played back to enable the respondent to understand how the mechanism operated, to satisfy his curiosity as to what was being recorded, and to ease "mike fright." Interviews ran from an hour to an hour and thirty minutes, often with short breaks. Efforts were made to restrict the interview to one person, but when others were present they were often included either at their own request or because the interviewer felt they had a worthwhile contribution to make.

229

Transcriptions were made of the recordings. However, in some cases extraneous noises interfered with the interviewing to such an extent that it was impossible to separate the two. In other cases, the recording was not intelligible for other reasons. These faults cut down to nineteen the number of transcriptions we felt were complete enough to use. Even with the deletions, we recognize that the transcriptions used are not always wholly accurate verbatim reports of what was said and that some portions, of unknown value, are missing. Nonetheless, we believe the material has value both in itself and as an indication of what can be done with this research tool.

These considerations seriously affect the validity and value of the materials to be presented. The comments accompanying the excerpts are those of persons trained in sociology who make no pretense of being expert in analyzing psychological data. The value of these comments, then, comes from the application of a sociological point of view to material perhaps more properly belonging to another discipline.

Both comments on and editing of the material have been kept to a strict minimum. Only where it was necessary to give understanding to the materials, or where a comment would make more explicit the reason for including the specific quotation, was any elaboration undertaken. We felt that the persons who had gone through these catastrophes could describe their emotional impact better than anyone else, and that they should be allowed to do so. Further, since the intention of the study was primarily descriptive rather than analytic, it seemed obvious that the participants' own accounts were the best means of carrying the emotional tone as well as the factual information.

At first we made an effort to have the respondents separate their descriptions of the two storms during the interviews, but when this was found to be impractical—if not impossible—we abandoned the attempt. Most of the material presented refers to the tornado—the more dramatic storm, of course—but it must always be remembered that these interviews were taken less than a month after the hailstorm and that memories of the tornado were not only revived by that second storm but were also interwoven with it.

It should also be made clear that this is not a description of mentally ill persons. Much of the highly emotional behavior related by these persons was also intelligently calculated to increase safety, minimize danger, or otherwise to serve rationally conceived and prosecuted goals of high utilitarian value. The construction and use of

230

storm cellars are a case in point. In these concrete actions both the emotional and the rational elements were highly important. At the same time, it is evident throughout that these are persons who were hard-hit emotionally by the disasters and who, in many cases, still showed emotional stress at the time of the interview. One of the informants was known to have been under treatment by a psychiatrist prior to the tornado. We made no effort to ascertain whether any of the others were psychotic or seriously neurotic before that event, but no mention of such a condition was made by those identifying these sufferers. Certainly they were not, in any sense, typical of their community.

Material from the interviews has been divided into three major portions. The first comprises those statements which have to do with the immediate reactions, the medical care sought or avoided, and the functioning of the family in these crises. The second part presents materials depicting the various forms of fear growing out of the catastrophes, and some of the consequences of this fear in personal, family, and community life. The third portion shows attempts to rationalize and integrate these experiences.

Here, then, is what these people had to say about what had happened to them.

A Different World

It happened so fast and all—not too excited. And then after it was all over with, I—just more numb, or something. I just got a numb feeling or something. I don't know how to explain it ... R[1]

The speaker was a woman trying to describe how she felt and acted immediately after the tornado. What she said is typical of many of the persons interviewed. They said they were numb; they were dazed, they did not know what they were doing; or in some way they expressed the general idea of inability to function normally. In most cases this inability existed for only a short time, often only a matter of hours; in other cases, a matter of a few days; in some exceptional cases, for still longer periods.

One of the persons told of picking up a stranger who seemed to be dazed and asking where she lived. The only reply she was able to get was, "Back up there, back up there." The rescuer took her to the

[1] Letters at the end of quotations refer to an identification code. Readers interested in a particular person may get a more complete picture by piecing together all quotations bearing the same code letter.

schoolhouse and turned her over to authorities there. But more typical was the reaction of the woman whose husband said: "She just kinda slumped down, you see, and I got her by the shoulders and shook her. And I said, 'We're not hurt; let's just hope and pray nobody else is.'" The interviewer asked who was present and whether she had screamed. The reply to both was, "I don't know."

A temporary inability to recognize close friends and even members of the family was revealed by one of the informants:

WIFE: . . . I don't know, so many people after they did begin to come out there they told me that they came, I don't even remember seeing them. His father came out and two brothers and sister-in-law and I don't even remember seeing his father.

HUSBAND: Other words, everybody was just in kind of a daze there for several days. They just, somebody—I know it did me—somebody would come along and tell me what they thought I ought to do or something; why it just—it got all over me 'cause I didn't know what to do myself.   N

A mother gave the following description of the refusal of her young daughter to talk of her storm experiences:

INTERVIEWER: Did she eat?

RESPONDENT: No, and she wouldn't talk to us. It was the third day before we knew really everything that happened. She—when they brought her in after my nephew found her she wouldn't say a word and she wouldn't talk about it that night, and the next day she just turned and walked off when it was mentioned. She just didn't want to hear anything about it or talk about it. She just wouldn't answer you. She would turn and walk off. And seemed like she just didn't hardly know what it was all about. . . . She wasn't her usual self. She, uh, just stood around and seemed like it was, something was on her mind. She didn't play like she usually does, or talk. She's quite a talker, she's her normal self. She—she chewed on her finger like she is right now. She stayed with us in the store and seemed like she didn't want to be by herself. Still she wouldn't talk about it.   H

Later in the same interview, this mother revealed that her own condition was quite similar to that of her small daughter:

I know that I couldn't concentrate on the store. It just seemed like I— have you ever been in a tornado? I—first two or three days I—I didn't, wasn't capable of talking to her at all, I was too upset myself.   H

Another mother revealed that she had repeatedly asked for her daughter, though the child was with her:

And I asked where Nancy was. And they says, "Well, she's right here; we will take care of her." Then some come and got me and throwed a quilt around me and was going to carry me to the ambulance. And I got up to start to walk, but everything turned black. I just felt dazed you know. And I turned my head down and shook it and I said, "Where is Nancy?" And she said—I just felt like I had to keep up with her because she wasn't there. She said, "Uh, are you scared?" I said, "I just don't know." You know, I was just so numb I was just . . . K

Another mother who was with her daughter kept repeating directions for what she thought would be safe conduct until the child said, "Mother, you sound like a broken record." The mother went on to give this explanation:

I'm sure that I must have been under shock. I felt a shock hit me after we got out of the closet and I didn't realize it but I know now that I must have been because my new camera was laying in the, in the living room—it had been in the bedroom, but it was in the living room now—then. And I picked it up. It was . . . but I picked it up and put it in the—uh—hassock. I said I didn't want it to get wet, but it was already soaking wet . . . E

There were two cases in which injuries of unknown seriousness were discounted or the injured person remained unconscious of their existence for some time. In the first case, evidently, the woman was so excited and worried that the injury to her leg never entered her consciousness:

Well, I don't remember feeling anything too much. I know that this door had fallen on my leg and I asked him if he would move it, if he could move it so I could get my leg out. I remember that my leg didn't hurt at the time, not a bit in the world. Until late that afternoon, it didn't hurt. But it was awfully bruised and there was for about two weeks that I couldn't walk very well. The main thing I was thinking about was to see if the children were hurt. F

The second case is that of a man who, under stress, was able to perform a muscular feat which he normally would be entirely incapable of. This man had had a rupture, and his exertion in raising a section of wall caused it to reopen:

INTERVIEWER: You hurt yourself?
RESPONDENT: Yes, sir. I raised something that two of us couldn't raise the next day. I was excited, you know, and I just got, I guess, supernatural strength. I don't know. But I raised that section of wall and looked under that for him. And I dug around other places and three men came up and led me off and I don't know who they was. A

When the tornado had passed, some people left in the devastated area felt they faced a new world. This is brought out by one person who revealed that he and his companion were physically disoriented until they came upon a familiar landmark:

We had to go over and see about our sister-in-law and we started off and we couldn't see any landmarks or anything. You know, we didn't know where we was until we got to the Fair Ground.   V

More often the lack of orientation was emotional or intellectual, as in the case of this woman:

Well, I thought I was—I have often heard that—it seemed that I was the only one there was and that I had a job to do.   E

And another informant expressed this idea of disorientation:

Well, it's a little bit hard to describe except that you just feel com——just, just completely lost. Well, it seemed like our whole life pattern, momentarily, that it was stopped.   I

The feeling of being in a new and strange world is even more vividly expressed by this person:

INTERVIEWER: When you stepped out of the closet, how did you feel?
RESPONDENT: I—I felt like I was in a different world.
INTERVIEWER: A different world?
RESPONDENT: A–a–a strange place that I had never been before. Now that was—I wouldn't say another world, but I could compare this anyway. But the thing was—when we came out there was no sound, there was not a breath of air, there was no one in sight, and the whole universe had changed.
INTERVIEWER: How did you feel then?
RESPONDENT: And then I felt like I was all alone. I felt like this little girl and I were the only people that had survived.
INTERVIEWER: What kind of feeling is that, Mrs. E?
RESPONDENT: Well, that would be hard to describe. It's the loneliest feeling in the world. To feel like you're the only person left in the place where you've lived for several years.   E

In some of the interviews, there is a strong indication that behavior in such a situation depends to a large degree upon social training. In the first of these, the informant stressed that he did not know how to behave because he had never had a similar experience before:

I just walked around. I just walked around in there, you know; I don't know, I looked, started to go in a clothes closet and I didn't know what to do because I'd never been in anything like that. Didn't know what to do.   R

234

The second illustration is perhaps more indicative. This is the case of a young girl with a long history of vomiting whenever she was even slightly disturbed. She did not vomit during the tornado, but she did during the hailstorm more than a year later. It should be noted also that she vomited after having supper on the evening following the tornado. There was, of course, ample opportunity between the tornado at about 2:30 P.M. and suppertime for the child to have been taught the expected behavior for such an occasion:

INTERVIEWER: Was she nauseated then, at the time of the first tornado?
RESPONDENT [*to daughter*]: Did you get nauseated then, Ion?
DAUGHTER: No, I didn't, because I had never been in a storm or anything like that and I didn't feel sick because I wasn't scared.   O

The experiences of these two informants suggest that even so primitive an emotion as fear is expressed not only because of the objective reality to which the person is exposed but also, and to a large extent, because of the social definition of that situation. These persons did not display certain emotional reactions because, in the first case, there was ignorance of the appropriate reaction; in the second, lack of experience prevented the child from knowing or having been taught what she should do in such a situation.

"If I Get Real Nervous, It Hurts"

Although only a small percentage of informants in Lake View admitted on scheduled interviewing that they or members of their family suffered illness as a result of the storms, a large number of those given a chance to talk freely did admit it. But again it must be emphasized that the persons interviewed intensively were not typical of the community, that they were selected because researchers had been told they had shown symptoms of emotional stress as a result of the disasters.

The reported illnesses can be divided into two major classes: those definitely biosomatic in nature, and those for which no definite biological basis was found and which may have been, therefore, psychosomatic. But in both classes, it seems likely that an undetermined portion of the suffering had been precipitated or aggravated by the stress of the disasters. The persons suffering such symptoms, whether biosomatic or psychosomatic, may or may not have placed themselves under the treatment of a physician. However, on the whole, residents of Lake View tend to shy away from using physicians, particularly when there is no evident injury. In some of the cases, too, the symptoms were too obscure and of too little moment to be classified definitely as "illnesses."

Typical of those who suffered vague, poorly defined ailments and who did go to a physician for treatment is this case:

INTERVIEWER: How has your health been this year?

RESPONDENT: Well, it went down hill but, uh, it didn't build up but— I think mine is just due—'cause I just wouldn't give up to go to the doctor. But, uh, and course, uh, strain of the tornado—it just went down hill but, uh, I've always felt good though, like that. It just seemed like I was just— uh, nervous.

INTERVIEWER: What did the doctor tell you?

RESPONDENT: Oh, he said I was just awful nervous and I was just going to have to get over it.   S

Certainly in the minds of these disaster victims, and perhaps from what they saw in the minds of the physicians attending them, there was a clear distinction between "real" illness in the biological sense and the sort of distress these people were suffering. This comes out strongly in the following interchange:

RESPONDENT: I went to the doctor along the first of the year and he gave me some nerve medicine. I took that and I seemed to be pretty good for a while, when I quit taking it. I thought I was doing real good—you know, I could do without it. But I guess I do feel better when I'm taking it. . . . Well, the doctor said there wasn't anything the matter with me, he gave me, uh, a good checkup and he said there wasn't nothing in the world wrong with me. Just my nerves. And that I was a little under weight.

INTERVIEWER: How do you feel physically?

RESPONDENT: Oh, I feel just fine.   X

It is to be noted in the above quotation that the victim waited some months before going to the physician and then dropped the treatment prescribed within a short time. This delay in seeking aid also appears in the following quotation and seems to be typical of the community:

I know there is one of my friends here that was in the tornado. In fact, the only thing that saved her was crawling between the mattresses on her bed, and a log fell down across it, you know. She has been going to the doctor lately and he tells her that that's what's wrong with her—her nerves. She's just going to have to learn to not think about it. And as I said, I can talk about it, I can just set here and talk all you want to about it, just so I don't have to stop and start thinking.   P

Mrs. E, quoted below, presents the interesting case of a person who evidently felt she could not discuss her emotional difficulties with her own physician. Nevertheless she felt the need for medical advice and went to another doctor. The advice given for the treatment of herself and her daughter certainly indicates that the physician was aware of the emotional stress she was enduring:

Well, it—it didn't make us sick—finally I went to the doctor. I guess about two weeks later I went to the doctor and I told him that, uh, that I was a little nervous and, uh . . . . Well, that was when I wasn't sleeping. I told him that I didn't sleep very good and he told me that—uh, that if I would take a warm bath—he said a pretty hot one before I went to bed and that if I would just lay there and clear my mind of everything that I would go to sleep. And the little girl had a night or two that she couldn't sleep and, uh, I called him about her and he said, "Is she limping?" and I said "No" and then he told me, he said, uh, "Don't mention this to her; just give her a hot bath and a drink of water or anything and . . ." I talked to my doctor about that and he told me that, uh, that it would be possible that, uh, for people to get sick after a shock. In fact, it was *not my doctor,* but another one, that told me—said that it was not . . . and I asked him for *my own particular reason,* I said, "I'd just like to know if you believe that a shock like that will make people sick?" and that's what he said—that it will.   F.

The next informant was evidently in serious doubt about whether his emotions could be the basis for his distress, in spite of his physician's diagnosis:

Well, of course, naturally, uh, it could be, you know we've had quite a bit of weather here lately. I don't know; I'm not a doctor. It could be that that had brought on me feeling bad. I've been sick this last week. I know the doctor said it was just an allergy and it could have been that. I don't know, but I wouldn't, you know; hadn't thought about it being. Course, naturally this kind of weather upsets anybody.   P

Several informants who had not sought medical aid discussed emotional symptoms with the interviewers. Often these symptoms were poorly defined and, perhaps for this reason, were not seen as constituting a real illness. Vagueness of the complaint was matched by the vagueness of the description offered by this informant:

Well, I don't know; you just feel nervous and you just feel trembly. I even sometimes . . . seems like inside of me just this way; shaky. And I'm shaky all over. Then the next morning I'll be feeling pretty good. Then maybe I'll be here just doing my work and then it'll come over me all at once, you know—just, I'm just so nervous I can't hardly—and sometimes my blood pressure don't go up at all. I don't know what's the matter.   P

But that this person was unwell there seems to be little room for doubt.

Other informants were more specific. One told of overeating since the disaster:

> INTERVIEWER: Do you have any trouble eating?
>
> RESPONDENT: No. Only trouble I have is I eat too much. That's something I shouldn't do.
>
> INTERVIEWER: Just since the tornado?
>
> RESPONDENT: Yes, it's been worse since the tornado. I had someone to tell me that it was my nerves that made me that way. I don't know whether it is or not. It could be. I know, used to I wouldn't—I didn't eat too much that way up till then. I would stay on my diet, you know, like the doctor told me.   D

At least two persons associated headaches with excitement or frustration:

> RESPONDENT: Excitement and things like that of the tornado I guess is what did it. I don't know, but more or less I've just been uneasy. Well, I don't know, I get kinda aggravated at things that gets on my nerves that didn't used to, and, of course, work in church—and Sunday school, and work in the beginners' department, racket of the little kids—seems like I'd come out more or less with a nervous headache or something that I never did. I have headaches quite a bit, but uh . . .
>
> INTERVIEWER: You do?
>
> RESPONDENT: It's more or less, uh, nervous I think; just my eyes and I had . . .   E

> No, I do have one if I get her—you know, if I get aggravated or something—or something exciting. I know right after the hailstorm I took a bad headache, but it didn't last long, I took an aspirin and it didn't last long.   T

Upset stomachs and vomiting were perhaps the most common ailment cited. In the quotation below, it appears that the interviewer, blundering, had injected the idea that vomiting might be the result of nervousness brought about by the storm. This idea is not wholly acceptable to the informant:

> RESPONDENT: They had upset stomachs quite a bit that night. Could be caused from them being a little more nervous than they used to be. I just hadn't even thought about it along that line.
>
> INTERVIEWER: This stomach doesn't seem to come from anything in particular?
>
> RESPONDENT: No, uh, yesterday this boy and my youngest one were sick all morning long. And there wasn't anything particularly that they'd

eaten that caused it. But I wouldn't say that it was due from something that happened a year ago.   P

The V family appears to have suffered an epidemic of undiagnosed nature. Whatever the nature of the illness, it obviously was associated with the tornado:

I had it first and I was in bed about a week . . . week before I could get up. I was just sick. I just couldn't get up. And then the next week, oh, just one of the children would take it and then another one would take it, and you know, they just—we just couldn't get over it. You know, was all tore up and we, uh, you know, we stayed down at my mother's about, uh, two weeks, I guess, till they got it back and dry, you know, and got everything dried up. And then, uh, we moved back up here and, uh, aw, I don't know. Then, we couldn't move the dead cow—we had to take the cow off and the chickens was all gone and then and you know we was just all tore up. We just couldn't get settled back.   V

A case that might be either emotional or biological is illustrated in the following excerpt:

INTERVIEWER: Did he have to see a doctor anytime after the ——?
RESPONDENT: No, no; you see, it just tore his nerves up because he couldn't find me. He just knew I had blown away. When they found me, why he was just almost out . . .
I still have a hurting right in there about, well, I'd say about the size of a quarter. It feels like it is just that big. And if I get real nervous it hurts, and I guess it always will . . . I wanted to get back home but I was awful nervous. But now time a cloud passes, oh, I don't know, I just get weak.
INTERVIEWER: Do you think this feeling is gradually leaving you as time goes on? Are you getting a little better, do you think?
RESPONDENT: I just don't know. I'm all right, only when those—when a cloud comes up then I get—get that way.   K

The community pattern of persistent refusal to seek medical assistance is indicated in the following husband-wife responses:

INTERVIEWER: Some of the people tell me that they themselves and their children too had upset stomach.
WIFE: She did, the oldest girl, and I did too. I was sick all that night; in fact, I collapsed when he came in.
INTERVIEWER: Nervous?
WIFE: Yes, nervous.
HUSBAND: She just was scared to death.
WIFE: But we didn't have to go to the doctor. I mean, the children had an upset stomach, I mean, and Marcia and the girls did, All night and the

next day there was one of them sick. But we didn't have to go to the doctor or anything—just upset stomach.

INTERVIEWER: Well, I think most people tell us that when they see a cloud, they get uneasy about it.

WIFE: Well, I don't know; seemed like I went on two or three months that I was just a nervous wreck, but I still didn't go to a doctor. I went to work around the house and over here, helping, and I finally overcame it but I still get nervous when I see a cloud.   N

Pride in her ability to work out her problem without medical aid and a feeling that repression was essential because of other family members are mixed in this quotation:

INTERVIEWER: During the tornado did you have any of the same feelings that you had when you had this thyroid condition?

RESPONDENT: Oh, yes, of course. Because you know the thyroid works so much on the nerves until naturally it would have been the same. And I would have hated to have had a doctor to take my blood pressure because it would probably have been *something*. Nervousness will usually run your blood pressure up and I had quite a bit of blood-pressure trouble with that thyroid trouble. And I'm sure my nerves that day probably run it up too. I was too upset over the hurts of other people to have time to consider myself.

INTERVIEWER: How long did this last, this upset feeling?

RESPONDENT: Oh, well, a day or two. I was nervous for a day or two, but not to the extent that some people I know were. In other words, I didn't have to have medical aid to overcome it. Some people that I know did. Of course, I was busy enough—I think most of those who had to have medical aid to overcome it were perhaps those who sat down and considered themselves first and foremost. I think when you have others to consider we can throw off our own feelings better.   O

"It Just Takes Time to Get Over"

Acting in terms of their particular community culture, several persons in Lake View failed to seek medical aid for conditions which would be thought to demand such treatment in many cities. Most of those who went to physicians showed definite physical symptoms. A smaller number complained only of "nervousness." Several who did not go to physicians said they had had definite physical ills. But the largest class of persons suffering from the disasters were those who presented emotional conditions of various sorts and who did seek advice or treatment. Even some of those who had sought medical aid clearly were embarrassed by the fact and permitted themselves only the minimum benefit from it; they took drugs, for example, until the acute symptoms had disappeared but not until they felt fully recovered. Such action seems to be approved by the West Texas ethos.

It was surprising that only one informant who suffered any definitely biological symptom as a result of either storm had sought the aid of a physician. A child was reported as having been sick following the tornado, though the nature of her illness is not sufficiently clear to make it certain whether it was or was not the result of the disaster:

Well, my little girl was awfully sick for a week. Ran a high temperature. She couldn't even talk, couldn't say a word, her throat was swollen up so bad. Doctor treated her for a week or more. Thought we was going to have to put her in the hospital, but she just finally got all right. And it really scared her. She's more excited over clouds now than my little boy, and he there was lots of them who was sick.   V

Several of the persons had, however, developed biological ailments. One man, for example, said he had stuck a nail in his foot but did not realize it at the time: "I just limped around here with that thing hurting and I never slowed down, never went to see a doctor. If it was to do over, I'd run to a doctor and have it fixed up."

One mother related that her daughter frequently vomited and that her husband had dreams associated with the tornado:

It didn't upset their eating except—that eleven-year-old girl. And everything that upsets her nerves, it immediately goes to her stomach and what she eats comes up. We made our first move in her school life last year. It took us six weeks to get her in school because she was frightened of her teachers. So, of course, naturally the tornado did upset her eating. But other than her nerves it didn't bother her. Now it upset my husband in his rest at night by reason of the fact that he would wake up thinking that he could hear the school children screaming. He could hear them screaming and all, you know, over the wind. He was in our car—that one that's sitting out there now—under the dashboard. He hadn't had time to turn the motor off when he got to the schoolhouse. He rolled under the dashboard as a two-by-four came through the windshield and then reached up and turned the switch key off. He would have been killed if he hadn't used what brain he had.   O

In two families, loss of weight was reported. One wife reported a loss of about eight pounds, while her husband, whose ulcers antedated the tornado, lost a greater, but unascertained, amount. The husband offered this explanation:

INTERVIEWER: Your wife says you have some difficulty with your stomach. Has it been worse since . . .?

RESPONDENT: Well, yes; in other words, uh, ulcerated stomach works on the nerves. It makes you nervous, in other words; I don't know—just—I guess I'm overworked because, trying to get back, you know, like I was. Course, I'll never get back like I was, but you know kinda—but, uh, I don't know. B

In the other family, the husband was reported to have lost about twenty pounds.

In another family, it was related: "We were all sick; we had dysentery and dropsy and we were all, every one of us, sick." However, this family did not seek medical aid and explained:

We didn't, uh, we didn't have, uh, we was just sick. You know, and they just said it was our nerves. They said it was . . . everybody's nerves; there was lots of them who was sick.   V

One woman who had put on fireman's attire and tramped through the rain-flooded streets throughout the afternoon of the tornado seeking persons in or under wreckage, directing traffic, and in similar activities, related how she developed a limp which may or may not have been psychosomatic in nature:

RESPONDENT: Course now—I didn't know at the time that I was limping, but I was. Something that I had twisted my hip or leg, or anyway I limped for three or four days and, no, I never did find a knot or bruises or anything on it.

INTERVIEWER: But you limped?

RESPONDENT: I did limp. And, uh, I didn't know but what it might have been caused from shock, that it would make you do that. Now I didn't know that to be a fact.

INTERVIEWER: Were you in pain?

RESPONDENT: No pain, no pain at all.

INTERVIEWER: No remembrance of the fact that you were limping?

RESPONDENT: No, I didn't even know it. They told me I was. I mean, couple of days later I did, and I noticed it got worse and I guess I . . .

INTERVIEWER: Any pain then?

RESPONDENT: Yeah, I knew I had a pain in my, uh, hip then, but . . . I didn't have a bruise or a thing. And it left me just in a day or two—I just didn't have it. So I don't know what—what caused it.   E

Hysterical blindness would seem to be a plausible diagnosis of the condition described by Mrs. P:

RESPONDENT: No, we didn't any of us have a scratch on us, you know, as far as, you know, physical. Uh, they tried to get me to go to a doctor later

242

because I nearly went blind in my left eye. But that was purely nerves, I suppose, just reaction, because it finally got all right. As far as being hurt in any way, we—we weren't.

My left eye seemed like for about a couple of weeks . . . just a–a film over it and I wanted to rub it all the time. And, uh, they, the nurses up there, you know the Red Cross workers, tried to get me to go . . .

I mean that was funny, just that one eye; the other one was all right, it just affected that one eye. And they kept telling me, "You might have got hit in that eye and didn't know it." I said, well, if I had got hit in that eye I would have to go to a doctor with it—oh, if it had gotten worse instead of better I—I would have.

INTERVIEWER: You could always see out of it some?

RESPONDENT: That's right. You know—Mother told me that it was probably a nervous reaction from—you know, 'cause more or less I guess everybody that was in that was in a sort of a state of shock for awhile. For the time being, I know I feel like I was.   P

Regardless of whether their ills were biosomatic or psychosomatic, whether they had medical therapy or not, most of the persons interviewed maintained an optimistic and hopeful outlook. Although the two persons quoted below admit they still suffer from the storm, both also feel that they have worked out, or will be able to work out, a means of protection for themselves and their families. It is interesting that one places his trust in God while the other reveals his plan to keep closely attentive to his radio:

It's just something that it just takes time to get over and I think I'm getting over it now a little bit. I tell you the way I feel about it in a way—of course, everybody's human. They get scared. But sometimes I feel like if it's your time to go, well, you'll go; and if it's not, well, you won't. Whether you've got a storm cellar or not. And, uh, of course, everybody's human—you're going to get scared when a cloud comes up even if you do feel that way about it. God give us sense enough to protect ourselves if we could.   O

RESPONDENT: Well, I think with us, everything's might near normal again, I hope. And you know, as I see it, these little upsets we have could be caused from what we went through then, and again it might be just another one of those things, because other people have them too, you know, other people that I know that were in the tornado still have them and . . .

INTERVIEWER: Well, you've had this sort of thing before?

RESPONDENT: Of course, uh, I'll still be glad when we get that storm cellar built and I'm going to put a bed down there.

INTERVIEWER: So if you need to go and stay a while you can be comfortable, huh?

RESPONDENT: If the clouds look too bad I might well, it'll be a good place to sleep, but until we do get it finished, well, uh, I want to keep him around close. I don't know, I'm just pretty well over being so terribly afraid, but I tell you one thing that I do do, I listen to my radio more often to the weather reports; I definitely do.   P

"But After Daddy Got Here, I Was OK"

The family as a protective group and the home as a place of refuge are concepts deeply rooted in our emotional culture. Just how firm an attachment to the family had been formed was demonstrated in many of the interviews with victims of the San Angelo storms.

Although their statements should perhaps be discounted somewhat since they were made more than a year after the tornado, many of these persons give a very clear impression that they were more anxious about the safety of other family members than about their own. Certainly they emphasized time and again their greater concern over the whereabouts and condition of family members than over the loss of property. Immediately after the tornado, these persons began to experience anxiety and to attempt, often frantically, to regain contact with family members. These sentiments appear in this statement by the husband of a badly injured woman:

All my mind was on whether they were living or not. It didn't worry me so much about the destruction, or what I lost didn't affect me a bit, ah, in the world. It was just their welfare was what I was thinking about— whether they were dead or alive. And, uh, but, uh, then my wife for, oh, ah, better than a week, we didn't know whether she was going to make it or not, and I, of course, I know I kinda got—uh, my mind on her so much I didn't think about and didn't care about nothing else at all. After I found out the boys was safe and the girls would take care of them I—I [was] with my wife and my mind was on her most of the time.   A

The next two quotations were taken from discussions of the hailstorm rather than the tornado. The first shows a high-school lad willing to go out into threatening weather to make sure that his sister was all right and to return her to the family:

He happened to look up and saw that it looked kinda mean and she was at a party and he said, "Mother, I'm going to go get Kathrine." So he run and got her and they just drove up out there when it started hailing and we went to the cellar. So he—he said he had seen that it looked kinda bad. In other words, it's just cautious. They're not really just plain scared to

244

death all the time, but just trying to be careful. We don't want to do like we did last time, just sit here and let it blow us away.   C

The next reveals a practice which appears to be fairly common in the community, that of getting all the children home when weather threatens:

INTERVIEWER: Then how did you feel? When you saw this hail cloud?
RESPONDENT: I'm afraid I was a little bit nervous—in respect, in the fact that, uh, one of my children was over next door at the other neighbor's house. . . . I called this child home.   O

Efforts to reunite the family were the first actions taken in many cases. Until this was done, everything else was postponed and often was reported to have been insignificant. Since many people in the neighborhood, perhaps most, had children in the school, it became the point of convergence for anxious parents. Some idea of how these people were driven in their efforts to reunite their family appears in this excerpt:

There were people that had children in that school out there that as soon as they heard about it they just almost went out of their heads. You know, didn't know what to say. You know, they'd just tear out there in their cars and whatever got in front of them in the street, why they would just try to climb right on over it in their automobiles, you know.   P

In another instance, the mother had started to the school from the home and the father from his place of work:

We started up to the schoolhouse and met my husband about halfway running, coming home. He had gone up to the schoolhouse from his work after our two children who were due to get out of school in just a matter of minutes. And we met him coming home and he said that the schoolhouse was torn up and that our car was wrecked. There had been another car set on top of it. We came around then back to the schoolhouse because, of course, all of us, the first thing we were interested in was those children. And the other two ladies had children up there in school, too. And that's when I got scared—when I thought of the schoolhouse and how it was torn up. And it scared my little five-year-old son very bad.   O

But not only were parents seeking children. In some cases, the children sought each other or/and their parents:

Well, see, he got out of school—he wasn't in the schoolhouse. They couldn't hold him; and he come on to the house right after he looked to see about the girls.   W

Tornadoes over Texas

After injuring himself digging through the rubble of his son's home in a vain search for family members, an elderly man began a further search which finally led him to his wife in the hospital:

Yes, I—I was very fearful that they were all killed, until I saw my house there, because I didn't know and there wasn't anybody to tell me, you know. They had all gone to hospitals and places of refuge down in town. The community gym and the Shannon Hospital and other places, you know. And, uh, so I did hear when we passed by over there, the lady stopped and I had to—I had to see if anybody knew and they didn't. And they was a fellow there said that there was a lady badly hurt there in the store and they were all going to the hospital. Well, she carried me, but he didn't tell me what hospital, ah, or anything. And, uh, so I went to the fourth floor of the Shannon Hospital before I, uh, found out where she was.   A

Apparent here is the breakdown of the community plan of communication by which a central headquarters was to have been established to disseminate information such as this man sought. Lack of effective communication also appears to be the critical factor in the failure of the K family to establish contact. Noteworthy here also is the injection of humor as a mechanism to ease tension:

RESPONDENT: See—all the wires was down and everybody said they couldn't, so it was nine-thirty that night before they found me. They were out here just turning everything upside down to find me. So they finally came to the hospital; well, they had been there three times. They even went to the funeral homes and everywhere looking for me. They just knew I was killed. So at nine-thirty, they came walking in. I never will forget how they looked. I tell you, of course, I looked awful; I tried to pass it off, you know. They had a little old thing wrapped around my head. I told them I didn't get an Easter bonnet, but now I got one after all.

INTERVIEWER: Got an Easter bonnet?

RESPONDENT: Yeah, an Easter bonnet. I tried to be funny, you know, where it wouldn't tear them up so bad. It sure did hurt my husband's nerves. He didn't ever, you know, be like he was anymore. Just any little thing just upsets him, you know, awfully bad. It seems like he's, just, I don't know, just can't take it anymore.   K

In another family something of the feeling of being lost, experienced by both the husband and wife, is conveyed in this account by the wife:

When he got close enough he could see the house was gone, he was afraid to come to the house and he didn't know what to do. So, he met some of our

246

neighbors over there and he stayed with them, and we looked for him at the schoolhouse over there and down at the community gym where they took the school children and then we, uh, looked, well, everybody, all of our neighbors and family and friends and everybody else was looking for him. And everybody said, "I saw him after the storm was over and he was all right, but I don't know where he is now." And finally we found him. He was in the car with these neighbors of ours out here. And really, I think that two hours and a half were worse than the tornado, wondering, you know, if he was all right or what had happened to him, because just—it seemed that unnerved me worse than anything else to—to not be able to find him.   F

When physical reunion was impossible, the victims substituted verbal contact, by telephone, telegraph, or by messages through friends. When a husband who was in another town could not reach his family by telephone, he made arrangements to be driven home:

My husband drives a truck. He was in the truck and he was out of town. He heard about it in about—oh, it had been about ten or fifteen minutes and he went to trying to call home and he finally got his mother's number and he talked about two or three minutes and the line went out. Got a man to bring him down here. He gave a man fifty dollars to bring him home.   R

Although the cost of the trip was undoubtedly high for the man quoted above, it was still less than that incurred by another man attempting to get in touch with his children:

Naturally, you know, when people's children were in danger like that—I know my mother and dad and brother live at Odessa and they started down here, Brother and Dad in my brother's pickup and my brother's wife and my mother in my dad's car. He gave her orders not to drive over 65 and he drove his pickup and ruined it. Didn't get here in it, driving 85.   P

For those families whose members were all in the immediate area, anxiety often ran high. Here a woman gives a glimpse of her concern when she was unable to check on the safety of her husband and son:

When the cloud had let up—of course, the first thing I thought of as the other children were here was to try to call the shop and see if Daddy and Son were all right. But their lines were out and all we could get down there was a busy signal as usual when the lines were down. Well, there was water too deep so I don't know how we expected them to get home. But we would walk from this window to the back window looking to see if Daddy and Son were coming home.   O

Not only did people outside the community attempt to reach

247

friends and relatives within it but people in the community realized the anxiety that would be felt by family members in other towns when they learned of the disaster. Here are two efforts to forestall such anxiety or to alleviate it if it existed:

I called my brother—I sent a telegram to my brother and his wife in California. And I called his [husband's] mother and daddy in Big Spring. 'Cause we found out that his dad and three brothers had come down here the night of the storm. And they couldn't find us. We didn't tell anybody anywhere around where we were going—we just didn't have enough sense to. And frankly everyone else was so torn up, they were just in the same boat we was in and they was looking for a place to stay.   J

In the other case, this reassuring effort was unavailing, for after receiving the call the husband drove some 450 miles during the night anyway to assure himself that his wife really was not in danger:

I called him in Pecos; he was—he was working—and told him that we were all right, that we had very little loss and damage. I said, "We don't have any flowers or trees or shrubs and part of the windows are gone, and I'm sure the roof has some damage," and I assured him that we were all right. However, at ten o'clock he drove in here from that 225 miles—he looked things over and said he was afraid maybe the windows might be loosened and he'd need to putty them up or something, and he said he'd feel better—he felt better—to come in and see if everything was all right. And he went back that night to Pecos and worked the next day.   E

Two short excerpts display two major facets of the feeling of security that came to these people when they were in their family groups at a time of danger:

I was just scared before Daddy and them got here, but after Daddy got here—I was—I was OK.   O

We were in the cellar, as I said a while ago. We were in the cellar, but our son was working—he wasn't here—we weren't all together. And that, you know, that means lots to me.   B

In neither case, it is to be noted, was anything sought other than the reuniting of the family to bring about this sense of security.

The uneasiness of a mother a very short distance from her family at a time of possible danger is related in this excerpt:

Well, I don't know. I know a while back we went down to visit my husband's sister and her husband. They didn't live but about four or five blocks from us. It was cloudy, pretty cloudy that night, and, uh, I didn't want to go in the first place, but I went. I had an uneasy feeling and our oldest boy and seems like one or two of the others stayed home. They wanted to watch a program on TV. I was uneasy and all the time we were down there I couldn't hardly wait to get back home. But people—you can't hardly explain your feelings like that, but, uh, you do have them. And you know, if you have a family, it's just—if they're going to be in any danger or if they're not, they like to all be together. I've always said if we're going to get blowed away we might as well all do it together. I think more or less the families that love one another, you know, feel that way too. They're going to want to be together whether it's good or whether it's bad.   P

That there may be some utilitarian thinking in the mind of the mother quoted above appears in this exchange between her and her husband:

HUSBAND: . . . then I think I've got to make a living, so if I have to go, I have to go. She usually throws a hissy about it. I don't think I could get too far off without taking her with me.

WIFE: Well, I tell you, where you have a bunch of children to look after—we have five—well, you just naturally need someone around to help you.   P

Sharing responsibility and receiving emotional support are evidently essential to this woman:

I guess if my husband was home all the time and used his judgment on the clouds a little bit I wouldn't be quite this scared, but I have to just—all the responsibility on me and I just get so excited I just—I don't know—I don't know—if he was here and let him look at 'em with me—I don't know.   R

The concern of one child for her brothers and sisters is related by their mother:

My eleven-year-old, she was very hysterical. She was just frightened to death about her little sister because she was out in this barracks building that was her schoolroom. Well, she just didn't see how it could stand. And my husband said when he went in the school building she was the first of our four children that he located because she was screaming at the top of her lungs, "I want my brother and my two little sisters."   O

This same mother said that when clouds become threatening, her children become frightened and come to her saying, "If there's going to be another tornado, I want my daddy." If one of the boys is absent, they say, "I want my daddy and brother."

The concern of a wife over the possible reaction of her husband to a tornado is given amusingly:

RESPONDENT: This hailstorm, now, tore him up quite a bit because, you know, he had dug pretty hard in the garden and everything and, oh, he sure was sick. We come home and everything was just beat down, you know, and it got, I believe, as bad on his nerves worse than it did mine.

INTERVIEWER: From the hailstorm?

RESPONDENT: Just from the hailstorm. I told him I don't know what he'd a done if he had of been in the tornado. I just don't know. I am glad he wasn't here because I would have got hurt a lot worse trying to take care of him. K

The following extended excerpt displays a situation where it would seem family unity was endangered insofar as the husband-wife relationship was concerned. There appears to be difficulty in the mind of this woman in deciding whether she is a wife or a daughter. Rather, she seems to have been unable to integrate the two roles harmoniously:

INTERVIEWER: Were you at your mother's when the hailstorm came up about a week ago?

RESPONDENT: Yes, sir.

INTERVIEWER: You'd been there how long?

RESPONDENT: Well, all evening. And, uh, he [husband]—he usually comes in about this time in the afternoon and all. Well, it hit right after he came in. I was thankful that he made it home before it did start hailing.

INTERVIEWER: When you go to your mother's, do you know what it is there that makes you feel better?

RESPONDENT: Well, I don't know unless it's just being around somebody. Course, my husband is kinda the quiet type and when we're at home we never talk very much. And he'll sit in here and read or watch TV or something. But I don't have anything to do; I just get—I don't care anything about the TV—I just can't sit still long enough to watch it.

INTERVIEWER: What difference does it make to you when he comes home?

RESPONDENT: I don't know as it makes any. As soon as supper's over, if it's cloudy, I get up and go back over to my mother's.

INTERVIEWER: Does he go with you?

RESPONDENT: Well, sometimes.

. . . .

INTERVIEWER: Have you ever had children?

RESPONDENT: No, sir.

INTERVIEWER: Do you want them? Do you think you would like to have children?

RESPONDENT: I don't know. I used to but I don't anymore, because I don't think I'm capable of taking care of them. Then again it might help me if I did. Y

250

As anxiety over the safety of other family members was high, so was relief when families were reunited. In some instances, informants insisted that from the moment they perceived the danger, their thoughts were of other members rather than of themselves. The joy of a mother at being reunited with her daughter is displayed here:

Well, I was so glad to see her that afternoon that I didn't think I would ever let her out of my sight. I guess she—I just thought that since I did get her back and she wasn't hurt other than just scared that I'd sure try to have more patience with her until she could get over it. And we did; we tried to take her mind off of it. Taking her to shows and letting her go to parties and things, tried to help her that way.   H

Inevitably, the question arose as to whether the loss of furnishings and houses loomed larger in the emotional stress accompanying the storms than did the safety of other members. This informant leaves little doubt about how she felt:

INTERVIEWER: But how about the house . . .?
RESPONDENT: It didn't enter my mind. It didn't bother me about what happened to the house. We could talk about the loss wonderfully; the loss wasn't anything to us. We still had all our kids. This other stuff, we weren't concerned. We salvaged so much of our stuff that we felt fortunate.   J

The same sentiment is expressed by another mother whose son was absent from home during the hailstorm:

. . . neighbors worrying about their house tops . . . and everything in the hail. And us, we weren't worrying about that. We were worrying about Son. Because their families were all there.   B

A schoolteacher expressed the opinion that the tornado and hailstorm resulted in greater family unity than had existed before:

And I believe the storm brought them closer together, and it intensified that feeling, perhaps, that they already had.   L

A family echoed the same sentiment:

We never have been a family that—we've always gotten along real well, never fussed, but it seems like we are closer together. Much closer. Just, we just don't like to be away from one another and as long as I have my brood around me, well, I—I'm all right.   C

Perhaps one of the elements in family unity is the freedom to act in an uninhibited manner within the family. At least something of this appears to be in the mind of this informant:

251

Well, I guess you know, naturally, anyone is going to get a little bit nervous if the weather is bad enough. And I guess maybe the way I feel I'd rather be at home where I can pray if I want to. And if I want to scream at my kids, I'm at home where I can scream at them, and I guess that's just about the way, maybe, I feel about it. I think more or less anyone feels that way; maybe their home is not safe but that's just where they want to be. P

"It's Just Not Like Home Anymore"

One of the outstanding impressions from our study of the intensive interviews made in Lake View is the importance of the home as a symbol. When the home was intact, the family was intact; when the home was destroyed, the family was in peril. Further, and interestingly, new houses did not mean new homes. Several informants had houses they felt were as good as their old homes or better, but they were far from being satisfied with them. In some cases, the difference between the new and the old was quite specific and was described in concrete terms. In other cases, as the one cited below, there seems to be nothing definite except the fact that the new house was not the old home. In this particular case, not only was the new house a replica of the old, but the furnishings were almost precisely the same:

RESPONDENT: Uh-huh, we built our house back just like it was and I'm just not satisfied since we've rebuilt. We have it up for sale now.

INTERVIEWER: I noticed that there was a sign up. Why aren't you satisfied?

RESPONDENT: I don't know. It's just not like home anymore. I've lived on this block all my life and, uh, it's just not like home anymore.

INTERVIEWER: Is it the way the house is built or the house is arranged or ——?

RESPONDENT: Well, uh, see, we had it built back just like it was and, uh —but I don't know, it's just not like home anymore.   Y

Another informant cited certain minor differences that made her new house seem not to be her home:

There was difference in furniture, house, and the outside surroundings and everything. Was just different; wasn't home.   B

In another case, it was the loss of small items of sentimental value that disturbed the person:

Yeah, it did hurt then. I lost all my pictures, you know, of my mother and my relatives, you know. Lost everything. And a lot of things I wouldn't have taken anything for. You know, they can't be replaced. I can't replace them. It's pretty hard to have to part with everything. Still we always have something to be thankful for, if we look at it that way.   K

This same woman and her husband had done much of the construction work themselves and thereby had built sentiment into their home. Thus, when the house was destroyed, they felt they had lost part of themselves:

INTERVIEWER: Well, do you think that, everything considered, you are pretty well satisfied with this place now?

RESPONDENT: Well, I guess so. You know, it still don't seem like home. You know the other place we had worked and built it ourselves. And it—it was just, well, we put the nails in there ourselves, you know, and that makes a difference. . . . Of course, I knew it was home all right, but just seemed like the house, I just felt like I was off somewhere and I'd go home after a while. That's just how I felt, you know. Of course, now I feel more—more so about the place than I did then. . . . I don't know if it was any stronger or not. I just sorta felt like it was, you know.   K

In the following excerpts, an elderly couple, who also had built their home and who took enormous pride in the sturdiness of its construction, tell of their heartbreak when their house was wrecked. To make matters worse, a son's house not nearly so sturdily constructed, in their opinion, came through with relatively slight damage:

RESPONDENT A: Well, I think it probably helped this community. We've all got nicer houses, better-built houses. Our other house was big. It had six rooms and a bath. . . . Everything fixed up real nice. Still a lot . . .

INTERVIEWER: It isn't the same house, is it?

RESPONDENT A: No.

RESPONDENT B: The other place was the first place we ever owned.

INTERVIEWER: The first one you ever owned?

RESPONDENT B: Actually, we were very attached to it. Something dear to us. Well, this one is, but . . . we both started and built it with our own hands, saved for it. I don't know, though. This one never has seemed like home.

INTERVIEWER: Do you think much about the other house?

RESPONDENT A: Yes, I did for a long time, but I don't think too much about it now, till I go off and come back.

INTERVIEWER: When you go off and come back?

RESPONDENT A: Yes, when I go off and come back, that's when it hits me. It was just the house. We both thought lots of the house. It was built out of this tile. There was no shaking, the sandstorms would roll around here, and it would look dark outdoors and you'd never feel a tremble out of it.

253

INTERVIEWER: It's as though this could never be blown down, isn't it?

RESPONDENT A: Well, now, I tell you what; my son out there and folks from plumb across over there, they come right in our house for protection from clouds—and their house was left. They was blown to pieces, of course, but—but the frames was all left and ours was completely demolished.

INTERVIEWER: Do your children live here?

RESPONDENT B: Yeah, all our kids live here but one. One boy lives right there. His house wasn't wrecked like ours. One lives right over there; his house wasn't tore down as bad as ours. You know, that just struck in spots. That house over there was just torn to pieces and then one right there was gone and never did see no pieces of it. And, uh, I'll get out there and get to looking at the houses and I'll think, "Well, we've got a much prettier place than we did have to live, but it just ain't home."   D

The following quotations are taken from the interview with a woman whose life was saved because she and her daughter took refuge in a closet. When the tornado had passed, only the closet remained. Such an emotional attachment to the closet grew up that when the house was being rebuilt, the husband and workmen schemed to get her away while they removed this symbol of her safety. It should be explained that the bricklayer mentioned in the excerpt is one of a crew of workmen who aided their fellow-bricklayer—the husband-father of the family—in rebuilding his home:

One of the bricklayers sent my husband over to me and he said, "Uh, you give this check to your wife and, uh—for your daughter and I want her to take her down there and buy her some clothes." Well, he—he gave me forty dollars and my daughter was here so she took me to town. We were gone about two hours and when we came back, well, uh, the [closet I] had been in was gone. That was the reason for sending us to town in the first place, I guess. Anyway, the closet we had been in was gone. They had torn it down. And, uh, we came up and I—I noticed it and I made the remark I said, "Well, my goodness, they've already torn the closet down." And my daughter said, "Well, what do you think I kept you in town for an hour and a half for?"

And I don't know that, course, it does make me feel kind of bad to have people to come up and see this big nice home and tell me, well, I'm better off than I ever was. Because I would say that, I'd tell them I'll trade it all back . . . if you'll take me back to the day before the storm and let things be just like they were then. I'd rather have the things I had then than the things I have now.   E

It is evident that the stratagem did not entirely succeed. In this case, as in others, it is clear that satisfaction is a nonmaterial thing; it cannot be assured through material provisions.

Plunged into a new situation for which none of their experiences had prepared them and for which their culture had no institutional solution, these persons felt lost. Then, reaching backward for their *status quo ante,* some of them refused to recognize somatic warnings, while others developed symptoms that would aid in fitting into this new world. On another plane, they made strenuous efforts to regain comfort and security in their families and their homes. Unfortunately both family and home had been so changed by the storms that these efforts were not always wholly successful.

13. There's a Fear You Can't Conquer

Fear is the constant companion of many people in Lake View. It may be recalled that approximately 40 per cent of the families in San Angelo had said they thought one or more members of the family were suffering emotional stress caused by the tornado. At the same time, more than four out of five of these people also said one or more members of the family showed undue fear of bad weather.

When we listened to the transcriptions of the intensive interviews, we got the impression that a much higher percentage lived with daily fear than was indicated by the scheduled interviews. In every case some member of the family was described as being badly disturbed when weather conditions were threatening, the degree of disturbance ranging from mild uneasiness on cloudy afternoons to stark terror during storms. As one person expressed it, "When it hit, it was just such a horrible thing that you couldn't believe it." This chapter presents material that shows the various forms of fear growing out of these two disasters, and how this fear affected the personal, family, and community life of the people to whom we talked.

A mother gave this description of her daughter's behavior when the ceiling of the room in which they had taken refuge collapsed under the weight of water pouring through the broken roof:

Of course, the hail was harder after the wind stopped—stopped blowing. It was really coming down hard then. And I told her that we could get under the table. The hail wouldn't hurt us like the wind would, when it was blowing so hard. So she began to calm down some, but when the ceiling fell she screamed "Daddy" and ran out the front door. She was really upset then.   H

Conditioned by her tornado experience, a high-school girl confided in her mother that her terror in the hailstorm was as great as it had been during the tornado or greater:

Well, my girl told me when she was at the drugstore—you know, when we had that hail? And there was another girl out there, and both of them were in the schoolhouse and she says, "Mamma, you can just about guess what I—how it felt out there with that hail hitting, going through the storm, I just wondered if I was going to get out of that building alive." And she says, "I got out of the high-school building alive, but I didn't know whether I'd get out of this little thing alive." S

Another young woman gave this description of her terror in the tornado and the resulting persistent fear:

I really was; I was terrified. I was like a trapped animal that didn't know what way to run. We had been planning a storm cellar and hadn't gotten one. And I don't know, I just—when those storms come up, I just—just feel like for sure this may be the end. That it could be a cloud that could swoop down before you could get to protection. They are murderous things. There's—there's a fear you can't conquer. A fear of storms. I used to enjoy a thunderstorm, a display of lightning. It just gave me a feeling of the importance of the Creator to watch it. But I don't now; when I see a storm coming now you always imagine there is destruction in it, even if it is a rainstorm. Just don't get over that fear. I have noticed two or three times that we've just walked the floor wondering if we would have to leave. And this past week did finally, we just couldn't constrain ourselves. We finally got in the car and ran from it. Just an instinct to try to run from it and get away. I

Fortunately, most of the expressions are of fear not so intense. A husband and wife described their feelings and those of their small son at the approach of the hailstorm in these words:

WIFE: Why, this little boy here, well, you know, that's, he's very—he's very frightened of clouds and things and, uh, the other day when that hail hit, why, uh, he—he—he was pretty badly perturbed.
HUSBAND: Well, I was very much shocked, I tell you—I couldn't hardly tell you, when I looked at that cloud, that was enough, I was—I was fearful then.
WIFE: And, brother, was I scared! A

One cause of fear at night seems to be that in the dark one cannot judge the configuration of clouds or their probable behavior. One person so explained his greater fear at night: "I can't tell much about a cloud at night at all. In the daytime, I can kinda tell what they look like; at night I can't."

One child was reported to have developed an intense fear of airplanes, believing they were about to drop atomic bombs on her home whenever a flight was heard. This fear grew out of civil defense training drills, according to the child's mother, though it seems quite likely that the meaning attributed to the noises of the planes must have been "explained" to the child by an adult.

Usually, younger children appeared to be less seriously affected than older ones. In one case, however, this appears not to have been true:

I thought the baby was going to be afraid, but I don't think he was afraid of that cloud the other day. He can hear a siren across town, and he can be outside playing and he's back in this house before I can hear it. I guess everybody that was in it, their feelings and all, was different for a while. We have a sixteen-year old boy—I—he was harder to manage than any we ever had for about two months after that. He wasn't interested in anything. We made a trip to San Antonio, you know, and all such things. I don't know whether it was just the nervous state he had gone through or what. He wasn't like he had been.   W

In several cases, it was said that all members of the family suffered from fear. A mother describes how she and her daughter became alarmed during the severe hailstorm and gives some insight into how she felt:

INTERVIEWER: How do you feel when this sort of thing is going on? How does it affect you?
RESPONDENT: Well, just seems like everything inside of me wants to come up and I'm just honest about it—I don't know—I just feel jittery or something. I don't know how to even express how I feel. It just makes you, well, I don't know what—just—I cried with her Monday night, I just couldn't keep from crying, and I cried and—and I prayed with her, and she was just a-screaming . . .   T

In the case of a young girl, there appeared an acute fear of being smothered or crushed:

She said the walls were fixing to fall in on her. Just a few days after it happened, well, I put her in a—made her bed in my room. She just—the wind was blowing just a little bit, and she was awful—afraid the walls— just crying that the walls was falling in.   R

But more frequently the fear seems to be in the form of anxiety not at all clearly defined:

Well, really, I don't know, only just nervous and scared—I was just afraid every time, you know, of a cloud. I wasn't scared about anything else. Seems like I was kind of jerky and uneasy, you know, if we heard a fire alarm or ambulance or something like that, well, it just more or less scared me, what I mean is—well, I don't know how to really explain it.   T

Something of the anatomy of fear is to be seen in the description given by this informant:

HUSBAND: One effect it did have on people down here, every time they see a dark-looking cloud a-floating around they generally hunt a hole in the ground.

WIFE: Yes, that's right. Well, I'm not as bad now as I was to start with, but I'm telling you, two weeks after that one we had another cloud that looked pretty muchly like a tornado cloud, and we were out there next door to our place that got tore up and we went in the cellar and they's a cellar out there. But I'm telling you, I just felt like someone was trying to tear my heart out, that's just how I felt at that time . . .

INTERVIEWER: Just real weak?

WIFE: Uh-huh, just something in here just like someone had ahold of your heart and was trying to tear it out. I mean, that's just the sensation I had, but of course, now, you know, it takes a little time to get over anything like that.   P

Another informant said she could not stand an air conditioner because of the noise and her memory of the tornado as a very great noise:

Well, I can't stand an air conditioner very much. I never could very well, though. I still say it just sounded like a million freight trains.   C

Often persons suffering from fear of bad weather sought the company of others to lessen their distress. Two short excerpts illustrate this:

She was alone and so was I and I'm afraid by myself . . . cloud, you know . . . so I didn't have a cellar and she didn't either.   B

INTERVIEWER: Now do you feel perfectly all right when you are with your father?

RESPONDENT: As long as there's somebody with me I'm all right, but when I get by myself, well . . .   Y

"I Never Knew I'd Be Scared of Clouds"

One cannot closely observe the people of Lake View without characterizing them as being a highly independent and rather fiercely self-sufficient group. These characteristics not only prevented their seeking aid from psychiatrists or other physicians for "nervous" conditions but, in some cases at least, also led to a sense of shame at the

259

fear they felt. In the following quotation, the interviewer—a stranger whom the respondent had never seen before and probably would never see again—was given an indication of an emotional state that had been denied the family physician:

INTERVIEWER: How do you feel when you talk about it?

RESPONDENT: Well, sometimes it makes me feel bad, sometimes it doesn't.

INTERVIEWER: And when it makes you feel bad?

RESPONDENT: Well, sometimes it will—I'll feel pretty bad. I never told the doctor the feeling.

INTERVIEWER: You haven't?

RESPONDENT: Oh, no. I'm ashamed of it.

INTERVIEWER: Could you tell me?

RESPONDENT: Well, that's about as near as I can tell you, what I've told you about it. That's more'n I've told him.   D

The reaction to fear extended beyond the San Angelo area for at least some of the people. The person quoted below either had extraordinarily bad luck in running into bad weather or was extraordinarily aware of such weather:

I know when we were living at Abilene we were back down here one week end visiting her mother and dad and we were getting ready to go back home to Abilene, you know, and there was some news came out that there was a tornado warning out for Abilene and Sweetwater and Wichita Falls. Boy, that was a pretty hard thing to do to get in the car and take off up that way knowing it was there! Boy, it's pretty nerve-racking to run right into something like that.

We were in a pretty bad cloud up in Denver City about three weeks ago—well, it was the night that it tore up that rig, you know, at—Andrews; you might remember hearing about it. That was the one that injured four men. And the cloud looked terribly bad there. We were driving from Denver City to Brownfield and it was an awful bad-looking cloud and that was the same night that it hit that rig and tore it up. We—we been catching it pretty well all the way around.

We run into something nearly every place we go. Used to be—I'll tell you, when we went out to Colorado last year right after the tornado, and we drove up the Peak and coming down it started raining. And that was an awful-looking thing to see and yet it was something I'm glad I saw. . . . I'd say we were four or five miles down from the top when it started raining and looking back up at the top of the Peak, it looked like a volcano because the clouds were so low they looked just like smoke and it was really something to see and it was scary too.   P

The pervasive character of the fear which blankets Lake View is nicely illustrated by one mother who described the reactions of the various children in her family to storms. After the hailstorm, she said, none of the family slept very much because there were clouds to be seen throughout the night, and each time there was a heavy clap of thunder, the older children would wake. These older children were a high-school son and three daughters, ranging in age from eight to twelve. The youngest child in the family, about four, was not disturbed, but for the older children, "let a cloud come up now and them be awake where they can hear it and it upsets them quite a bit."

INTERVIEWER: What happens when they get upset?

RESPONDENT: They'll go to crying and wanting to know if it's going to be another tornado like that one last year. Thunder usually wakes the twelve-year-old girl and the son, of course. And how it wakes that boy I'll never be able to figure out, because it takes his father and I thirty minutes to get him awake of mornings, normally. So I know it must have made quite an impression on him though he doesn't—a cloud doesn't seem to upset him, you know, emotionally other than the fact that he wants to know to take precautions. You know, to get things in that might be damaged, or to see that the neighbor's windows are closed, or something like that.

INTERVIEWER: Well, what does he do then?

RESPONDENT: The small boy cries and wants to know from Mamma what to do. And, uh, the eight-year-old girl, that is usually the way she does. She'll go to crying and want to know what to do. But now the little girl who's ten says, "Well, goodness gracious, we came through the other tornado all right—what's the matter with ya'll, don't you have any faith, and confidence, at all?" And she more or less helps to calm the others, including Nancy, I'm afraid. She's more calm and collected than her older sister. She just has a different nature, you see, that controls herself better. And the son, he was telling me the other day after we had this hailstorm, said, "You know, Mother, I didn't know what it meant to be scared of clouds until we had that tornado." But he says, "I don't feel like I want to get panicky or go to running around or nothing like that." He said, "What I want to do is just watch and try to stay in contact with the radio station." O

The older girl, well, just anything upsets her—if we get a, uh, message you know, or if serious illness is in the family or anything she takes it much more serious than any of the rest of us. Or she can hear some of her friends —some of her little playmates and chums, she can hear they're sick, well, that upsets her. Someone, uh, gets hurt, well, first thing she does is get upset over that and go to crying. And that doesn't help a thing in the world and especially for her.

INTERVIEWER: Yes, and then what happens when she gets to crying?

RESPONDENT: She starts vomiting; she'll lose everything that's in her stomach. I have, uh—a prescription that the doctor has given me that I give her when she gets upset. It'll calm her nerves down and quiet her stomach down and everything's all right.   O

Thus, in this family, there seems to be only one person who remains calm during stormy weather, unless perhaps the father does so. His behavior was not described.

It would almost seem as if Mr. R was speaking for his community when he said, "And I never knew I'd be scared of clouds, but I don't know. I guess I will be from now on."

Several persons reported that they had been able to go through the storms without suffering but later on had found themselves having difficulty. In each case, it is to be noted, the person was no longer in danger, and all but one had relaxed somewhat. Typical is the experience of the wife and husband quoted below, except for the short interim before the reaction set in. Something of the wife's dependence upon her husband is also revealed:

Yes, he had left that morning. He said you'll never know how it feels to leave in the morning and everything all right and come home at night and everything gone . . . And it was pretty bad—I just went right on through it all right till that night, I collapsed a little bit, I guess—I had a rigor—you know, just been going and not even thinking and it—it is a wonder that there weren't more people killed—I don't see how . . .   P

The husband had returned home and had worked calmly for two full days attempting to salvage what was left of his furnishings and his house. It would appear that a full realization of the extent of his loss did not come to him until the incident he related:

RESPONDENT: The first two days it didn't bother me a bit, and then I started over here one morning to work. I had rented a little place over there on the east side, and I was coming over here to work, and I got up here close to the schoolhouse and I just turned sick.
INTERVIEWER: You turned sick?
RESPONDENT: Just sick and nervous. It all just hit me, you know—how bad everything was gone—what shape we was in, and it, it just, I don't know, all that day I couldn't work. It—I just seemed like I cracked . . .   P

That relaxation plays an important part in such a delayed reaction is indicated in the following quotation:

And, of course, after, I say, after I drove all that distance and let everybody know that I could think of that we were all right, I got to my cousin's house and got me a cup of coffee and sort of relaxed a little bit. And then is when it hit me the hardest. I got to remembering what I had seen. And I thought that half the people in Lake View would be dead and, of course, you know, everyone, you know, they'd laugh at me and they felt sorry for me too; I'd cry awhile and then laugh awhile and I guess I did act silly, but, uh . . .   P

That such a reaction may take place much further away from the event in time than is commonly believed is one indication of the following quotation:

Oh, I'd just think about it all over again, you know; I mean, I'd live it all over again from the beginning. If I just had time. Of course, as I said, I didn't have much time and then I was so tired at night . . . I guess that was the reason that several, well, three or four months later, you know, I relaxed enough to think.   B

"I Just Kept Fighting It—I Never Have Give Up"

Although the recorded interviews were taken more than a year after the tornado and from two weeks to a month after the hailstorm, they uncovered abundant evidence of the persistence of emotional conditions associated with the tornado. How much longer this state persisted is, of course, something the evidence secured cannot answer. However, at least one of the informants believed that his son was permanently affected:

I would think, uh, that it would be that way—that, uh he'll never forget this incident. It put something in him that he'll always be fearful.   A

Although the next speaker mentions a six months' duration, it is evident that the condition she describes still existed at the time of the interview:

I think for six months after the tornado, well, of course, I didn't—I guess —well, I don't know as I think of anything only just kinda live the tornado over. And as I say, the clouds—you can ask him about me and the clouds. He gets kinda aggravated at me now because I get so upset, you know, when there's really not anything to be upset about, when it's cloudy.   B

Fear of unusual weather appeared to be endemic in the San Angelo area. Here it is coupled with doubt as to the possibility of ultimate recovery from the tornado experience:

And course now we try to listen to the weather forecast every time it

263

comes on, and when a cloud comes up that looks unusual we can't help but be kinda nervy about it like in a reaction of—it's something that—I don't know—it's about that I don't know if I'll ever recover or not because, uh, of seeing and knowing what I did.   W

One person, who seemed to have attained a very good understanding of her condition, was also, fortunately, rather vocal and expressed herself with a conciseness not common to all the interviews. For this reason, a considerable portion of the conversation with her is reproduced:

RESPONDENT: I—I try not to pay too much attention when they start talking about it, you know, because I know how upset I get. And, uh, mostly she talks about the hailstorm, you know. Course, my mother—when she gets to talking on the tornado, well, she can recall everything, and the sooner I forget it the better off I'll be.

INTERVIEWER: Do you think about the tornado often?

RESPONDENT: Yeah, I guess I do. I don't suppose there's a day passes that I don't think about it and think about something that's gone that I hadn't ever thought about before. You know, keepsakes or something like that.

INTERVIEWER: Do you have dreams about it?

RESPONDENT: No, that's something I'll say. I've never had any, uh, bad dreams about it. I guess I don't go to sleep long enough to dream about it. Even if the sky is clear and the wind is blowing I can't sleep. I stay up all night before I close my eyes.

INTERVIEWER: Do you get out of bed to watch the weather?

RESPONDENT: Yes, if it's cloudy or if it looks too awful bad. Course, I usually stand around to see what's going to happen next. Even if the moon's a-shining and the wind's a-blowing.

INTERVIEWER: How do you feel about your future?

RESPONDENT: Well, I don't know. I haven't give it much thought. I guess, uh, when we get away from here, uh, maybe I can take time out to stop and think about a few things if I get away from out here instead of seeing things that keep reminding me of what has already passed. . . . Sometimes—at times—I act like I used to before the storm and, uh, then again seems like that's just all I do—you know, just sit around and think about what I went through and everything.

INTERVIEWER: Then you think . . .?

RESPONDENT: Well, just a whole lot, I guess—'cause anybody can say anything to me—oh, I just get mad, you know, and—I didn't used to be that way.   Y

If storm-induced emotional conditions persisted, they were met by many Lake View residents with a perseverance and determination that more than compensated for the handicap. Optimism was one of their outstanding characteristics. Discouragement and a determination to overcome the obstacles encountered seem to be expressed about equally by this elderly couple:

HUSBAND: Well, she kinda gets, gets disheartened at times, I think kind of wonders what's the use. When that hail struck here, you know, why she had flowers all around the place here and the hail beat them down. I kind of thought for a while she was going to break down and cry over that.

WIFE: Well, I had worked so hard out there on —— Street, on my yard and garden and I said that I'd never try again so hard, but, of course, a person will, and then just as our dahlias and gladiolas and everything started blooming—well, what's the use? I said once before that I wouldn't try it again and yet I have and I guess I'll keep on. . . . Then we were looking out the window, you know, and seeing everything beat to the ground and I said, "Well, God didn't promise us anything else, except that we'd work by the sweat of our brow over and over again to have the things we want and so there's no use in setting down and crying. Although you feel like it sometime. P

It would be hard to find a better expression of perseverance than this:

I just kept fighting it. I never have give up. I guess I'd just have to be dead to give up. D

But the man who made the statement following appears able to match his fellow-citizen in perseverance and to add to it a consciousness of the dependence of others upon him. Attitudes such as these go far to justify the opinion expressed by many persons in Lake View that their community was better for having gone through this tragic experience:

. . . if my wife would get out of there [hospital], I would be just as content as I ever was. I never was a man that would—uh, think, "Oh, well, I just oughta go ahead and quit," or anything like that, because they ain't no use of that. A man that's raising a family, if he just gives up, throws up and quits, why he wouldn't get anywhere, and, uh, for their sake I've got to keep on keeping on. A

The emotional impact of the storms sometimes took the form of intense feelings of desolation, of depression, of loss, or of apathy. Sometimes the feeling of desolation is described as sweeping over the person when he discovers what happened to his home and his belongings. In one case, this feeling was so intense that the inform- ant said she "didn't have the heart to pick up some of the stuff that was there" for more than a week after the tornado. Another woman described her feelings in these words:

It's such a horrible emotional shock. I'm afraid I, more or less, had a hysterical spell. Not for long. Not for . . . You more or less break down to know everything's gone. Yes, I cried very hard. That's a very desolate feeling to know you haven't anything left except what you have on your back. We had no insurance on anything we had. So we had taken a total loss of everything we had. Were at that time expecting our first child and were just building a home and were living in a house trailer. A nice trailer, but, of course, we wanted more space with our baby on the way. And it's a pretty bad feeling to go back and look at the pieces.   I

The depression following the second storm is described by one of its victims:

RESPONDENT: And it hailed—I think they said fifty minutes that it never let up. I knew we didn't have nothing but still it didn't—it didn't bother me. It didn't seem like it bothered me a bit in the world till the next morn- ing.
INTERVIEWER: And then what happened?
RESPONDENT: Well, I just kinda felt blue and didn't care whether I did anything or not and didn't want to look outside. Stayed in the house all day, didn't even go out there, I don't think. It was late in the evening. I've been a whole lot worse—I wasn't near that bad before the storm. This storm just tore me all to pieces.
INTERVIEWER: Did you have any of this before the storm?
RESPONDENT: No, not so bad.
INTERVIEWER: But you did have some of it?
RESPONDENT: Yeah, just once in a while I'd take these—well, I always called it the blues.
INTERVIEWER: Could you tell me about these blues?
RESPONDENT: Just—you just get blue. Well, you just don't care about nothing, I don't reckon, in a way. It's just been that way—and seems like when it's a storm or hail the other evening . . . Why, still right at the present time now . . .   D

By some accident, the recorder did not secure what it is that happens "still right at the present time now."
  Another housewife reveals her inability to force herself to perform a simple chore:

. . . it's so hard to gather yourself together again and start and—I'll tell you

266

the truth, it's just a lot of things that I have, that I have, that still—are not straightened out from the tornado. I've crammed things back in my chest of drawers, things that need to be maybe thrown away, and I just haven't had the heart yet to dig it all out. And that's true. I haven't got completely straightened up yet. I started last week before I got sick and haven't done too much since.   P

"Apathy" appears to be the only appropriate term to describe the feeling revealed by the two women quoted below:

Just rather stay home. Course, I get tired of it sometimes. I get so tired of it, it seems like I've got to go somewhere and pass off the time. If I can just ride around a little bit and come back home, I'm all right.   K

INTERVIEWER: What do you do while he watches TV?
RESPONDENT: Oh, I usually go out in the yard and piddle, or go over to my mother's. I don't care about going anywhere. I'd just soon stay at home as go somewhere.
INTERVIEWER: What I'm getting at is, how much change has come about because of the tornado?
RESPONDENT: Oh, well, we did quite a bit of visiting. We'd go to the show three or four times a week—had company and I'd always enjoy it and now when somebody comes I—I just can't hardly wait for them to go home. I don't know. And other times I don't feel that way.   Y

Obviously, Mrs. Y had changed her mode of living rather radically.

"I Dream of a Tornado"

Interference with sleep as a sequel to the storms appeared most often in comments about watching clouds through the night, or the need for one member of the family to keep watch while others slept. A few comments on this effect, however, were more direct. In reply to a question about how he had slept after the storm, one informant said, "I didn't sleep. I imagine thirty minutes was all the time I slept that night." A mother reported that her daughter had always slept soundly until the tornado struck. After that, she slept fitfully, even when the wind was not blowing. But this difficulty had subsided when the second storm hit. After that, the child "hesitates about going to bed and she wakes early in the morning." Others reported they had had difficulty sleeping, though they were not aware of any particular worry. One wife said her husband was often unable to sleep when "nervous":

RESPONDENT: And he can't sleep at night, you know. Whenever he has

267

those nervous spells, he just can't sleep. Complains about his arms and legs hurting him and things like that.

INTERVIEWER: He had these complaints before the tornado?

RESPONDENT: Yes, but it wasn't as bad as it is right now. Some nights he don't sleep any. He just gets up and walks and gets out on the porch and sits out there. Sometimes he sits in a rocking chair.   K

When asked what kinds of things kept her from sleeping, another respondent gave this picture of worry induced by minor events:

INTERVIEWER: How did you act when you couldn't sleep?

RESPONDENT: Well, just rolling, tossed, got up, set up a minute in the bed, lay back down, and, well, I was just wide-eyed. Nothing hurt me, but I just couldn't sleep. Ever since the tornado there's just lots of nights I don't sleep, but especially if I've had a hard day or, what I mean, uh, just, uh, oh, get excited over something or something or nother, well, I just . . .

INTERVIEWER: What do you get excited about?

RESPONDENT: Well, about, you know, oh . . . if I see a wreck or something—if the ambulances go out and things like that—they just bother me.   T

Whereas the insomnia of the person just quoted seemed to result from outside stimulation, that of another came from stimulation within his own mind:

Well, maybe some of it will be just something that's happened around the place or some little old something anybody else I don't think would pay any attention to. Maybe I'll be studying about something on the outside, something about the chickens, or something about like that. And I just get my mind on that and can't go back to sleep. And, of course, that tears my nerves up.   D

Certainly the two persons just cited made a direct connection between their difficulties in sleeping well and the storms. So did another who reported disturbing dreams:

RESPONDENT: I generally sleep well. I don't necessarily have bad dreams. I had one this last week, but I have them every now and then anyway, whether there is a storm or not.

INTERVIEWER: Could you tell us something about that bad dream?

RESPONDENT: I'd rather not go into detail on that. It was rather gruesome. For the most part I don't dream much. I sleep pretty good. Even when I'm having a headache I sleep pretty good.   I

This person said she also had bad headaches, especially when she was worried or under stress, and had had one following the hailstorm.

It seems safe to say that disturbed sleep was one of the concomitants of these disasters for some of the persons exposed to them.

"Just Want to Get Away"

The desirability of Lake View as a place to live was discussed by almost every person interviewed. Opinions ranged from wholly favorable to entirely negative. All but one, however, said there had been discussion in the family about whether it was wise to remain in the area. This exception declared:

Oh, I love it, so far as the community; I—I like it because my kids can all go to the same school, and I don't have them all scattered around. There is no one out here that's, uh, so uppity; you know what I mean? We're not in the high cotton district or anything. Most of them are like us, working people.   J

There were definite reservations in most of the other answers, which were, however, favorable in over-all tone. In some this takes the form of defensiveness:

We don't feel like that—that it's the community we live in like a lot of people we hear say they wouldn't live in Lake View. They just wouldn't buy; the property out here is reduced a thousand dollars per place. Well, we don't feel that way; we just feel like we're . . .   T

Not only was the hailstorm reported to have reduced the price of real estate in Lake View; it also brought despondency:

I almost gave up. I thought, "Well, what's the use?" I thought maybe we was living in the wrong part of town. Seem like its Lake View when we do have anything bad like that—it always seems to be North Angelo. I don't suppose it is. This is the third one that we have been in since we've been living here. Third time we've roofed the house, and it's been beat in.   H

However, to one person at least, the fact that the hailstorm struck a great portion of the entire city mitigated somewhat the sense of oppression and made it more acceptable:

Of course, it hit up town as bad as it did up here, I think. The main part of town. But I still felt, well, we're getting a little more than our share. But, but as long as it wasn't any worse than it was, I didn't let it worry me too much. We may always have more hailstorms out here. I don't know. It seems that people think that. As long as it's hailstorms, I'm not going to worry about that.   C

Most often danger was accepted because of a belief that since it

269

is impossible to predict such a disaster, the peril must be accepted:

> We had friends that tried to get us not to rebuild on this lot. I said, "Yes, sir, that's home to me and I'm going to rebuild right there." "Well," they said, "aren't you afraid to?" I said, "No, I'm not afraid." Well, how can you be afraid to live in one spot on account of weather? There's nothing anyone can do about it, unless—nobody knows where it's going to hit next. Where would you go?   E

The possibility of a minor conflict in the family is apparent in this excerpt:

> RESPONDENT: You know, I just wouldn't feel at home no place else. I have lived here so long. I have lived here about fourteen years.
> INTERVIEWER: Does your husband feel about the same way?
> RESPONDENT: Well, I don't know. He didn't want to come back, and I told him he didn't have no place else to go.   K

A woman who had persuaded her husband to move to Lake View so that she might be near her parents was making a half-hearted attempt to sell her home so that she might live in another section of the city. Somewhat reluctantly she admitted her fear of remaining:

> INTERVIEWER: How do you feel toward Lake View now? You said you grew up right here on this block.
> RESPONDENT: Well, I, I don't have any grudge against it. I just—I don't know—just want to get away from out here, though. I don't know, might want to come back if I ever get away. Just never can tell.
> INTERVIEWER: And you think that it is a result of the tornado?
> RESPONDENT: Yes, I do, because otherwise, I think I would have been perfectly satisfied here the rest of my life.   Y

Another respondent also associated her fear with the tornado and the location:

> RESPONDENT: I don't know—it's just a nerve-racking place to live in.
> INTERVIEWER: How long have you felt like this?
> RESPONDENT: Well, I've been worse for the last year.   D

Some informants had moved short distances from their pretornado homes but were still within the area covered by the storms. The feelings revealed by these persons assume importance because they are representative, perhaps, of those who were entirely eliminated from this study because they had moved away from Lake View. Something of the community loyalty and personal pressures to remain appears in the case of one family who moved. Perhaps there is also an overtone of defensiveness:

WIFE: Well, you know it takes a long time to get things back to normal. Things aren't back to normal here. You can drive out in Lake View and around out in there are a lot of places that they haven't done a thing to. We sold ours—we didn't even try to build over.

HUSBAND: We talked about it once, building back, you know, and she didn't act like she was so happy about it, so I thought maybe it'd just be better and take a lot off her mind if we didn't and just moved somewhere else, you know.

WIFE: Well, someone asked me the other day if I was sorry we sold the place, because we had a wonderful well of water out there and . . .

HUSBAND: We had five acres out there, you know. We could raise anything we wanted to and had plenty of water to water it with.

WIFE: And they built a real nice place back out there. And I said, "Well, no, I'm not sorry." I said, "I still feel like that I would have been uneasy." I said, "That is a silly way to feel." But I said, "Every time a cloud would come up, I believe I would have felt a little more uneasy out there." That is a silly way to feel because if it hit anywhere else it would probably not hit out there again. However, they claim that towns do have tornado areas. P

"Named It Our Tornado Club"

The large number of families in Lake View who built storm cellars between the time of the tornado and the hailstorm bears witness to their value both as a place of physical safety and a symbol of refuge. It is not unlikely that the latter is their more important function. This was nicely expressed by a wife's conversation with her husband, who was going to another town to work for a short time:

I laughed and told him when he was thinking about going . . . I said, "Well, if you leave here, you're going to leave me a good storm cellar and you might as well make up your mind to finish it before you leave . . ." And I said, "Well, we're either going to have you or the storm cellar, one." P

Need it be added that the only function a storm cellar and a husband have in common is that both provide psychic security? Two other informants made the security of the storm cellar very explicit:

You know, a cellar helps your nerves a lot in any storm. I knew that before, because I had gone in cellars all my life when I was growing up, you know. And I guess that was one reason that I needed a cellar so bad. I just couldn't stay by myself at nighttime until the cellar was finished, if it was a cloud. B

271

I don't get what you call real scared or anything like that, but I just get weak. I want to go somewhere. I don't want to stay here at all. I go look for a hole in the ground.   K

Others explained that for one reason or another—usually the rock-like soil—they had been unable to construct a cellar. One added: "If I had me a good cellar out here, they couldn't run me off. That's where I'd be every time it thundered. That's just the way I feel about that."

This is not to imply that the storm cellars are constructed but not actually used. They are. One person disclosed that she commonly spends two or three nights each week in the storm cellar. She was asked how long she remained there after the hailstorm:

Let's see, I must have spent the night in there that night. I think, yeah, I did because we were—then we went over and got my grandmother and brought her over here and I stayed down with her that night.   Y

Often, it seems, social interaction is involved in flight to the storm cellar. In one case, the attempt of a husband to keep his wife above ground was thwarted when a neighbor unwittingly intervened:

And so it began to roar back this way. And I told them, I said, "Gee, that cloud's a-roaring." He said, "Oh, it's just rain." Trying to keep me from being scared, I guess. And I said, "Well, Mrs. —— is going to the storm cellar and I am too."   K

Another interview brought out a more serious disagreement between family members over going to the cellar:

But if it even blows slightly I go to watching [clouds]. I'm ready to take off to the storm cellar. Course I haven't went in there but twice, I think. I got——[husband] up out of bed one night—running a high temperature and taken him. We'd had some bad storm warnings here. And some people —I got up and looked at the cloud. I didn't think it looked so bad—wouldn't do anything but rain. But some neighbors came over and I thought they'd gotten some more information on it. So I got him up out of bed and went to the cellar. But he didn't like that very much.   R

Commonly trips to the storm cellar were reported as pleasant oc-casions because of contact with friends and neighbors. In one home, it was reported that the cellar would accommodate "about fifteen. In fact, we have had as many as twenty-seven in there at one time. . . . When we're down there we just talk and laugh. We have a club meeting down there. . . . Kiddoes named it our Tornado Club." An-other housewife reported:

RESPONDENT: Yeah, we've been pretty well on the lookout ever since. It took us about thirty days to get that storm house out there fixed up where we could go in it, and we have a lot of company when we go in there. We had twenty-two the other night in it.

INTERVIEWER: Really? Is it that large?

RESPONDENT: Well, it's uh, it's really not that large. It's nine-by-eleven. But you know something like that; a lot of people can get in a small hole. N

One of the schoolteachers reported that a colleague planned to take her entire class to her own storm cellar whenever a warning was issued that the school building might be hit again. An older mother explained the frequent visits of her married daughter:

RESPONDENT: She doesn't say so much about it. But she said she'd just feel safer if she was in a storm cellar. That's the reason she comes up here.

INTERVIEWER: She comes here when there is a storm or when it looks like there might be a storm?

RESPONDENT: Yes. She was at home the other day when the hailstorm hit. They said they just had to hold her; she just like to went wild. A

But the use, or even approval, of storm cellars is not universal in Lake View. One informant seemed to be debating the issue with herself, expressing the ambivalence often noted in comments of victims of these disasters:

Fear must not control you, and you must not run everytime you get scared. Sometimes it's better to stay in the house. Now as far as running to the storm cellar I had one lady tell me that she'd rather be in a tornado than close to the storm cellar because she was afraid of snakes. I said, "Well, just give me a stick I can fight the snakes for an hour or two, but I can't do nothing about a tornado." I'd rather be in the storm cellar. But I think a person that won't go to one is very foolish. E

One person traced her antipathy to storm cellars to early experiences:

Our house was blown off the blocks when I was three weeks old, they tell me; but it didn't frighten me. You know it frightened my mother. And she always dragged us to a storm house and I said, I never knew it to do any good. We always had to go back through the rain and the mud, and we always lost a lot of sleep, and I never could see any use. . . .

I never shall forget going to the storm house one time. It was covered over with logs, you know, up at top, and Mother always had a bed down there for us, but I never went to sleep. I had a sister who could lie there and sleep and everything, but I always had to stay awake and know what was going on, and I looked up and saw a great big snake up over us, you

273

know, just between the logs. You know, you could see the snake up there. And I was even afraid to say anything about it, you know; I didn't even tell them about it that evening. But it frightened me to lie there and look at that thing.   L

Others gave other reasons why they did not use storm cellars in times of danger. One reported that their cellar had flooded in the hailstorm and subsequent rain and the family would have been forced to flee during the storm had they gone there. "I'm nearly as afraid of a storm cellar as I am of a cloud." Another declined to join a party on their way to a cellar on the plea that he had to get sleep so that he could work the next day. A small boy in the party said they were going to have drinks and things to eat and a place to nap if they got sleepy, but even this was not sufficient to change the man's decision.

But those who refuse invitations to spend time in storm cellars when clouds look threatening in Lake View appear to be in a distinct minority; and they probably are considered either a bit "queer" or somewhat "uppity" by their more security-minded neighbors.

"If I Could Go Off"

Physical flight from the scene of their tragic experiences was rejected by the vast majority of the Lake View residents. Many ties made a change of residence difficult, and this appears to have been an important factor in deterring some who wished to live elsewhere. But also evident was the fierce determination expressed by those persons to fight back, to prove their ability to "take it," to persevere, in regard both to leaving the stricken community and to seeking medical aid for emotional difficulties. Either would have been considered an admission of weakness.

One informant who had fled in his automobile before both the tornado and the hailstorm felt the need to rationalize his actions:

The street we lived on was very muddy when it rained, so when it first started to raining we closed everything up and jumped in the car and took off for downtown because we didn't want . . . didn't want to leave the car there because it would get stuck in the mud.   I

Later this man, in telling of his flight before the hail, freely admitted fear at that time. A mother whose children were described as being "just so frightened . . . they were more or less hysterical" during the tornado were sent to relatives in another town for two weeks and were "pretty well reconciled to it. But still, a year later a cloud or

274

wind still upsets them. And upsets me, too, for that matter." Another parent was more optimistic about the recovery of her daughter:

Well, she got over this hail. She went to my mother's that night and spent the night. My mother has a storm cellar, so she spent two nights out there with them so she could go to the cellar if it was necessary.   H

Another woman managed to combine a bit of humor with her admission that she wanted to get far away from Lake View. She had just told of another member of the family who wanted to live elsewhere:

INTERVIEWER: She wanted to leave this place and go somewhere else?
RESPONDENT: Yes. I do too, now. Do you know of a good spot [*laughter*]?
INTERVIEWER: There is much in what you say. Let me ask you this, then. We'll come back to this later. You people would like to move?
RESPONDENT: I would. I don't know about my husband, but I am ready just any time [*laughter*]. Not anywhere in this town, though. No, sir. I want to go to Oregon. We didn't have such as this up there.
INTERVIEWER: You aren't from Oregon?
RESPONDENT: No, sir. But I lived up there about three years. I loved it. No thunder, no lightning. It was heaven.   J

Within the physical limits of the community, one high-school boy seemed to have found space enough to escape, at least to some extent. This lad was listening as his mother was being interviewed. When the mother admitted fear of clouds, the interviewer turned to the boy and asked whether he felt the same way. He assured the interviewer that he felt more fear than his mother, and added:

SON: I'm never home, anyway. I stay gone from this part of town. Only at nights at about eleven o'clock to about three in the afternoon.
INTERVIEWER: You just don't want any part of it, huh?
SON: Not in the afternoon, especially if there is a cloud in the sky. I just want to get out of this neck of the woods.   K

Recognition of flight as a means of regaining composure also seems indicated in the following exchange with this youth's mother:

RESPONDENT: I'm satisfied at home.
INTERVIEWER: Satisfied here?
RESPONDENT: Yes, until a cloud comes up and then I want to go.
INTERVIEWER: You are ready to take off?
RESPONDENT: Ready to go. But I want to come back after the cloud's gone.   K

275

Fear of remaining in the home alone to an extent suggestive of claustrophobia is expressed here:

When I feel good and get out and go, you know, be outside a lot, I just don't—don't worry. But when I'm in the house and don't get out, it seems like every little thing will worry me. Don't make any difference what it is. That's the reason I think I'd be better if I'd get up and travel some, if I was able—I just can't travel—we can hardly live at times. As long as I'm going, as long as I have company, you know, around, I'm not that way.   D

In this case the effect of being in the presence of others suggests security in a social situation as contrasted to fear when isolated.

Several of the persons had sought surcease through vacations. A husband explained:

Aw, she was, she was pretty well shook up after that tornado. And we spent quite a bit of money on just vacationing around—went out to Colorado and New Mexico and came back, and she still hadn't completely gotten over it, so then we took off down to Louisiana, and that helped her out more than anything—just getting away from here and traveling around.   P

One wife assured the interviewer that she had found relief through travel. Pertinently, she indicated a significant difference in the effect the wind had on her when she was at home and when she was away. It should be added that this respondent had commented (as had Respondent C also) that she could not use an air conditioner because the sound of the motor was too much like the sound of the wind:

RESPONDENT: I think I might be a lot better off if I could—wouldn't think about it. Now I know when we were on our vacation I didn't have a worry in the world. I was, well, I was somewhere different, you know, and I, I didn't even think about wind blowing or anything out there. But when I'm here at home I sure do.

INTERVIEWER: You felt fine while you were gone?

RESPONDENT: Yes, I didn't think about anything back home, I don't guess. I really did enjoy myself. Sometimes I think if I could go off and stay about a month somewhere like that I might feel a lot different when I come back. Last summer I went out with my husband's sister and her husband and stayed a week out there with them. Course I wasn't satisfied then because my husband wasn't with me. You know, it just makes a lot of difference when you're both not together. That was in August. Of course, I was still quite torn up, but I didn't enjoy—as long as I was riding, out on the highway, I was all right. But when I'd get still I was ready to go again.

INTERVIEWER: What about the wind out in Nevada?

RESPONDENT: Well, it didn't bother me so much. At night, it didn't really blow hard, not while we were there. Course during the day it did. But it didn't bother me.   Y

One family moved to a nearby city for a time but returned to San Angelo because the husband, a carpenter, found it easier to get work in the area where he was well known. The wife explained that she had moved both times "so we could all be together. This old staying by ourselves and something happening like it did before. . . . I don't want that to happen again." The husband added that whenever he mentioned the likelihood that he might work in another town for a time, his wife "has got her suitcase packed and ready to go." This strong desire for all family members to share whatever may come was one of the most frequent findings of our study; it has been developed in the preceding chapter.

A wife who spent much of her time away from her home felt that if she could live in another part of the city, it would be a solution to her problems: "I guess every time a cloud comes up I'll run to the cellar anyway, but I think I would be, uh, I'd stay at home more and be more interested in my work. . . . I just don't keep house like I used to. . . ."

A schoolteacher saw the problem as community-wide and suggested a somewhat drastic means of meeting it:

. . . these poeple are all so stirred up, and what I think, the only thing can actually cure them is not to go back and live in the same place and go to the same school, but make a change. Honestly, I believe they should make a change.   X

But an actual move is not always necessary for relief, as is illustrated by the woman who reported:

It affected my nerves awful bad and I'm still nervous from it. It took me quite a long time last year to get over the nervous shock. It was a big shock. It upset my nerves. A doctor treated me quite a long time last year from it. Well, I couldn't even talk about it last year. If I'd go downtown, people would go to question me, I'd jerk at them half the time. Couldn't talk about it last year. People in stores would go to asking me questions and I got so I didn't even want to go to town. Before I'd get through answering what few questions I had to answer, well, I'd get to jerking and I'd feel like . . .   R

It is likely that a psychiatrist could interpret this woman's statement more adequately than we are able to do, but it appears that she had built up a means of keeping the tragic event out of her thoughts and resented others breaking down that separation and forcing her to recognize and deal with this painful episode by asking her questions which could be answered only from her memory of the disaster. This forced her out of the psychic retreat into which she had fled.

"You Have to Kind of Hold Yourself Down"

Restraint is the obverse of coin of which flight is the reverse. As might be expected from the rather stern ethos of these people, restraint was more often resorted to as a means of meeting a situation seen as dangerous than was flight. How far this restraint goes, in the form of self-control, is well illustrated by the following comment:

> I could see parts of trees going by. But I didn't say anything to any of the kids. I kept it all to myself. That wind was terrific that day.   J

Not even in West Texas are there many days when one looks out the window and sees branches of trees going by.

Curiously, something that might be called restraint also functions as one form of flight. At least three informants stated they made conscious efforts not to think about storms and, particularly, not about tornadoes. The person quoted first had been asked whether he often found himself thinking about the storms and the danger in them:

> Well, not as much as I did. I try to not to think like that. Catch myself thinking about them, why, I try to forget it, and not study about it any more. Course, I do, yet still think about it some. Pops up in my mind, but I usually try to think about something else right quick. But I don't think you should study about it and I try not to let it—think about it any more than I can help. . . . I'd like to forget entirely about it all, if I could.   R

But the evasion through purposeful ignoring is most clearly expressed by this informant:

> Of course, we don't have a storm, uh, storm house and, course, we don't watch clouds here on that account 'cause, of course, if we don't watch them we don't know how bad it's going to be. So we don't ever watch them.   S

Several of the parents said they forced themselves to remain calm for the sake of their children. It is to be doubted, of course, whether the parents actually remained calm. It is entirely possible that they ascribed greater weight to their concern for their children than was really the case. Calmness, for the safety of both the adult and the children, is pictured in the following excerpt:

RESPONDENT: . . . because, you know, you've got to be calm around the children; why, it'll help you to be.

INTERVIEWER: How does it make you feel to know you have to be calm?

RESPONDENT: Uh—I think it's a good idea to know you have to be for the simple reason you won't let yourself go and you always feel better afterwards. It's a better feeling afterwards.   E

Another mother frankly admitted her fear but spoke of her efforts to repress it for the sake of the children:

Well, uh, yes, I was afraid; I'm still afraid of them. You have to kinda hold yourself down where there's children. You can't let them know you're afraid. I know they're afraid, too.   W

Some parents in Lake View consciously passed on to their children this technique of repressing fear toward weather conditions:

. . . when she's that way I do my best to keep her calmed down so she won't make the others cry. The day of the hailstorm, now, we had a little trouble here. She got scared wanting to go somewhere and there wasn't anywhere to go. You'd come nearer getting hurt getting out in it than staying in. She knew we couldn't go. We didn't have any way to go. She said, "I wish we could leave here. I wish we could leave here." I said, "I wish we'd left here a long time ago [*laughter*]." I was scared that day, and my oldest girl was, too. But I told her, I said, "We just got to keep ourselves so we won't un-nerve the little one."   S

That such teaching is sometimes successful is attested to by the young girl speaking here:

INTERVIEWER: How did Mary feel during this [hail]?

RESPONDENT: More calm then than I was in the tornado.

INTERVIEWER: You didn't feel upset then?

RESPONDENT: Well, I was awful upset, but I didn't say anything because I knew if I did Bob and Nell would go getting more frightened.

INTERVIEWER: How did you feel when you felt scared?

RESPONDENT: I don't know; I just felt nervous and just shook all over.   O

In instructing her daughter in the art of restraint, the mother of this child adds to the more usual appeal of coming through a bad situation in better shape, the utilitarian appeal of keeping oneself in condition to give help to others:

Just—uh—trying to sit down and reason with her and telling her that if there was to be something that she personally could do to help, if she allowed her emotions to run away with her she won't be in any condition to do anything. So the first thing for her to do is learn to keep herself under control and then she might render some aid in some way. But she certainly can't help anyone else as long as she needs aid herself. And you can get your emotions so upset until you're physically ill, as she knows.   O

The tactics described above are often successful. One mother told of her small son's going through the hailstorm without being frightened because they had played a game around the idea that the hailstones were rocks someone was throwing at them. When the father came in, the son greeted him with, "Daddy, you know what? Somebody was throwing rocks at me." Another reported that she had carried her small son through the experience by telling him the hailstones were frogs hopping around. A third mother said that the schoolteacher in charge of the room of first-graders with whom her daughter spent the period of the tornado was so successful in keeping the children calm that when her husband went into the room for the child, she greeted him with, "Hi, Daddy, what are you doing up here?" According to the mother, the child was unaware that anything out of the ordinary had happened. A high-school lad convinced himself that since tornadoes, like lightning, never strike the same place twice, he would be safe since he had been through one already.

A high-school boy said that during the tornado he had slapped a girl. He had been taught in Boy Scout work, he said, that sometimes a slap is an excellent means of bringing a person out of hysteria. When the girl attempted to force her way by him and out of the building where she might have been seriously injured, he stopped her with a "good sound slap." He reported the technique was effective; the girl began to cry, then went and sat quietly with the other children.

These persons obviously feel that restraint is a means of meeting a dangerous situation satisfactorily. Such restraint may take the form of self-control or, if self-control is insufficient, of control imposed from the outside.

But that excessive restraint may be dangerous is recognized by the mother quoted here:

. . . you can't make her hush, that's one thing you can't do, I don't suppose. I suppose it would do her more harm to try to make her—I know it would me—it would just—then—so we just talked to her and she said, "Oh, mother, please pray." And I knelt right in there on the floor beside the bed and I prayed to God to save us and spare our lives, and then she was just screaming just as loud as she could scream, "Oh, God, please stop that, God, please don't let it hail," and she just screamed like that for forty-five minutes.   T

Here is a vivid picture of self-imposed restraint by a mother who obviously was as frightened as her children were:

INTERVIEWER: Well, I guess then she was pretty upset when that hailstorm hit here the other day?
RESPONDENT: Yes, she was awful upset. She was really scared. If she had been in the house, she wouldn't a-been scared because I know last fall we had a—clouds and high wind. I was scared myself. But I didn't let on because I couldn't. The children—they was awful scared. The wind blowed pretty hard and it rained pretty hard for a while. And they was so excited I had to try to keep calm myself as I could. I didn't let them know anything about it, but I was just shaking all over when it was over with. They were really scared.   R

"We Run from a Pocket Cloud Now"

Clouds are a convenient focus for the fear which is endemic in the San Angelo area generally and epidemic in Lake View.

Nothing upsets me so much as a cloud. Just a cloud. I mean that's all that really excites me, you know. As far as, of course, I'm nervous, I know; more nervous generally than I was.   B

This is a basic expression of the pervasive fear of clouds voiced by almost every person we interviewed. The intensity of the fear varied greatly, as do the social arrangements that have come into existence because of it. As will be noted presently, distinctive family patterns have been worked out to aid in meeting this problem.

Just how much emotion and how much ordinary caution are mixed into this custom of scrutinizing clouds is impossible to determine from the data of these interviews. For example, the following excerpt begins on a rationalistic basis but ends with an indication of a highly emotional reaction:

No, I don't worry any. If I see a cloud coming up I just—I watch it, you know, and I wonder if it's gonna turn into a thunderstorm or a duststorm or what, but, frankly, I think I'll know the next time I see a tornado. I don't believe that anybody could ever make me forget that million jets that were roaring up there in that cloud. That's just the way it sounded, absolutely, and I didn't have sense enough to know that it was a tornado—the most awful roar.   J

Fear is nakedly disclosed in the comment by a mother on the behavior of her daughter during the hailstorm as well as in the following confession by an adult:

. . . and then when that cloud came up last week, well, she just went all to pieces. It was all I could do to keep her calmed down. She was just really scared.   H

No, I don't sleep on a windy night. I just sure don't. I walk the floor in the dark lots of times. I can hear the wind when it gets up, you know, but it doesn't keep me from watching.   W

Often humor is resorted to as a means of aiding the person to keep his composure and to aid others in meeting difficult situations. The former is illustrated by the woman who joked:

We run from a pocket cloud now [*laughter*]. Dry-weather clouds, you know.   J

Humor, possibly unintentional, is also in the pun made by another:

We've been having some good weather, but unsettled weather, and in unsettled weather I'm unsettled, and I don't know what makes it.   D

In some cases, cloud-fear is recognized, but efforts to escape it are without success:

I'm always scanning the skies. And I think, "I won't be scared when the next one comes." But I am . . . I just have a sort of weak feeling. And, of course, I get over it pretty soon after the cloud goes past us. I guess that's just nerves. . . . Each time I think, "Well, now I won't be as frightened next time," and next time, well . . . you know . . . when a cloud gets to looking . . . you know . . . well . . . I do.   B

Another person tells of a change in behavior since her tornado experience:

I never before the tornado, never—I don't care how dark it looked, how hard it rained or anything—I could sleep or I could go right ahead with my work regardless of whether the wind blew or what happened. It didn't bother me. But now I can't do that because I have to stop and watch the cloud. I have to see . . . I can't do my work when it's there . . . any storm clouds of any kind. I just, I just have to watch to see what it's going to do.   F

Where clouds are symbols of fear, storm cellars are symbols of security. The normal pattern of behavior is to take cover in the cellar when the cloud becomes too threatening. But occasionally these

282

two stimuli do not initiate such a pattern; rather, they interfere with each other:

INTERVIEWER: Do you often spend the night in there [cellar]?

RESPONDENT: No, not, uh, oh, well, not at night, we don't . . . 'cause we're usually staying out seeing what's going to happen next.

INTERVIEWER: If a cloud comes up, you watch it pretty closely?

RESPONDENT: Yes.

INTERVIEWER: Well, how much cloud does it take to cause you to go out and watch it?

RESPONDENT: Oh, I don't know. I watch them from . . . from the time they start gathering.   Y

But perhaps the most revealing observation in the comment quoted above is contained in the last sentence.

As a result of constant study, some people in the area believe they can tell from the appearance of a cloud the extent of the danger associated with it, and thus judge whether to be alarmed, take refuge, or ignore it. But even those who have acquired such skill may sometimes be in error, as one informant confessed:

RESPONDENT: Well, if I see a cloud coming up I go out and look at it, and then I can pretty well tell what it's going to do. You can kind of study those things and discover what they're going to do. You can tell. However, I will say this: that tornado cloud did not look bad from out here. Not as bad as some others did. And, uh, when you do see one that you think is . . . now just like this one we had last Monday . . . I saw that twister when it took off from the clouds, and I saw it when it hit the ground . . . saw the dust just fly . . .

INTERVIEWER: Can you describe your actions then?

RESPONDENT: I stood and watched it. I knew that it wasn't coming this way. It was going in another direction, because you can tell when they're coming toward you. But I will say this. If you have been warned by good authority that there is a tornado in your area, go get in a storm cellar.   E

It is not always convenient, or even possible, for a person to keep close watch on how clouds are forming and how they are moving. In such a contingency, another person is sometimes given this duty for the family or other group. This seems to be indicated in the following:

. . . some friends of mine were here too. Mrs. —— and Mrs. —— and her children. My boy phoned home and told me about it, but I was in bed, you see, and I had this lady to watch the clouds. She said, "Oh, it's just going to be a dust storm." You know, said we have had jillions of those and

283

so I got up and dressed. I said, "If I am going to be blown away I'll have my clothes on."   K

In the following comments by a father, not only is the family fear of clouds made clear but there is also a hint of his using the fear imputed to the children as a "reason" for doing something he wants to do anyway:

Well, now, they kind of rely on me. I . . . now the other night, night before last or night before that, well, we had a storm cloud in the west and in the direction of most of our storms come, you know, and of course, they depend on me and they ask me if I'll watch that cloud. They'll go on to sleep.

The clouds a-rolling, this one back here was a big cloud all right and it was doing lots of rolling, but I presumed it was a hailstorm and would pass on to the east. Well, I was a-watching back that way when all at once some big hailstones began to fall here, and I told the boys, I said, "Well, we better get in the storm cellar." I said, "Let's go and get the coats and . . ."

Well, I went as much for their sake, I didn't want to excite them, but they was already excited, and so I thought now that's what I built it for, as a place of refuge, you know.   A

One family seems to have adopted the practice of having one member, seemingly the mother, keep watch on the weather while the others sleep:

We never, we never have been nervous about sleeping. Now when a cloud comes up . . . now we won't go to sleep, not any of us unless we know that one of us is watching the cloud, if it's bad. My husband usually goes to bed. He says, "Well, I know that you'll watch it, so I'll go to bed. I have to work tomorrow." And the children, they depend on me too, so, uh, they sleep all right, I think . . .   C

However, fear is certainly expressed by the children also, if the word of their elders may be trusted. One mother said of her young daughter: "Just the idea of a cloud . . . just to see a cloud coming up, as a general rule, is about all it takes for her. Then she will start crying." Another mother said that she or her husband try always to be with their children when it is cloudy "because we think that our presence lends moral support, if nothing else. Helps them to get their nerves calm. . . . We don't want them to go through life frightened of every little cloud that comes up." Equally concerned, but less optimistic, was another mother, recounting the experiences of her family during the hailstorm:

. . . now like when it hailed last Monday. I don't know if you were here or not. But we had an awfully hard wind, about 65 miles an hour. And they just walked the floor and cried, "What is it going to do, is it going to be another tornado?" But when they act like that it makes you wonder if they ever will really forget or get to where they were like they were before the tornado when the wind didn't bother them. Now this spring when they were having some sand storms, Tommy [five years old] here, he wouldn't play outside. They was about three weeks that if there was just the least breeze he wouldn't go outside; he played in the house all the time. He'd say, "The wind is blowing." I'd tell him, "It's just a breeze; there's not any cloud; there's not any storm in sight, just go on and play." He said, "Well, we didn't think anything was going to happen when the tornado came, either." And he wouldn't go outside. And I thought "I'll just put him out and let him stay out, and he'll . . ." you know, he'd just forget about it. But he'd stand holding his hand to the door and cry and beg to come in the house.   F

"We Have a Very Unusual School"

It might logically be expected that children who were in the school building at the time of the tornado would hesitate to return to this particular building. The evidence, however, does not bear this out. In fact, more children transferred from the San Angelo system into the Lake View system than vice versa during the year following the tornado. Although the two systems are in the same city, they are entirely independent.

One of the teachers said that the staff had been told that they should be more tolerant of undisciplined behavior on cloudy days than they ordinarily would be because "these students have been through quite an ordeal." The fear of clouds does seem to have been a more or less seriously disrupting factor in school. One teacher commented on increased absences when the season for clouds rolled around:

However, later on, now when the clouds began to get here there were some absent who stayed out on account of that. That happened throughout the school, I know.   L

Two sisters used a subterfuge to escape when a cloud threatened:

I had twin girls, juniors, and one of them, as soon as the cloud came up, came to my room and knocked on my door. And she said, "Mrs. ——, would you forgive me but I have to talk to my little sister." And finally they came and asked me could they go call their mother—they had forgotten something. They made some excuse and so they went home. That's what they did. They never did go telephone. They were supposed to go to the office, but they went on home.   X

Those pupils who had been in school during the tornado were sometimes so disturbed by clouds that their work was interrupted:

Every time the wind comes up, some of those girls go haywire, or they will be sitting there and one of them will see a dark cloud and will start crying. Now the boys are just as bad. They are just as bad. They watch the window and they cannot recite. That is true; they cannot recite. And the way I approach the situation, I have some form questions, you know, workbooks. They were called achievement tests, all in a folder. Of course, I did not have to give all of them, but I said "Now let us start on these." And I knew they would not do any good on it, so I wouldn't grade that one, you see. But I kept them halfway employed during the time.   X

One teacher said that many students were frightened when clouds were in sight, but she was convinced that this was more the result of parental attitudes than of the children's fears. She told of one mother who came to get her son when the first cloud of the school year appeared. The boy said to the teacher: "It's Mother. She's down there just shaking right now."

There was evidence of emotional upset in some of the school children, and even more, perhaps, in some of the parents. A mother reported:

INTERVIEWER: How has your son been taking this? How old is he?

RESPONDENT: He's eighteen; he graduates this year. Well, he's been taking it pretty good. Of course, he got over it. He was very upset for a few months. He was very tense about everything. And I think all the school children were, you know, they—of course . . .   B

Fear on the part of the parent is evident here:

RESPONDENT: . . . he's happy to go back to school. He really is. It doesn't seem to bother the children, as near as I know. Course, they know that I'll come get them if we have a tornado warning; and I will. I go down and get them out of their classes—get them from school if we get a warning. That eases their mind a lot. They know that they can go to the cellar.

INTERVIEWER: Have you ever had to do this?

RESPONDENT: One time we had a tornado warning for San Angelo. And they let me have them without any trouble.   C

In this excerpt, apparently the fear is on the part of the child, though it must be remembered that it is the parent reporting:

. . . the little girl—several times we had to go to the schoolhouse and pick

286

her up if the wind was blowing the least bit and it was a little cloudy. Well, she'd just call and want to—she was scared.

School officials accepted this situation, and teachers offered no objections when parents asked to take their children out of school because of unusual weather. From a teacher:

The parents are affected as well as the children. Now believe it or not, uh, they may not own up to it and they say we have overcome it. But we haven't overcome it. You take the superintendent's office; he isn't with the children. And he isn't with the parents. And these clouds come and the wind seems to change or you hear a report there is a wind or a storm— parents are going to come after their children.   X

A teacher also reported there had been tacit agreement between teachers and administrators that children would be promoted the year of the tornado whether they had mastered their work or not, "because we didn't want any doubt in the minds of the parents, you know. We didn't want them blaming it on the tornado that they didn't get promoted."

Some concern was reported about the safety of the reconstructed school buildings; however, informants assured us that when parents saw the new buildings, they were perfectly satisfied that they were as strong as they had ever been or stronger.

There was one instance of a child seemingly unable to do work of as high quality as she had done previously:

RESPONDENT: The children would say to me, "That girl used to be so bright. She was so smart last year, and the year before she attended San Angelo school downtown. And said she made A's there. But since she came out here she just acts like she just is asleep all the time. And she is always watching out the window, just the least little flurry. . ."

INTERVIEWER: Had she been in the tornado?

RESPONDENT: She was in the tornado. Her mother was injured, or something.   X

The most noticeable effect upon the school was the improvement in discipline problems and the fine *esprit de corps*:

We have a very unusual school. It's the most unified school that I ever saw in thirteen years. It's the best school I ever taught in and with the best superintendent.   X

I understand they have more group activity in the high school than they did. And, uh, they tell me their discipline has been much better in the high school than it was heretofore. And I think they believe it to be due to that.

287

I know, uh, they didn't let them in the halls in high school at noontime last year. And this year they have not made any rulings about that. They have left them free; if they want to go to their locker or go down the hall of the building, they have gone. And they tell me it has been much quieter and nicer and, uh . . .   V

One teacher reported an increase in absences during the year following the tornado but attributed it to an increase in disease rather than to emotional disturbance of the children or parents.

One of the cherished stories in the community is that of the warnings to the Lake View schools with the consequence that no pupil or teacher was seriously injured. Here is an account of the incident in the words of a parent who probably heard it from her children as well as from others:

. . . his teacher says, "Well, I'm going downstairs to see what we can do about this—it's coming." And, course, they didn't have but about two minutes to do it in. So he ran downstairs and he ask the, uh, superintendent, "What can we do?" He says, "Well, get them all off the top floor down in the hall as fast as you can." So he ran up and said, "Children, just march down this hall just as fast as you can but not where you'll stumble down the stairs." So he ran from door to door and told all of them except one door— so one door he couldn't open—when he got there he couldn't open it—so they all went downstairs. Well, this one in this, uh, door he couldn't open happened to be his wife's room, so when this, uh, uh, tornado was over—I mean where they could open the door—well, her pupils—she had gotten them to get between the desks and she got under, uh, her desk and so when the roof fell, it fell on the desks and then they crawled out and then she came out but she was the only teacher that was badly hurt up there. Her ankles were hurt. I don't know what hit her.   S

The above description does not jibe entirely with other accounts; however, there is no doubt that the action taken was certainly effective. A parent gave glowing affirmation of this:

I met the grade-school principal in the corridor there. I asked how the little ones in the first grade were. He said, "Mrs. ——, they don't even know that this has happened." I said, "Well, that's just wonderful. I'll just wait till the rain lets up a little bit to go around there and get those two girls." They were both in the first-grade-room building. They had one second grade there. I have one—one of them was in the first and one in the second. And honestly they have no idea what the tornado was like. Those teachers held them so calmly.   J

Obviously, these teachers performed superbly. Also clear, but not quite so obvious, is the implication that in a situation of this sort, the social factors greatly impeded and muffled the innate, natural reactions to fear.

To Keep Informed

If cloud-watching is prevalent in the San Angelo area, so is listening to the radio for information about what the weather may do. Time after time informants said they nearly always remain within hearing of the radio. But they were divided as to whether this added to, or detracted from, their composure. The person quoted below is very definitely of the opinion that broadcast warnings make people fearful:

INTERVIEWER: Do the boys talk about the tornado very much?

RESPONDENT: No, sir. No, sir, not hardly any of them without it comes up a cloud or something like that, you see—a storm cloud. And—well, now our station has been broadcasting quite a bit about tornado warnings, and that's one thing without we can do—I guess it's a good thing to keep us leery and all that, but that has a tendency to put fear in people, I think. And, uh, they do that over the radio. Uh—night before last and night before that they had warnings of tornadoes in the Lampasas district and in East Texas—you know, to be on the alert. Well, most people are naturally fearful, and they're not—they'll be on pins and needles until they find out that . . . A

Resentment of, and sarcasm toward, the weather bureau and radio stations are evident in the reaction of this person:

RESPONDENT: But they tell us to "keep informed"! To keep informed! "Don't call your weather bureau; don't call your radio station. They'll give you all the news Leave the lines open." I know why they do that. Because in the early spring, when we had some bad clouds, why, I'm sure that others did like I did. They'd call and ask about the weather. I guess they got tired of answering people's questions.

INTERVIEWER: Do you watch clouds quite often? That sort of thing?

RESPONDENT: I try to, but I can't. I'm not very good on telling what a cloud is going to do.

INTERVIEWER: A person can't. Do you listen to weather reports?

RESPONDENT: Yeah! All the time that it was hailing we had our radio going. "No tornado warnings—just a scattered thundershower." We got that twice, and it was blowing a gale and it was just a-hailing like everything! I told the kids, I said, "They just don't want people to know what it's doing." But it wasn't doing it out there at the weather station.

I know one day they told us, "No tornado warnings for this vicinity."

289

Well, that afternoon one hit in Ballinger and hit at Norton. My mother lived just—oh, well, it hit in the next block from my mother's house. But it was a very narrow one. It kinda skipped over the town, and it didn't do a terrific damage. Just one or two or three or four houses, I think.   J

Persistent listening is certainly indicated in this case:

I don't know, I kind of think that is more or less the reason people kinda like to stick around home now, because they can listen to their radios, you know, and anything comes up, you know, well, they would be warned of it, when if they was off visiting somewheres they'd be a-talking and wouldn't be a-hearing no news nor nothing.   P

However, there is always the danger of misunderstanding broadcast warnings:

Even here, people, uh, catch, hear a little bit of the news maybe about a tornado somewhere else and they think it's here, especially older people, you know. They, I don't know—get things mixed up. I know there's been several, you know, that [thought] there's a tornado warning out.   P

Another informant gives an actual example of such misunderstanding. A child had listened to a radio program about how to take shelter in case of an atomic bomb attack. Whether as part of the program or whether sirens actually were sounded and planes were heard overhead is not clear. But, whenever such sounds occurred, this child panicked badly. The family attempted to dissipate her fears and thought they had succeeded until the hailstorm occurred. "Then she wouldn't listen to nothing. She just didn't pay any attention to us. She just screamed as long as it was hailing."

One teacher said that after being out of her room for a short time on the afternoon when there were heavy clouds, she returned to find a group of boys huddled in the back of the room. When she asked why the huddle, the boys replied by asking her, "You mean you're not afraid?" According to the teacher, "They were back there, so they were prepared. They were going to squat right where they were when the tornado happened." This incident followed a radio report that there was a possibility of tornadoes in two nearby towns.

Fear wears many faces in Lake View, plays many roles in the lives of those who live there. Out of the two storm experiences they have learned to know well the hag who lives in the clouds.

Sometimes this witch strikes them with sheer terror; again she afflicts with a weakness that makes for impotence. Still again she is seen in vague chronic distress or in less painful apathy. More actively, she drives some persons into wakeful watching that robs of restful sleep. Or, still more actively, she may send those she pursues into physical or psychic flight, into the refuge of "scare holes" in the ground, or sudden illness, or into the security of a loved family circle. From some she forces unwilling expressions of distress; on others she lays the heavy hand of restraint and repression. Family and school in Lake View do not function in quite the same way as in most communities. They acknowledge and make allowances for Fear.

Fear is a part of life in Lake View.

14. It Could Have Been Worse

LAKEVIEW WAS SORELY DESOLATED. It is not surprising that some of those who had been through two storms should develop a fear of clouds and winds; should seek refuge by developing ills psychosomatic as well as biosomatic; should feel themselves lost when they were faced with dangers without the support of their families and their homes; should seek explanations for their suffering in supernatural and nonunderstandable sources; should, for a time at least, forget the pioneer tradition which is so dear a part of their culture. But it must be emphasized again that these were the reactions of a small minority of the disaster victims; for most of them, it was a matter of pitching in and restoring their former way of life insofar as was possible, of accepting and making the best of what they found when the winds and the hail had gone.

Even as these people were struck by a feeling of desolation and began to count their losses, they also expressed thanks for not having been killed or more seriously hurt. This resulted in an ambivalence expressed in the following comment:

I think overwhelming is the sense of being glad we're alive. Now and then, about my household duties, I don't know, you miss the things you had and, uh, once in a while you can't help feel tears come to your eyes, but overwhelmingly you think, well, it could have been my life, not my possessions, and, you know, after all, life is so much more important than material possessions. You feel almost absurd to cry over something that you cherish when you've got your life. And every time I look at my child I think how glad I can be because it could have been me. It could have been the child. I have him. I

The next excerpt combines thanks with perseverance and a determination to overcome new obstacles:

INTERVIEWER: How do you feel inside?

292

RESPONDENT: Well, I'm not going to let it get me down. I'm going to do the best we can and redo everything and try again. I almost gave up. I had a lump in my throat that seemed like just wouldn't go away for several days, but now I'm determined to go ahead and start all over again.

INTERVIEWER: Any other feelings?

RESPONDENT: Well, I'm very thankful that it wasn't a tornado, this last one. It could have been much worse.   H

A third limited her comments to an expression of thanks:

Well, uh, I just feel like it is wonderful because there wasn't any of us hurt. And I also feel good because there wasn't any more people injured in it than there were. It was pretty bad and covered quite a bit of territory not to have injured any more than it did.   P

One mother compared the relative value of material possessions with the safety of her family:

RESPONDENT: The kids was uppermost in my mind. I told—they said, "Mother, the house is gone, our clothes are gone, this is gone." I said, "Yep, but we got ourselves, and we are all together. That's the main thing to be thankful for. We can get these material things back; but lives you can't."

INTERVIEWER: You remember then feeling more thankful?

RESPONDENT: I was more grateful to my God than I have ever been in my life—for having spared us.   J

Something of the same spirit appears in the comment quoted below. In this case, the informant voices the commonly accepted ideas of religion, but as she talks, it may be noted, she comes more and more to emphasize material loss and to drop religious content from her thoughts. The indication is clear that she, like others, was in a highly ambivalent state at the time of the interview:

I think it has made a woman out of me. And a great deal more. I don't know, it—it seems like after you've gone through a thing like that . . . a more mature attitude. I don't know. Uh, it teaches you reverence, for one thing, that you never have had before. It teaches you appreciation for your friends. And it does teach you that you can start out from nothing. It leaves you with a sense that material things are not everything in life. Even though you might treasure them, though they might make life easier and living a lot easier, they're not everything in life. Because, you know, you could have all the wealth in the world; without life itself it would be no good. And that's the way we always try to look at loss. If you had a lot you can start over and perhaps even have more than you lost. Because we have had to rebuild, we're—seems like we're getting used to it. Material possessions themselves—of course, financial loss—it's hard on a family to always be starting over again. And there are things you think about you could have, you could provide for your child, that you can't have when you have to rebuild all the time.   I

"By the Grace of God We're All Doing Fine"

Although the statistics display no startling effects of the storms on the religious life of the people of Lake View, it is nonetheless evident from the intensive interview material that in some cases there was a pronounced impact. Part of the pervasive optimism of these people appears to have its foundation in religious faith:

INTERVIEWER: How do you feel when these storms hit? Do you feel that your number is coming up?

RESPONDENT: No, sir; as long as there's life there's hope. And until they tell me that I'm dead or I meet St. Peter or Satan I'm gonna still think there's hope. I don't know, I never have, I've had several narrow escapes but I still feel like there is something left for me here.   J

Something of fatalism is mixed with religious gratitude in this:

The only way you can feel is to pray it won't happen. I don't know, that's the only—there's just the higher power that took care of all these people out here. And I think—I think they were left for a purpose, I don't know. A good one maybe; I hope.   W

Emotional impact plus an implicit plea for help appears in this comment:

I feel like we're all—by the grace of God—we're all doing fine and trying to hold up under it and not let our minds give completely away.   T

At least two informants saw active intervention on the part of God to bring about changes in behavior through these disasters:

Well, of course, I don't know about actual experiences, but I have heard tales about it bringing about salvation for a lot of people. Course, I don't really know. But I have heard things to that effect, that it would make people want to live a lot better. I think, more or less, that a lot of people took it as a warning that they weren't living exactly right. I, I just really don't know, but I have—you know, have heard talk to that effect. Course, you know, lots of times you can hear things that are just tales that start. No reason for you to quote anybody, but I, I have heard them.   P

In the mind of one woman, the disaster evoked an image of a God of Wrath, the Jehovah who cast down the walls of Jericho:

Well, uh, I told Mrs. —— the time when they, the people down there in the city made us go in the city limits in a crooked way, I told Mrs. ——, I said, "Listen, I don't know what it is but something's going to happen to this city that's going to take it all in and I don't know what it is." Well, see, after the tornado happened in two or three days I went over there and I said, "Mrs. ——, I guess this is what happened . . ."   S

More frequently, the response was one of thanksgiving. Several persons expressed a belief in a miraculous deliverance from harm. A curious mixture of faith and dependence upon the laws of chance appears in this comment:

. . . this middle little girl of ours, we have, uh, in Sunday school and church and all, they have learned to have faith, and have faith that everything will be all right. So they do. They're trying to apply that to their clouds as well as the other phases of their life. 'Cause, goodness gracious, if we don't have any faith in anything being right, well, chances are it'll more likely not—not be more often than if we expect the right.   O

More direct intervention is seen in the belief of a mother who was absent when her house was destroyed. Elsewhere in her interview, she had said that during storms her sons and their families usually came to her home because it was built more strongly than were theirs:

I believe—I believe that God had a hand in that, 'cause if we'd been here, if He hadn't had us away from here, I believe that us and both our sons' families probably would have been killed right in this house.   D

Two cases of seemingly miraculous protection from harm were recorded:

. . . it seemed the rest of their house blew down all around and that particular spot stayed, you know, where she and the little girl were. And, uh, she told me another interesting thing, I thought, that, uh, that her husband was Baptist and she was Catholic. And she said, not any of their religious things were destroyed. She said she had his Bible and, oh, some Catholic book, I believe she said in a box and everything else around was wet and ruined and those things weren't. This Bible and these Catholic books were not hurt and she had two rosaries, one of which, uh, was, uh, oh, uh, a keepsake. Her sister who died had had it and it was, I judge, a very ornate one. I don't know much about rosaries or the Catholic religion, but anyway, uh, this one was found, you know, in the debris, not hurt in the least. And she also found hers which she had always had, and it was not hurt. And I think those were about the only things that were not hurt in all that they had in that whole house.   L

. . . it's just nothing but providence—it wasn't meant for anybody to be killed—because look at the many funny things that happened out here— wherever the people went—that's what was saved. If the people were in the corner, the whole house went except that corner. Well, uh, a mother and daughter were in a closet—the whole house went except that closet, and then a mother and dad and eight children got in the living room. Well, you see, the whole house went except that living room and left them sitting there right in the middle of the floor. All they had a—they had a dining table—not a dining table, a library table, and they all got down under that library table. There were just as many in it out here as in Waco, but it just wasn't meant for them to be taken—and some that were taken in the storm wouldn't have been taken if they had done right.   S

An alternate explanation offered for the occurrence of such disas- ters was that they were caused by explosions of atomic bombs. In the excerpt that follows, these two explanations are in conflict in the thinking of the informant. The religious interpretation, reinforced by the knowledge of a seemingly miraculous occurrence in another por- tion of the state, finally is accepted:

Well, it [religion] keeps me from being afraid and all that. And I read a whole lot and hear a whole lot about the atomic bomb and things like that, but I—I don't think it'll—it'll ever be permitted to be used until, well, something . . . I believe that the Lord didn't want his children to suffer. I believe they'll be saved; I really do. I've seen things happen that cause me to believe that. My wife's grandmother was living in East Texas and they was right in the path of a tornado that destroyed everything, passed right over their house. This old lady, you know, she, you know, her age, and she couldn't go to the storm cellar. And her son is a Baptist preacher, and my father-in-law, he stayed with her, but he didn't know the roaring just when it passed over and it destroyed buildings on each side of them and everybody in the country said, "Well, the Lord just protected that woman and that preacher." She trusted in the Lord. She couldn't help herself and everybody agreed that she was saved by her life.   A

Teachers in Lake View School were greatly interested in the rapid growth of the Youth for Christ movement. Two of them gave these descriptions of it:

Now they organized what they call the "Youth for Christ." That is on students' time really. There is no—we didn't have an activity period this last year. This following year we have reorganized the schedule in such a way that they will have an activity period. But these children would rush through lunch, be out of the lunch room, be back in the auditorium and I counted 103. I didn't know, I thought it was just for children, see, and I didn't go. And one day I liked their singing, so I just stepped in. And, oh,

296

they were so happy and they would come and get me from that time forth. They would say, "We are so happy that you came to our Youth for Christ." X

Oh, they read the Bible, and they have confession and witnessing for Christ, and you would be surprised some of those boys that would go—get up and witness for Christ, and too, they brought in the tornado too. They knew that Christ was with them during that time or they would not have been saved, and if they hadn't prayed for it, there hadn't been enough prayers for it, that it probably would . . . L

Well, now, Jim —— is in the—is a sophomore—and I doubt if he is over fifteen years old and he is one of the preachers at the revival. And another boy here who had been playing the piano at honky tonks and so forth became an elder during their revival and has been doing wonderful church— been going to church. X

Religion undoubtedly aided in their acceptance of losses, though many accepted their situation without this aid. Some persons seem to have had a belief in fate, or luck, instead of the religious belief of their fellow-citizens.

A feeling of desolation, later replaced by one of thanks for help, is displayed in these two excerpts from one interview:

I just, you know, I just seem like I just drew up in a knot and felt bad all over. The more I studied about it, the worse I felt about it, and I just wanted to get up and walk off and leave it.

.   .   .   .

We happened to be away and when we got home we didn't have any home. It was pretty tough on us coming here and seeing everything tore up and we didn't have any insurance. We didn't know what we were going to do and got in touch with the Red Cross. Everything worked out pretty good. D

The following woman seems to be making a matter-of-fact statement of what happened rather than giving expression to emotion. The interviewer had just commented that her young child, reported to be badly upset, had dropped off to sleep during the discussion of her condition:

Yes, she's asleep; it doesn't bother her to talk about it before her any more than it does to—we've tried that. Fact of the matter, I said we'd just talk about how we've come through, how lucky we are; it's not the first time we've lost a home, or lost a garden, we've been hailed out and beat and burned out and . . . T

297

This statement also seems matter-of-fact:

That just happened, one of those things, and might as well take it and go on, and so I made up my mind that there wasn't anything I could do about it only just build back, get back in there, and trust that in . . .   A

This respondent more freely displayed the emotional impact of his loss:

. . . losing your home and everything after twenty years of having—collecting things, you know, and losing them in a matter of minutes; well, of course, it's a different feeling. It's all still a nerve-racking feeling.   B

Something of the puzzled resentment of the person who has but little and loses that little appears here:

It hurt me awful bad to think that our home was gone, because we had been ten years accumulating enough to buy us a home to have to raise our children in. And we didn't have a fine home. It was—it was comfortable. It was large enough that we had plenty of room and all such as that, but it wasn't anything fine. But we were awfully proud of it, and it hurt mighty bad to think that it was gone.   F

The following is perhaps more typical: a firm realization of the damage coupled with an equally firm determination to rebuild:

Well, I think I'm over that storm last week and it's just, oh, I don't know, it's just been so hard to try to start all over. We had such a mess here. We'll have to redo every room because all the ceilings had water in them and seems like it's going to be—oh, you always give up, but I have made up my mind that we're going ahead and do it and start all over again. Not let it get us down. That's the only way I can figure it. And it could have been much worse. I always think of that when I feel real low. It could have been worse.   H

Added to this determination is a note of thanksgiving for the safety of the family:

If it should happen again, why, we will start over again without—we're not worried about what might happen in the future because we—we know very well that whatever does happen, why, we will be able to recover. We'll be able to go right on as long as we have our lives. That's what we consider the most important thing. We're not worried too much about what might happen in the future, but we're, uh . . . . We're doing the hard things, but we don't mind doing that as long as our family's OK. That's the important thing to us.   A

"Just to Get It off My Mind"

Opinion in Lake View was markedly divided on the question of whether talking freely about experiences in the disasters was good therapy or not. Some adults said they got release by talking; others said they found it impossible or painful to talk about their experiences. Similarly, some parents said their children could not talk about what happened to them, while others said they encouraged them "to get it out of their system." There is evidence also that those who had gone through these experiences formed an in-group and felt themselves set apart from the out-group, who had no knowledge based on the actual experience. Both the therapeutic value of talk and the growth of a small in-group appear in the conversation of Mrs. K:

RESPONDENT: And there we were, all three neighbors in the same room at the hospital.
INTERVIEWER: Well, did this seem to make it a little bit easier to take if you could talk to your neighbors and . . .?
RESPONDENT: Yes, I enjoyed talking to them.
INTERVIEWER: It didn't make it seem quite as bad, then?
RESPONDENT: No. Then they would bring in some more victims, you know, that was hurt in the storm and we would have them to talk to. Of course, you never met them before but anyway, you know, you just felt close to them, 'cause they was hurt. And you would talk to them, too.   K

This same informant told how she used conversation, somewhat reluctantly, to aid a fellow-victim. Interesting, too, is the ceremonial remembrance of the disaster:

Sometimes I talk about it, you know, just to get it off my mind. You know, I think that's best; you talk about it and get it off. So when —— came and spent the day with me—you know, she was the one that got hurt the worst—and she came out and spent the day with me. It was in May and she talked about it with different people, you know. And I'd try to change the subject, you know, to get her to talk about something else. I thought she might feel better. But she wanted to talk about it, so I got to where I'd answer her and tell her the best I could. We enjoyed the day very much. She eat dinner with me on the eleventh and then I think it was the twelfth she come and eat dinner with me again a year after. Of course, we had to celebrate. We didn't drink anything. We had a good dinner and talk about old times.   K

In the following passage there is an indication that talking aided a child to regain composure. Finally she was able to make of an incident in her tornado experience something of interest to visitors and a means of occupying the limelight:

People came in talking and talk before her and she'd tell them "Well, we took shelter," and talk about it. And, uh, everytime she'd see a cloud she'd ask if that wasn't just like the tornado cloud. And I'd say, "No, that's not like it," or try to, you know, get her mind off of it. That was, about it, that was, about the cloud coming up. But we did let her talk about it and we still let her talk about it. And she will tell people about her cats and that they were spared . . . T

The in-group–out-group division is demonstrated strongly in the following excerpt where the children in the family apparently feel free to talk about their experiences among themselves but refuse to talk about them to strangers:

If someone comes in from out of town or something and we talk about it, well, they'll say, "Let's don't talk about it," because they—it reminds them, I guess. They'll say, "Don't—don't talk about it." But still they'll talk about it among themselves and not seem to think so much about it. But if they hear older people discussing it, well, they—they'd rather you didn't talk about it. . . . If they talk about it, maybe they'll become more accustomed to the idea of it and not, not be so nervous about it. So if they'll talk about it I just let them talk. F

Not only does this respondent feel puzzled about what course is the best to follow, but she indicates a prevailing disturbance among the children of the area:

Some say you shouldn't talk it before the children so much, so they'll forget it. Well, I think my children have forgotten it better than a lot of children and we've gone to the cellar when we've got ready and we've talked about it when we got ready. Some will whisper around and not let the children know they are kinda nervous over a cloud. Oh, I don't know which is best. C

In one case, at least, the in-group feeling became so strong as to cause a loss of interest between persons who formerly had been friends:

There are some people that were not in that [disaster] out there that were sort of friends of ours. I know I talked to them afterwards and they seemed altogether different, you know. Well, it seemed like they just drifted away from you; they didn't pay no mind to you talking to them nor nothing, you know, and of course, you—you nearly know that that was the reason of it. Go through something like that, being tore up . . . P

300

The fear of not being believed points again toward the consciousness of in-group and out-group feelings, accounting for the refusal of this person to discuss the disasters:

I think the reason that she did stop talking about it—one reason is because if you talk to people that were in the area, uh, and tell them things that happened, they believe you, but you can talk to someone out of the area who has never been in a tornado and you don't know, you kind of get the idea they don't believe you.   E

In the next quotation, however, the refusal to talk is obviously based on an emotional feeling of this speaker:

RESPONDENT: I don't ever say nothing about it.
INTERVIEWER: Do you find it very difficult to say anything about it?
RESPONDENT: I don't never talk about it. But I think it will wear out all right.   H

If talk is sometimes a therapeutic measure, it is also sometimes a means of transmitting fears. In discussing her experience in the hailstorm, one woman said, "I believe I was more nervous after my neighbor came and called my attention to it." This woman also said that she never did get frightened during the tornado, but she had developed nervousness about storms since then, particularly concerning members of her family who were not at home. One mother was acutely aware that she was largely responsible for the fear in her children:

INTERVIEWER: What about the children after the storm? Did you have any trouble with them?
RESPONDENT: Not a bit of trouble with them. They, of course, they were scared; you know, after that every time they would see a cloud. And probably I made them more afraid than they would have been. You know, children get over things a lot easier than grown-ups. But naturally me being afraid—well, I talked it a lot too much I guess, and I think they are, more or less, about over it by now. They don't seem so scared when a cloud's coming up. I usually have to make them get in the house if it looks very bad or something.   P

"Friends Just Mean So Much More"

The absence of panic in both Waco and San Angelo was one of the unexpected findings of this study. Furthermore, self-preservation did not appear to be the primary concern of many of the persons involved, or, perhaps more accurately, as soon as their own safety was assured, their thoughts turned to others. Most often these "others" were members of the family, though this was not always true.

I saw a lady carrying a baby, and I thought, "Well, I'll see if I can't help her out." I could tell she was hurt, and I stopped and picked her up and I told her that if she'd stick with me 'til I came home to see about how my three at home were—something just told me—Providence told me that my kids at school were all right—to get home to see the ones at home.   J

The mother just quoted left a wrecked home, got into a badly damaged automobile, and drove over rubble and live wires to search for her children. Another person welcomed aid because of his somewhat dazed condition:

That man came in. He was the only one that came in and helped me. He was the only one who offered to help. Course, if he hadn't offered I wouldn't have known what to do. As I said, I wasn't thinking.   R

In at least one instance altruism took the form of pity, expressed through a seeming refusal to aid. The man mentioned below could not bring himself to take part in the emotional crisis which he was sure would follow when the mother learned of the death of her children:

I got out there. I was going to see if I could get a ride and they wouldn't nobody let me ride. They wouldn't nobody stop, they wouldn't nobody do nothing. See, they was going on. I stopped one man that was coming down this way and I asked him. It was Mr. ——, and I asked him to take me to school and he, oh, he didn't have time and so, uh, he went on. He had got his little boy so then the next day—my husband knew him, I mean he was raised out there where he was and he had known him always—he came by and he said, "I'm sorry about not taking your wife to school, but I heard all your children was killed and I didn't want to take her . . ."   V

More material aid, extending over a much longer period, was offered by members of the family, other relatives, friends, and organized relief institutions, such as American Red Cross and the Salvation Army. How members of one family aided a victim is displayed in the following:

Well, of course, my mother came and stayed with me—was it a week?—after that. And that helped a lot to have her here and we moved into her little house—over here next door to this place. And my brother had a three-room house vacant and we had to move what we had left over there. And we were quite busy for a week trying to get things straightened around and save what we could and get things cleaned up, what part didn't blow away. It just messed up everything—quilts water-soaked. There is quite a lot to do to keep you busy after a thing like that hits.   P

The same sort of aid seems to have been even more essential and more appreciated in another case:

We knew we had to get back here where we could work and get it so we could live, 'cause my husband had to take off from work (And, uh, we didn't have any money)—and get it presentable see, for us to live in, because we couldn't afford to pay rent and probably couldn't have found a place, anyway. We had to get it fixed up so he could go back to work. It'd be—if we hadn't had help, friends and relatives, I don't know what we would have done because they all come out, you know, and worked so hard. Oh, they just worked awfully hard. And that's the reason we came back, on account of them.   C

The promptness with which neighbors volunteered is shown here:

Now, uh, I was really scared, but I felt like that we were going to be protected; we were going to pray and ask God to help us and I really felt like we were going to be protected, and after it was over with, well, I didn't seem so nervous—when it was first over with until the neighbors, they came to see about us from both sides and they ran—this one over here ran over and—and, uh, this one across the street, they came wanting us to come to their houses . . .   T

In this case, the work of the husband had brought him in contact with the persons who came to the assistance of his family:

As I said, I have never seen such co-operation or people get together in such a crisis as fast as they did in this town. I don't know what you have heard from others, but that's my opinion. Where my husband works they— If there is a disaster in the family—say, a person needs hospital care, or they have a heavy load of sickness or just anything like that—they always make up a pot. Well, there were five families that were working, their husbands, you know, worked over there and they made up a pot. And I believe it was on about Wednesday or Thursday that they contacted us and told us that they had been trying to get us to come over there—wanted to see ——. And they had made up that money and divided it between the families. And it was—well, our part of it was two hundred dollars, and they divided it equally. So you can imagine how that group of men . . . Then people from Ballinger and Big Spring, Ballinger's where his sister, and my folks, live over there. She brought a carload of stuff to us from Ballinger that was given to her to give to us. People in Big Spring sent us money. People that he knew out on his route where he delivered to these little stores around—they gave him money. His brother that was in Waco, even though they had a terrible disaster there, he was not harmed whatsoever. Well, he wired his sister some money to be sure to give to —— because he knew that he wouldn't know where he was. His money came in; and it all went, too! S

Much of the long-term aid came through organized agencies. The agency involved in the incident related here is not revealed, but certainly the gratitude with which it was received is:

This was an awful torn-up place, but still everybody went to work and got their shoulders to it. I got in there trying to clean up my home and it looked like I wasn't making no success—just me by myself. One morning, well, there was a Mexican who came up and said, "Is this 1957 Blank Street?" And I said that it was and he said, "We came to help you." And I said, "Naw, it's too much like Santa Claus." And he said, "Santa Claus came to help you." And in just a little while, they had all these ruins cleaned up and then we started building back. You can see the home that we have built back. D

Curiously, none of the persons we interviewed intensively voiced derogatory opinion of either the Salvation Army or Red Cross. On the contrary, many expressed appreciation:

INTERVIEWER: They came out and put up kitchens, didn't they?
RESPONDENT: Well, the Salvation Army and Red Cross both put up kitchens. The Salvation Army—boy, they worked day and night at it! J

Since Red Cross was the agency that aided in rebuilding homes and, in doing so, demanded proof of need, checked bank accounts and debts, and supervised the construction work, it is to be expected that a more critical evaluation would be given its activities. There is a notable lack of enthusiasm in comments on Red Cross, but there is appreciation for a job well done. In the first of the following comments, it is evident the informant made a distinction between local Red Cross workers and those brought in from other areas:

INTERVIEWER: The Red Cross workers—did they seem to know how to meet the situation?
RESPONDENT: It seemed to me like they were very efficient. The ones that didn't know how to meet it were these that were from here in town and were up there helping distributing stuff. But we didn't ask for any of that. The only thing that we asked for was bedclothes, since ours were all wet. J

A somewhat reluctant admiration plus gratitude for a workman-like job appears in this excerpt:

The Red Cross helped me look for my home and, uh, helped me in, uh, in, uh, and provided me a place to stay until my home was built—that's right. I had not, uh, nothing to reflect on anybody else in my case—that's right. I, uh, think I was pretty well taken care of—that is—beyond my expectations. I am telling the truth.   A

In the next quotation there is something of a tendency to depreciate local effort:

But you take these case workers that the Red Cross brought in here—they are trained to work in disasters. They know how to handle the situation. True there is red tape to it, but they wanted to be sure that the money was going to the right places and for the right cause. And I could understand why they—why I had to go up there every day for two weeks with different kinds of papers and this and that and the other. . . . Red Cross did a wonderful job, and these other agencies, in distributing this money. You leave it up to an individual, well—well, "I know So-and-So," or "I'll just give him a little more than I do So-and-So. I don't like him." But the Red Cross showed no favorites.   J

The general feeling of neighborliness that enveloped the Lake View area seems to have extended into relationships between it and the rest of San Angelo:

Friends just mean so much more to you, and, uh, at the time it seemed like everyone loved one another. All the neighbors felt the same way. We talked about that, that we just had more time for one another, it seems. And we're still that way.   C

. . . and I said, "Since the tornado," I said, "haven't you noticed that the people in San Angelo are far better and nicer to us today?" I said, "I can go down the street now and if I say I'm from Lake View, they're far better to me and nicer to me than they used to be." And I said, "It just took that—it took the tornado in order to wipe out their indifference or big gulf between the city and us."   S

It may be remembered that there had been some ill feeling between Lake View and the rest of the city because Lake View had been taken into the city limits against its will.

Lake View is a community of workingmen in the sense that work is considered a virtue as well as in the sense that most of the inhabitants either are employed or are small businessmen. Hence, it was to be expected that many would choose hard work as their way of eradicating emotional difficulties resulting from the storm experiences. A husband admitted quite frankly that he worked his wife as hard as possible as a therapeutic measure:

You know, after the first night I figgered the best thing could happen to her is to, you know, kind of keep her busy or something and keep her mind off of it. Because I just kind of figgered if she ever got settled and nothing to do and got to thinking about it it would be just twice as hard on her as it would be otherwise. So I put everything I could off on her to keep her busy.   P

Being forced to work, however, was not necessary in most cases. The person suffering emotional stress was often as eager to find the relief that work offers as anyone else could have been to provide work for such a purpose:

Well, she felt like I ought to go and visit my sister or get away from here while they were cleaning up and rebuilding. I said, "No, I'm not going to leave." I said, "My husband has got to do this work and I'm going to stay right here and help him." And we did; we stayed right here and worked together. From daylight to dark, about fourteen hours a day. And I don't know, I think that was better. I know some people who did leave, and they were no better off when they came back; their problem was still there.   E

Another woman used work to escape from thinking:

Well, I slept pretty good, because we worked so hard out there trying to clean up and everything . . . day after day. And we'd come out here and work all day till about eight or nine o'clock. Of course, there wasn't anything else to do but sleep, you know . . . but, uh, work all day. And I just didn't have time to think, you know.   B

Mrs. C appears to have found in work a means of escaping the feeling of desolation born of her property loss. This is implied in the intensity with which she describes her unremitting work and the apparent satisfaction it gave her. Although she does not say so, it may well be that the absence of worry over material loss was due to the satisfaction she gained from work:

INTERVIEWER: Do you remember, Mrs. ——, whether, oh, shortly after the tornado, did any of you have any trouble getting to sleep at night?
RESPONDENT: No. It seemed that we were always so tired after working that we didn't have—we just slept. . . . I just worked like mad. I never stopped. And I know if it had been any other time I'd probably been in bed. But I just worked; just never did stop. And I had a sister-in-law that did the same thing. She wasn't even in it. But she never did stop until she almost collapsed. I think she just knew that I had to have help. She and I would take the scoop shovel and scoop the mud and glass out and then we'd scrub and wash and scrub, and nobody can imagine how much dirt there was, to get out. There wasn't anything in this house that wasn't cov-

ered in mud, and that needed scrubbing and drying and picking up. It was awful. . . . I felt that maybe if we didn't have all that work to do we could have set around and let ourselves think about it. And could be that it would have made us more nervous. But we didn't have time. And we weren't worried in the least about what we lost. In fact, we just, you might say, lost about our life's savings, earnings. But it didn't worry us one bit. We were just happy to have been alive. And to have the children not hurt. That it didn't—it didn't even—you know, you'd think—we'd go home and see everything gone and it'd hurt you—but it didn't . . .   C

Work seemed effective not only as a therapeutic measure immediately following the disaster but also as an aid to emotional stability later on. Although the money with which to reduce the debt was undoubtedly one of the motivating factors in the work of the woman quoted below, it seems fair to say that the work itself was of equal, or perhaps even higher, value:

I got me a job this year and went to work. We had so many bills that I had, you know, I thought I could help with the bills, that I had, you know. . . . No, I never had worked out, but I thought maybe it would, well, you know, it would help us with the bills. Then, too, I didn't like to set here, you know. All day by myself.   V

That work is an aid toward emotional stability is expressed even more explicitly by this person:

For a while till I started back to work this year seems like I was awfully easy upset, but, long as I'm working, I'm all right.   N

The passages above have to do with work outside the home, but the same principle is applied by at least one informant to work in the home. Indicated also is a slight conflict between working as a therapeutic measure and religious doctrine:

Seems like Sunday is my hardest day. You can't do very much on Sunday that you want to. But a lot of time I do. Just to pass the time off, I'll do something if I can't go nowhere.   K

The prevailing belief and the persisting problem of many persons in Lake View were voiced here:

RESPONDENT: Just get to work at something, I don't care what it is if it ain't nothing but running the sewing machine, or ironing, or washing, or just anything. I'm all right just as long as I'm working. But when I'm sitting down with nobody to talk to, or nothing . . .

INTERVIEWER: Do you have many people around you?

RESPONDENT: Yeah, we have lots of people around, but they're all just like I am.   D

In the stern ethos of the Western Plains, work is not only a duty which is not to be laid aside lightly, but more positively it is a therapeutic measure, a means of combating the ills which beset the body and the mind.

Our work with the materials from Lake View left certain definite impressions which cannot be supported by acceptable scientific evidence but which, nevertheless, are so persuasive they clamor for expression.

When we compared the data obtained from the intensive interviews with those obtained by the schedules, we were forced to conclude that the formally structured interview does not go deep enough for this type of research. The tone and color in the open-end interviews gave life to the statistics caught in the schedule net, and often added dimensions not included in the schedule. Sometimes the two sets of data do not jibe closely; but it must be remembered that intensive interviewing was done only with persons known to be suffering greater emotional reactions to the catastrophes than were the majority of their neighbors.

Within the year between the tornado and the hailstorm, the community of Lake View had undoubtedly arrived at a fairly definite consensus about the tornado, about what should or should not be said about it. The replies given the interviewers were probably more stereotyped than the material excerpted indicates.

In spite of these limitations, there are some tentative conclusions— perhaps they should be called hunches for proof or disproof in further research—that seem of sufficient value to pass along:

There is an abnormal and epidemic fear of threatening weather in Lake View. This is, of course, rational as well as emotional. Persons in an area frequented by storms would be foolish indeed not to make every effort to gain accurate knowledge of current weather conditions. But no one can read the words of these people and not be struck by the intense emotionality manifest in their comments on clouds.

Anxiety appears in other areas, also. In some cases there appeared to be a free-floating uneasiness and disquiet that found expression in various vague complaints. Specifically, the emotional stress of at least one mother seemed definitely projected to her small daughter; the child appeared to be the much more stable emotionally.

Storm cellars are an excellent example of a combination of a utilitarian provision for safety and a symbol of security. Often, in West Texas, they are referred to as "scare holes." Normally they are considered valuable places of refuge in time of storms, but obviously in some cases they take on emotional connotations beyond this utilitarian function. In some cases this connotation was negative.

Work was an effective therapy for several persons. In some cases, this stratagem postponed emotional disquiet until the immediate task of reoccupying a home had been completed. In other instances, it was deliberately used, and successfully, to cope with emotional distress.

The importance with which these persons regard the family cannot be overemphasized. Several informants insisted that they were more concerned for the safety of other members of the family than for their own. The effort to reunite the family was ordinarily the first made. In minor crises, it was essential to the peace of mind of others that all members of the family be present, or accounted for; and it was within the family that much of the therapeutic "talking out" of emotional difficulties took place. It would be hard to concoct a better demonstration of the importance of this fundamental social institution than is provided by these informants.

Hardly less striking is the importance some of these persons attach to the home as a symbol of well-being and security. Losing the home clearly meant more to several persons than merely losing a place of shelter: in two families at least it meant the loss of years of effort and the object of their pride in workmanship as well as possession. Notable, too, was the importance placed on articles of little intrinsic value but of high sentimental significance which were lost when homes were destroyed. Obviously, here was a major focus of emotional health.

Perhaps the most important finding uncovered by the entire study of the disasters in Waco and in San Angelo was the unfailing optimism of the people. These people displayed courage and perseverance, a prideful ability to "take it," and a determination to build better lives on the ruins of their old ones—an attitude that is reassuring in a time when doubts are often being voiced about the stamina of the nation. But even more pertinent, they spoke their faith that they would accomplish the task of creating a better personal, family, and community life.

15. Toward a Theory of Disaster

Disasters are commonly thought of as tragic situations over which persons, groups, or communities have no control—situations that are imposed by an outside force too great to resist. Disasters render ineffectual the customary behavior patterns, often nullify previous efforts, and block or drastically change the course of events. The loss of life is an essential element. Survivors are suddenly given a feeling of impotence. Institutions find themselves facing new tasks of undeniable immediacy which must be accomplished if survival is to be assured. On the community level, the situation can be described as one of acute disorganization; at the personal level, there is a high degree of frustration.

But lives are rebuilt, groups are formed and operate, communities plan their budgets and other activities on the assumption that events in the future will follow the patterns that were effective in the past. Changes are expected to come slowly enough and to be mild enough that they can be assimilated without destroying those patterns. Nonpredictability may be an essential characteristic of disaster.

We do have records of tornadoes, of floods, of drought conditions, and other disasters from which we could construct probability tables for any given city or person. But we do not, and for two very good reasons: the cost would be high, and we recognize there is only a very small chance of a disaster affecting a particular community or family or person. In other words, disaster consists in the occurrence of conditions for which no protective plan has been put into effect to prevent their occurrence, not in the knowledge that conditions exist that could bring disaster.

NOTE. The material in this chapter first appeared, in substantially the same form, in the *American Sociological Review*, Vol. 21, No. 6 (December, 1956). The author gratefully acknowledges his indebtedness to that journal for permission to reprint the material here.

In the case of tornadoes, there are no known protective devices that can be used to prevent their desolating the community. Most persons living in areas subject to tornadoes make wry jokes about the possibility of their being involved but do not see the threat as serious enough to call for preparatory action beyond, perhaps, equipping the home with a storm cellar.

When a tornado strikes, then, it is unexpected, and no plan is possible for its prevention. Plans may, of course, be made for meeting the catastrophe after it has occurred.

Because of lack of preparation, its unexpectedness, and the lack of adequate safeguards against it, the tornado is a disaster. As a disaster, it is irresistible and for that very reason the more frightening and disorganizing. With no plans made, or with plans which often prove to be wholly inadequate, the first reaction may be one of dazed bewilderment, sometimes one of disbelief, or at least of refusal to accept the fact. This, it seems to us, is the essential explanation of the behavior of persons and groups in Waco when it was devastated in 1953.[1] It explains why citizens and officials alike had to have time for a minimum reorientation before going into action. On the personal level, it explains why a girl climbed into a music store through a broken display window, calmly purchased a record, and walked

[1] The material here was developed in an effort to summarize and synthesize a descriptive study of the disasters in Waco and San Angelo, without special reference to other studies of disaster. But this is certainly not to say that resemblance to conclusions reached by others doing research in disaster was coincidental. Many of the basic ideas have been available in the sociological literature since the pioneering study in this field. See Samuel Henry Prince, *Catastrophe and Social Change* (Columbia University Studies in History, Economics and Public Law, 1920), Vol. 94, No. 1. Prince expresses or at least adumbrates many of the ideas found here. Nonetheless, the opinion of Irving L. Janis, voiced in 1954, is still substantially correct: "As yet, little advance has been made in the direction of developing any kind of theoretical framework that systematically covers the effects that disasters are known to have on individuals, organizations and communities."—"Problems of Theory in the Analysis of Stress Behavior," *Journal of Social Issues*, Vol. 10, No. 3 (1954), p. 13. Janis has done as much as anyone to remedy this situation.

For a review of the literature in disaster research, see Anthony F. C. Wallace, *Human Behavior in Extreme Situations* (Washington, D.C., National Academy of Science–National Research Council, Committee on Disaster Studies), Disaster Study No. 1 (Academy-Council Publication No. 390).

Much of the recent literature on disasters has been developed in the form of reports to this organization. The author is grateful for having been given access to the following unpublished reports: John W. Powell and Jeannette F. Rayner, "Progress Notes on Disaster Research"; John W. Powell, "Preliminary Observations: Waco, Texas, Tornado of May, 1953"; Jeannette F. Rayner, "Role of the Military in Disaster."

out again, even though the plate-glass front of the building had blown out and articles were flying through the air inside the building. This may explain, too, why institutions set up for the relief of human suffering seemed to suffer a paralysis, their functionaries unable to assign tasks to others who were anxious to go into action.[2]

Such lack of action may be explained in terms of two factors that seemingly reinforce each other. Psychologically, such a drastic event seems to have a narcotizing effect that temporarily prevents the person from comprehending the extent to which his world and his position within it are changed, i.e., he has a lowered level of perception. Sociologically, it also appears that such a person is, in a sense, disoriented. He does not receive the customary cues from his surroundings or from his associates. He is unable to assess his situation through communication with others.[3] This may explain why many people often display more upset or "shock" after they have talked with others than they do immediately after a catastrophe. Similarly on the institutional level, functionaries are obviously dependent on reports of the changes which have taken place before they are able to make decisions about what, and how great, an effort is required of them.

How long this period of inactivity lasts,[4] if present, seems to vary with persons and institutions, and its duration is probably related to organizational factors. It may be postulated that the rate of recovery at the personal level is associated with such factors as past experiences with the same or similar types of events, the degree of emotional involvement and/or emotional stability, and the way in which the situation is defined. In groups and institutions these same factors appear to operate, but here additional elements also seem important. Some of these may be the personal factors mentioned as they affect individual institutional functionaries, the traditions of the group or institution, the degree of preparation in the form of realistic plans and practices, the accumulation of needed supplies, and established relationships with other institutions. But more research is needed to

[2] Cf. Prince, *op. cit.*, pp. 36, 49, 61.

[3] Much of this idea has been expressed in conversation and in an unpublished paper by Anthony F. C. Wallace, "Disruption of the Individual's Identification with His Culture in Disasters and Other Extreme Situations." Wallace gives to the term "maze" much the meaning that is usually given the term "culture."

[4] The primary source for the notion of a series of stages as used in this paper is L. T. Carr, "Disaster and Sequence-Pattern-Concept of Social Change," *American Journal of Sociology*, Vol. 38 (September, 1932), pp. 207–218.

delineate accurately the parts these factors actually play in disaster situations.

This phase of immobility lasts for an indefinite, but short, period. Intense activity quickly follows—an effort to effect reorganization by the use of physical strength and vigor. This is the rescue period in a disaster sequence. The situation still is not seen clearly and rationally, but action is demanded as a means of reasserting control. Leadership begins to function. If the titular leaders do not assume control, others take over. Orders are given and obeyed with no clear understanding on the part of anyone of what the orders are to accomplish; perhaps they are given more for the cathartic effect of the action or the ordering than for the accomplishment of any consciously held goal. "For God's sake, *do something!*" seems to be the prevailing sentiment.

This demand for activity is met not only on an impromptu basis but, within a short time, in more organized and directed ways. This reorganization has been described by Rosenquist:

Such organization as exists under these conditions [of impact and immediately after] is impromptu and temporary. Usually it is quickly replaced by the organized agencies of the community, which have command over the local resources and can proceed more systematically. If the situation is not soon brought under control by the community, aid will be tendered by Red Cross. This organization, having disaster relief as one of its primary objects, is prepared to meet every kind of emergency. Its long and successful record of relief-giving has earned for it a public confidence which enables it to secure cooperation easily and quickly.[5]

During this second phase, persons and institutions submerge their particular aims in a common effort. Old rivalries and conflicts are forgotten, or at least become subliminal, in the face of what seems to be an overwhelming task. Almost complete selflessness and great generosity are the emotional climate of this time. The giving of material things or of physical effort is a way of doing something. Merchants in Waco opened their stores and gave any supplies requested by any person, with or without authority or responsibility, without asking whether or not the materials could be used effectively.[6] Indeed, it may well be that this desire to do something to aid in setting the situation to rights is a primary factor in the outpouring of dona-

5 Carl M. Rosenquist, *Social Problems* (New York, Prentice-Hall, Inc., 1940), p. 248.
6 Cf. Prince, *op. cit.*, pp. 41, 57.

tions in such a situation. More plausibly, it would account for the thousands of sandwiches and the piles of clothing and bedding that appeared as if by magic. At the same time it accounts for one crew's throwing debris and rubble into the path of another when the intention of both was to clear away obstacles.

Social-welfare agencies in Waco placed their personnel and resources at the disposal of American Red Cross and the Salvation Army, recognized and experienced leaders in such work. Military units in the area moved in with needed supplies and men with no apparent thought of protocol. Within less than twenty-four hours a task force composed of persons from numerous federal agencies was on the scene, working as a newly created institution. Red tape was disposed of after the manner of the Gordian knot, at least for the time being. But organization was at a minimum, and the little there was, was largely confined to small work-groups and functionaries of institutions with past experience in disaster situations.

Because of the magnitude of rescue operations in a disaster such as that at Waco, and partly because of the frenzy with which effort is expended for the sake of "doing something," it becomes apparent only after some time that this type of action is not restoring the *status quo ante* and that not all the activity is productive of desired ends. In Waco this realization came after about three days. It may begin to look as if the problem is too big to be solved, that defeat is inevitable. By the time leaders and workers have reached this conclusion, they are becoming physically and mentally fatigued, and the keen stimulus of the possibility of saving lives has been dissipated. In this phase, the frustration may produce aggression or it may produce apathy.

This tendency toward disorganization and frustration is furthered by the necessity for leaders to issue orders which are not always understood but which must, nevertheless, be obeyed. Often such orders run directly counter to the wishes or judgment of those receiving them. In Waco, by way of illustration, merchants were ordered to remain away from their stores. At the same time demolition crews were knocking over walls that had been pronounced unsafe. Everything in the training and experience of the merchant bade him protect his property, but this he was forbidden to do.[7] His hostility found expression in a mass meeting of protest. The next day

[7] The idea of role conflict has been developed by Lewis M. Killian, "The Significance of Multiple-Group Membership in Disaster," *American Journal of Sociology*, Vol. 57 (January, 1952), pp. 309–314.

the military withdrew its heavy equipment from the task of removing hazardous structures. In such a situation, it would seem, orders are likely to transgress the values of some groups, resulting thereby in expressions of hostility. Similarly, when welfare agencies apply impersonal, universalistic values to the local situation, they may incur enmity if it appears they are ignoring or transgressing local standards. And when they give orders or issue instructions whose underlying reasons are not known, the hostility is aggravated.[8]

It is at this point that serious planning for reorganization is undertaken to bring the situation under customary controls, to restore community authority, and to protect community interests for the future as well as the present. An effort is made to meet criticisms either by pointing out their unfounded nature, or by remedying situations that transgress community standards. The "reasons why" are made explicit, and the need for compliance with instructions is stressed.

At this stage, persons needing and seeking sympathy and understanding may face requirements which they do not understand and which may appear heartless, arbitrary, or directly opposed to the principles that should prevail. Their losses become apparent, and they begin to seek someone to blame for their losses. With institutions, things are not going smoothly in spite of their intense efforts. Search for a scapegoat on whom emotional tension can be released may begin. Old conflicts are revived and fanned into new life; new ones are created. Institutions, even religious ones, active in rescue and temporary relief-work, are attacked and accused of being heartless, of selling supplies donated for relief at exorbitant prices to the sufferers who must have them regardless of cost; or of shipping out relief supplies to be sold in other cities. Political campaigns may be undertaken to fix blame and assess punishment for failure to solve the problems the community faces. The old world is gone; the new is strange and frightening.[9] People argue that they did nothing to deserve such a fate; therefore, someone else *must* have. That someone else must be exposed and castigated.

This "brick bat" stage is the beginning of the period of reorientation. And it is critical. What will happen to the person, family, insti-

---

[8] Perhaps the most thoroughly sociological study of a disaster yet to appear is in William H. Form, Sigmund Nosow, Gregory P. Stone, and Charles M. Westie, *Final Report on the Flint-Beecher Tornado* (Michigan State University, Social Research Service, 1954). The report discusses factors making for or against the acceptance of activities of organizations in that disaster situation.

[9] Prince, *op. cit.*, built his entire study around the central notion of the disaster as a socially disorganizing event which was followed by reorganization.

tution, or community depends on how the situation is redefined and how plans are redrawn to attain goals newly set. There are several possibilities. The belief may persist that things cannot be restored to any desirable state because of the malevolence of fate or of other persons or groups, or the refusal of others to take necessary action, or the ineffectuality of existing institutions. If this occurs, an accommodation may be made on the assumption that the disastrous consequences are permanent, the situation unsolvable, and further effort is only a waste of energy. This is adjustment on the lowest level. In persons, this position is often accompanied by regressive behavior involving the loss of discriminatory judgment. In institutions, the sense of failure may be so great that contributors withdraw support, or voluntary dissolution is undertaken.

Physical withdrawal is another possibility. Individuals may move out of the community or the damaged area. But flight from unacceptable reality may also be symbolic, as, for instance, in the refusal to participate further in civic affairs. Institutions may withdraw from fields of activity.

Withdrawal may also be accomplished through rationalization and projection. If no satisfactory resolution to problems can be found, solutions may be labeled as unworthy of attainment. Persons may accomplish this adjustment partly by an increased interest in religion, with its central symbol of the suffering God. Or withdrawal may be accomplished by projecting one's own feelings to another and then reacting to the other as one cannot to oneself. Finally, there may be repression to the extent of a steadfast denial of suffering and deprivation, a refusal to acknowledge that anything or everything is not what is desirable and wanted.

But the redefinition of goals in terms of what is seen as attainable is more normally the reaction. Resources are estimated, and where they are clearly insufficient for the desired goal, replanning is done to bring the resources and goals into consonance. Here the group comes into emphatic importance, with its ability to smooth out personal differences and to synthesize varying desires through such processes as compromise, arbitration, and conciliation, thereby replacing emotional reaction with rational consideration.

Leaders have important roles to play in this process of reorganization. They take the lead in leveling out differences between persons and within institutional groups. They also assist in fixing the attention of all participants on a common focus, thereby securing concerted and co-operative action. Through their former experience, reading, or discussion with experts, leaders may be able to present information or theories which aid in seeing more clearly what is possible and what is impossible. Tasks are assigned in accordance with the known abilities and interest of the various persons and institutions. A team effort is developed.

The closer the new plan is to the former, but no longer tenable, behavior patterns, the more quickly and easily it will be accepted and acted upon. From this it follows, too, that the nearer the goals and activities of persons and groups coincided before the crisis, the more co-operative effort there was in the past, the less will be the difficulty in attaining team play for the new plan.

The reorganization of aims and agreement about how they can best be pursued are the necessary first steps in the rehabilitation process. Once these are established, the process is one of planning and working in a fashion quite similar to that which prevailed before the disaster, but with the added factor of a conscious, over-all purpose motivating the entire community. A city plan may state these aims explicitly, or it may consist of tacitly accepted goals of re-establishing the *status quo ante*. In any case, the process of rehabilitation becomes much more institutionalized and group-centered than was the immediate reaction to disaster; the shattered social structure reasserts its priority, and social controls, formal and informal, assume their former dominance to a greater and greater degree. This is illustrated particularly in new ordinances, such as building codes or provisions for the demolition of dangerous structures.[10] Institutions set up new patterns of co-operative working arrangements, and new institutions may be created to meet foreseeable needs in future emergencies.

But the process of rebuilding, of maintaining and strengthening new relationships, of reorienting and reorganizing ways of living, both on the personal and community levels, is a slow and painful one. If and when it has been successfully carried through, a new social structure will have been produced that permits a return to normal living.

And rehabilitation will have been accomplished.

[10] For an excellent substantive study of physical problems of community reconstruction, see Fred C. Ikle, "The Effects of War Destruction upon the Ecology of Cities," *Social Forces*, Vol. 29 (May, 1951). Gordon W. Blackwell and George E. Nicholson, Jr., have applied minimax theory to defense against disaster. The same theory obviously has equal, or greater, applicability to rehabilitation.

Index

Index

Displaced Survivors—*Continued*
—residential movement of: *see* Residential movement

Donations: 153–181; as related to dramatic appeal of disasters, 153; generosity of American people, 153–154; records of, 153–154, 155; and emotional impact of disaster, 154; geographic distribution of, 154, 157t.; local committees for, 155; total amounts, 155; amounts of, 155–157; classification of, 157–158; as listed in *Waco Times-Herald,* 158t., 160–161; time pattern of, 159–161, 159t.; stories about, 161–163; variety of sources of, 161–162; motives for, 163–166, 164t.; role of communications in receipt of, 164–165; distribution of, by local committees and by American Red Cross, 165; restrictions on use of, 165; relation of, to emotional climate of rescue period, 310–314; expenditure of, *see* Expenditure of funds

Donations, San Angelo: local committee for, 30, 156, 165; over-all picture of, 153–181; geographic distribution of, 155; effect of previous donations on, 218–219

Donations, Waco: 153–181; by American Red Cross from national disaster fund, 155; geographical distribution of, 155; stories about, 161–163; support of local donations committee, 165

Driskill, William: 68

East Waco Church of Christ: 104

East Waco Elementary School: 70–71, 73–76

Emergency reactions, emotional: *see* Emotional consequences of disaster

Emigh, Harry: 68

Emotional consequences of disaster: family evaluations of, 88–92; general, 109–114, 112t., 133–135, 133t., 143, 228–255; of the aged, 143; response to disaster through donations, 154–155, 165–166; permanent effects, 210–211; construction of storm cellars, 211; emotional stress, 211;

reluctance to seek medical aid for, 211; flight to storm cellars, 213; stress after storm warnings, 213; reassurance through social contact, 214–215; reluctance to admit stress, 215; serious impact of hailstorm, 215; movement from storm area, 217; worst aspect of storm, 217–218, 218t.; reactions of children, 218, 256–291 *passim;* emotional-practical aspects, 231; concern for home, 251–255 *passim;* persistence of, 263–265; refusal to talk of disaster experience, 299, 301; reactions accompanying rehabilitation planning, 315–317

—and health: effects of disaster on, 235–244; illness, psychosomatic, 235–240; illness, emotional and biological, 239; illness, biosomatic, 240–243; attitudes *re* illness, 243

—emergency reactions: 228–255; rationalization of fear, 231; various forms of fear, 231; unreality of actual world, 231–235

—emotional therapy: 299–301; *see* American Red Cross as means of emotional therapy; Salvation Army as means of emotional therapy; Talk of disaster experience; Work as means of emotional therapy

—family concern: 244; family as a protective group, 244–252; home as a refuge and anxiety for family members, 244–252; union of family, 245–250; lack of communications, as emotional factor, 246–250

—*see* Adjustment to disaster experience; Attitudes toward disaster experience; Fear; Interviews, second study (series); Residential movement; Weather, fear of

Employment, San Angelo: suspension of, compared with Waco, 93–95; of displaced survivors, 127–128, 128t.; of the aged, 143; Negro, 148

Employment, Waco: effect of tornado on, 46–52, 47t.; outside workers, 46–47; nonagricultural labor force, 47; labor market, 47–51; and insurance, 47–49; diversion of, 49; return to normal, 49; in construction, 49; retail, 51–52

Index

Waco Disaster, The: 5

Waco Disaster Relief Fund: funds for reconstruction, 40; relationships with other agencies, 87; church contributions to, 105–106; analysis of funds received by, 155; donations by, 162; donations to, 162; expenditures, estimated, 172t.; policies of expenditure, 173–176; staff, 174; illustrative problems of, 175–176

Waco, economy of: and volume of business, 32; conservatism *vs.* progressivism in, 32–34; economic division expressed in politics, 33; unity of, in disaster, 33; economic loss, 45–55; *see also* Businesses; Damage; Rehabilitation

Waco Relief Committee: 155

Waco–San Angelo Disaster Study: factual data on the three storms, 3–36, 206–227 *passim;* substudy, legal and intergovernmental problems, 67–87; substudy, donors and donations, 153–181; substudy of communications, 182–193; substudy of newspaper reporting, *Waco Times-Herald* study, 194–205; comparison of data from first and second series of interviews, 308; conclusions from, 310–317; *see also* Interviews, first study (series); Interviews, second study (series)

Waco Times-Herald: as reporter of the Waco disaster, 39, 45, 56, 74, 155, 160–163, 185, 205; *see also Waco Times-Herald* study of newspaper reporting of disaster

Waco Times-Herald study of newspaper reporting of disaster: 194–205; method of study, 194–205 *passim;* distribution of classes of content by space, 195–197, 196t.; analysis of disaster-related content of paper, categories of, 198–205; distribution of categories by type and time, 198–205, 198t.; quantitative ranking of categories, 200t.; distri-

bution of categories by space for first year after tornado, 202t.; factors in selection of tornado "news," 201–203; use of emotional appeal, 203–205; effect of tornado on circulation, 204t.

Warnings, tornado, San Angelo: 3, 25–27; value in saving lives of school children, 27–28

—Hailstorm, San Angelo: by weather bureau, 212; media for, 212t.; need of other media for, 212; effectiveness of, 212; reactions to, 212–215; to Lake View School, 288–289; interest of survivors in, 289–291

—Tornado, Waco: 3, 189

Water Department, San Angelo: 29

Water Department, Waco: 70

Weather, fear of: 112–113, 113t., 134–135, 134t., 150–151, 209–210, 256, 259; conclusions concerning, 308; *see also* Clouds, fear of

Weather bureaus: New Orleans, 6; *see* Warnings

Wesley Methodist Church (Waco): 104

Western ethos: *see* Spiritual and ethical values, Western spirit

Wichita Daily Times: 164–165

Wichita Falls Record News: 164–165

Wolf, Ralph: 68

Wolfenstein, Martha: 228n.

Work: and ethos of the Western Plains, 308; conclusions concerning, 309

—as means of emotional therapy: 305–308; Lake View as workingman's community, 305; eagerness for work as relief from emotional stress, 305–306; emergency and long-range value of, 307; Lake View philosophy of work, 307–308

Youth for Christ movement: 208, 296–297